Niki de Saint Phalle, *Golem*, Rabinovich Park, Jerusalem, 1972

1

The Playground Project

Gabriela Burkhalter

Kunsthalle Zürich

jrp|ringier

2   Kinder spielen auf den Armierungseisen der verlassenen Baustelle einer Kirche / Children playing on armoring irons of an abandoned construction site of a church, Rione Traiano, Neapel / Naples, November 1972

Vorwort

Warum sollte eine Kunsthalle eine Ausstellung über Spielplätze organisieren? Ich bin der Überzeugung, dass sie viel voneinander lernen können und im Grunde wesensverwandt sind. Beide entwickeln ihr Potential als klar abgesteckte Freiräume, als Orte des öffentlichen Raumes und als Experimentierfelder für Ästhetik. Beide laden Laien und Eingeweihte, Kinder und Erwachsene dazu ein, sie als Laboratorien zu nutzen, um ihren Gedanken und Bewegungen freien Lauf zu lassen, um Neues zu erfahren und Unbekanntes auszutesten und um Beziehungen einzugehen. Es mögen Nischen sein, hinsichtlich Subversion sind sie jedoch nicht zu unterschätzen.

Dabei fällt auf, dass die Geschichte von Kunsthallen und allgemein von Kunstinstitutionen vielfach dokumentiert ist, die der Spielplätze jedoch kaum. Das ändern wir nun mit dieser Publikation und der Ausstellung, die sie begleitet. Warum aber interessiert sich niemand für den Spielplatz? Ein Grund ist wohl, dass man mit der Gestaltung eines Spielplatzes keine Karriere machen kann, weder als Architekt noch als Künstler, Stadtplaner oder Designer. Das Gleiche gilt für Historiker: Das Thema bringt weder Prestige noch Lehraufträge. Weil sie weder als Bauten, noch als Landschaft, Kunst oder Architektur wahrgenommen werden, hat man sie auch nie unter Denkmalschutz gestellt. „Zum Glück!", sagen wir, denn dadurch konnten sie sich fortlaufend verändern, verbessern, verschlechtern oder auch einfach verschwinden.

Seit einigen Jahren recherchiert die Stadtplanerin Gabriela Burkhalter zur Geschichte dieser urbanen Nische und macht ihre Funde und Erkenntnisse auf der Website www.architekturfuerkinder.ch weltweit zugänglich. Das von ihr aufgespürte Material erwies sich als so einzigartig, dass wir beschlossen, daraus eine gross angelegte Ausstellung zu machen. In einer ersten, kleinen Version eröffnete *The Playground Project* 2013 in Pittsburgh als Teil der *2013 Carnegie International*. Drei Jahre später wird das Projekt nun erstmals umfassend in der Kunsthalle Zürich gezeigt, inklusive Spielskulpturen für die jüngsten Besucherinnen und Besucher. Ein Füllhorn von Ideen, Entwürfen und tatsächlich realisierten Projekten leert sich über uns aus. Nicht nur entdecken wir, was alles gemacht wurde, sondern auch, was sein könnte und was es noch zu tun gibt. Die Ausstellung befragt zudem aus unerwarteter Perspektive die Rolle von Kunst im öffentlichen Raum und ganz allgemein das Verhältnis von Kunst und Gebrauchswert. *The Playground Project* konsultiert die Vergangenheit und Gegenwart, damit wir eine bessere Zukunft gestalten. Ich kann Gabriela Burkhalter nicht genug für ihr Engagement, ihre Recherche und Grosszügigkeit danken.

Ich möchte allen, die an diesem Projekt beteiligt waren, ganz herzlich für ihr Engagement danken, nicht zuletzt auch dem Team der Kunsthalle Zürich für seine beflügelnde Energie. Mein besonderer Dank geht an die Autoren Vincent Romagny, Sreejata Roy und Xavier de la Salle sowie an den Grafiker Dan Solbach und an Rahel Blättler für die Redaktion. Den Leihgebern, die ihre Werke zur Verfügung stellten, und allen Personen, die unsere Institution unterstützen und tragen, bin ich zutiefst verpflichtet. Für die Förderung der Ausstellung möchte ich der Ernst Göhner Stiftung herzlich danken sowie der Stadt und dem Kanton Zürich und der Luma Stiftung für

Foreword

Why should an art museum organize an exhibition about playgrounds? I am convinced that the two can learn a great deal from one another and are fundamentally similar in nature. Both develop their potential as clearly defined free spaces, as public places and experimental fields for aesthetics. Both invite non-professionals and insiders, children and adults to use them as laboratories in order to give their thoughts and movements free rein to experience new things, test out the unknown, and enter into relationships. They may be niches, but their subversive potential is not to be underestimated.

And yet it is striking that the history of art museums and art institutions has been thoroughly documented, while the history of playgrounds remains to be explored. This is now changing with this publication and the exhibition that it accompanies. But why is no one interested in playgrounds? One possible reason is that you cannot build a successful career by designing a playground—neither as an architect, nor as an artist, city planner, or designer. The same is true of historians: the topic is neither a route to prestige nor to teaching positions. Since they are neither perceived as buildings nor as landscapes, art, or architecture, they have never been designated for preservation—luckily, we say, since this has allowed them to continue to change, improve, become worse, or simply disappear.

For several years, the city planner Gabriela Burkhalter has researched the history of these urban spaces and has made her findings available to the world through the website www.architekturfuerkinder.ch. The material she has discovered has proven to be so unique that we decided to turn it into a major exhibition. In an initial, small-scale version, *The Playground Project* opened in 2013 in Pittsburgh as part of the *2013 Carnegie International*. Three years later, the project is now being shown for the first time in full at Kunsthalle Zürich, and includes play sculptures for younger visitors. It presents a cornucopia of ideas, designs, and realized projects. Not only can the visitor discover all the different kinds of things that have been done, but also what might be and what remains to be done. The exhibition examines the role of art in public spaces from an unexpected perspective, as well as the relationship between art and its function. *The Playground Project* consults the past and the present so that we can work for a better future. I cannot thank Gabriela Burkhalter enough for her dedication, research, and generosity.

I would like to thank everyone who was involved in this project for their dedication, and not least the team at Kunsthalle Zürich for

ihre treue Unterstützung der Kunsthalle Zürich. Der grösste Dank aber geht an alle Gestalter, Architekten, Aktivisten und Künstler, die unseren Kindern Treffpunkte bauen, wo sie lernen, Risiken einzugehen, Verantwortung zu übernehmen, Konflikte zu bewältigen, Spiele zu erfinden und Freiräume zu erschliessen.

Daniel Baumann
Direktor Kunsthalle Zürich

their inspiring energy. Special thanks go to the authors Vincent Romagny, Sreejata Roy, and Xavier de la Salle, as well as the graphic designer Dan Solbach, and Rahel Blättler, the director of publications. I am deeply grateful to the lenders who provided their works for the exhibition, and to everyone who supports our institution. For their support of the exhibition I would like to thank the Ernst Göhner Stiftung and the city and canton of Zurich, as well as the Luma Foundation for their loyal patronage of Kunsthalle Zürich. And my greatest thanks go to the designers, architects, activists, and artists who build meeting places for our children where they learn to take risks and responsibilities, overcome conflicts, invent games, and claim free spaces.

Daniel Baumann
Director, Kunsthalle Zürich

The **Playground Project**

Gabriela Burkhalter

4   Spielende Kinder auf dem / Children playing at the
Washington Park playground (Hill District, Pittsburgh), c. 1908

„Mein erster Besuch des Emdrup-Spielplatzes verblüffte mich zutiefst. Die Erkenntnis traf mich wie ein Blitz und ich realisierte, dass ich etwas Neuartiges betrachtete, etwas, das unzählige Möglichkeiten bot."[1] So beschrieb die Engländerin Marjory Allen, Kämpferin für Kinderrechte, ihren ersten Eindruck 1946 angesichts von Carl Theodor Sørensens Skrammellegeplads (Gerümpelspielplatz) in Emdrup, Dänemark. Ähnliche Momente des ungläubigen Staunens erlebte ich, als ich mehr und mehr von der Geschichte des Spielplatzes erfuhr. Was erst als unwichtige Nische schien, entpuppte sich als Experimentierfeld im öffentlichen Raum, als Reibungsfläche zwischen innovativen und etablierten Vorstellungen und als Projektionsfläche für Erwachsene und Kinder – kurz: als Ort mit subversivem Potential.

Der Spielplatz ist ein Nebenprodukt der industrialisierten Stadt des 20. Jahrhunderts. Bis heute ist er hässliches Entlein und viel umworbener Raum zugleich. In ihm kondensieren Vorstellungen von Erziehung und Kindheit, von Stadtplanung und öffentlichem Raum, von Architektur und Kunst, von Kreativität und Kontrolle. Dabei entzog sich der Spielplatz immer wieder der institutionellen und ideologischen Vereinnahmung und trug seine eigenen, zuweilen anarchischen Blüten. Dieses Nebeneinander von unterschiedlichen Erwartungen, momentanen Errungenschaften und radikalen Entwicklungen macht diesen Ort überhaupt erst spannend. Da Spielplätze fast nie als Teil des kulturellen Erbes angesehen wurden, ist vieles davon in Vergessenheit geraten oder kaum noch nachvollziehbar. Dabei haben wir alle nicht selten präzise Erinnerungen an diese Nische: Dort trafen wir unsere Freunde, gingen unbewusst Risiken ein, wagten stolz Neues, lernten mit Konflikten umzugehen und sie zu schlichten.

In der Entwicklung des Spielplatzes im Laufe der letzten 150 Jahre sind vier Paradigmenwechsel erkennbar: Anfang des 20. Jahrhunderts holten Sozialreformer das Kind von der Strasse auf den Spielplatz. Zu Beginn der 1930er Jahre kam die Idee auf, dass Kinder weniger auf Spielgeräten, sondern vielmehr mit natürlichen Materialien spielen sollten. Im Jahrzehnt der Selbstverwaltung und des Do-it-yourself, in den 1960er Jahren, glaubte man, dass Eltern, Kinder und Nachbarschaftsgruppen am besten selbst aktiv werden. Die 1980er Jahre kündigten mit dem Ende der gesellschaftlichen und politischen Utopien auch eine Krise der Spielplatzgestaltung an.

Dieser Essay macht sich zur Aufgabe, ein möglichst komplettes Bild der vielseitigen Wechselwirkungen und oft parallel verlaufenden Entfaltungen sowie der ihnen zugrundeliegenden Kräfte zu geben. Der Fokus liegt dabei auf Spielplätzen im öffentlichen Raum, wo sie den spannungsreichsten Situationen ausgesetzt sind. Er spricht Entwicklungen in den verschiedenen Ländern an und würdigt die wichtigsten Akteure und ihre Beiträge. Trotz mehrjähriger Forschung ist diese Geschichte bei weitem nicht abgeschlossen, denn noch immer tauchen unverhofft neue Gestalter und Beispiele aus anderen Ländern und Kontinenten auf.

1. Sozialreformer und die Anfänge der Spielplatzbewegung

Bereits am Ende des 19. Jahrhunderts gab es in den industrialisierten Städten Englands, Deutschlands und der USA

"I was completely swept off my feet by my first visit to the Emdrup playground. In a flash of understanding I realized that I was looking of something quite new and full of possibilities."[1] This was the English children's rights activist Marjory Allen's first impression on seeing Carl Theodor Sørensen's Skrammellegeplads ("junk playground") in Emdrup, Denmark, in 1946. I had similar moments of unbelievable astonishment as I learned more and more about the history of playgrounds. What at first seemed like an insignificant niche turned out to be a realm of public experimentation, a cause of conflict between innovative and established perspectives, and something for both adults and children to project their desires onto—in short, playgrounds are sites of subversive potential.

The playground is a byproduct of the industrialized city of the 20th century. Even now, it continues to be both an ugly duckling and a coveted space. A focal point for ideas about education and childhood, urban planning and public space, architecture and art, creativity and control, the playground has repeatedly resisted institutional and ideological appropriation and grown in its own sometimes quite anarchic ways. The coexistence of contradictory expectations, moments of temporary progress, and radical developments makes playgrounds so exciting. Still, as hardly anyone sees playgrounds as part of their cultural heritage, much of their history has been forgotten or can barely be understood anymore—even if all of us often have quite precise personal memories of this niche where we met our friends, took pride in new things we dared to do, braved danger without thinking about it, and learned to confront and resolve conflicts.

There have been four paradigm shifts in the development of the playground over the course of the last 150 years. First, at the beginning of the 20th century, social reformers took children off the street and onto the playground. Then, at the beginning of the 1930s, the idea arose that children should play with natural materials rather than playground equipment. In the 1960s, the decade of autonomy and do-it-yourself, parents, children, and neighborhood groups began to take charge of playgrounds themselves. Finally, in the 1980s, with the end of social and political utopias, a crisis in playground design began.

With a focus on playgrounds in public spaces, where they are subject to the most contradictions, my goal is to provide as complete a picture as possible of the multiple feedback loops and often parallel developments in the history of playgrounds, as well as the forces underlying them in a wide range of countries, and the contributions of the most important individuals. Despite several years of research, this story is far from

Spielplätze. Diese standen im Dienst der Volksgesundheit und der Überwachung der Kinder, sollten sie vor den Gefahren der Stadt schützen und Kriminalität verhindern. Kaiser Wilhelm II. mahnte auf dem Berliner Schulkongress 1890: „Wir müssen eine kräftige Generation haben!", worauf sich Einrichtungen zur „Förderung von Spielen und körperlichen Übung" mehrten.[2] In den USA führten Einwanderung und Industrialisierung zu einer katastrophalen Wohnsituation in Städten wie New York, was entscheidend zur Entwicklung des Spielplatzes beitrug. Mit der Reglementierung der Kinderarbeit ab Anfang des 20. Jahrhunderts stellte sich immer dringender die Frage, wo Kinder ihre Freizeit verbringen sollten. Zudem waren viele Arbeiterkinder tagsüber ohne Aufsicht. Die amerikanische Spielplatzbewegung nahm 1868 in Boston ihren Anfang: Nach deutschem Vorbild richtete man einen Sandhaufen für das Kinderspiel ein – eine Idee, die bald Nachahmer in anderen amerikanischen Städten fand.[3] Der Bostoner Philanthrop und Spielplatzpionier Joseph Lee (1862–1937) war bemüht, den idealen Spielplatz zu entwickeln, und sorgte für dessen Verbreitung. Damalige Plätze sahen wie Freiluftturnhallen aus, waren betreut und mit Geräten zum Klettern, Schaukeln und Rutschen bestückt. Von privaten Vereinen initiiert und auf Mass angefertigt, erscheinen sie uns heute kühn (Abb. 3–6). Angeregt durch die Erfahrung in Boston nahmen sich auch in anderen Städten – New York, Chicago, Philadelphia – philanthropische Gruppen der Situation an und bekämpften Armut und Vernachlässigung, wollten aber auch Einfluss auf die Erziehung und Sozialisierung der Kinder und Jugendlichen nehmen. 1890 setzte sich Charles B. Stover (1861–1929), der im Settlement House Movement der philanthropischen Sozialreformer aktiv war, für die Schaffung von Spielplätzen auf leeren öffentlichen und privaten Grundstücken in New York ein.[4] Deren Erfolg brachte das Parks Department dazu, 1903 den ersten von der Stadt finanzierten Spielplatz zu eröffnen, den in der Lower East Side gelegenen Seward Park. New York übernahm nun die Führung unter den amerikanischen Städten im Bezug auf Spiel- und Freizeiteinrichtungen, die sowohl in Parks als auch auf Schulgeländen angelegt wurden. Die Spielplatzbewegung vernetzte sich und tauschte sich regelmässig an nationalen Kongressen aus.[5]

Seit den 1930er Jahren lösten preiswerte, solide und unzerstörbare Stahlrohrgeräte ab Katalog die bis anhin individuell gebauten Spielgeräte ab. Zudem wollte die öffentliche Hand auf die Dauer nicht für die Löhne der Spielplatzbetreuer aufkommen.[6]

Als 1934 der Politikwissenschaftler und Politiker Robert Moses (1888–1981) vom New Yorker Bürgermeister Fiorello La Guardia zum Parks Commissioner ernannt wurde, begann eine Zeit tiefgreifender Veränderungen. Wie kaum ein anderer hat Moses den New Yorker Stadtraum geprägt, Strassen, Brücken und öffentliche Grünanlagen sowie Einrichtungen für Sport, Freizeit und Spiel gebaut. Er standardisierte das Design der Spielplätze und setzte eine flächendeckende Versorgung mit Spielraum um: Allein im Central Park liess er 20 Spielplätze anlegen. Die Kinder fanden gefängnisartige *pipe frame exercice units* vor: nach Geschlecht und Alter getrennte Spielbereiche mit standardisierten Geräten aus Stahlrohr auf asphaltiertem Untergrund. Bis zu seinem Amtsrücktritt 1960 blieb Moses diesem Konzept treu, wofür er jedoch zunehmend Kritik von Spielplatzexperten und Stadtplanern erntete.

being closed, for even now unexpected new faces and examples from other countries and continents keep coming to my attention.

1. Social Reformers and the Beginnings of the Playground Movement

At the end of the 19th century, there were already playgrounds in the industrialized cities of England, Germany, and the United States. They were meant to promote public health, to prevent criminality, and to supervise children and protect them from the dangers of the city. In 1890, Kaiser Wilhelm II announced at the Berlin School Congress that, "we have to have a strong generation!" This led to an increase in facilities for "the encouragement of games and physical training."[2] In American cities like New York, immigration and industrialization created catastrophic living conditions, which were decisive in the development of playgrounds. As child labor began to be regulated at the beginning of the 20th century, the issue of what children should do with their free time grew more and more urgent, with many children in the working class being completely unsupervised during the day. The American playground movement had actually begun in Boston in 1868, when a German model inspired the creation of a sand garden for children to play in.[3] The idea soon had imitators in other American cities. The Boston philanthropist and playground pioneer Joseph Lee (1862–1937) tried to develop the ideal playground and promote their diffusion. At the time, they looked like open-air gymnasiums, with supervision, and with swings, slides, and things to climb on. Custom-made by private associations, they seem quite audacious from our perspective (ill. 3–6). Encouraged by developments in Boston, philanthropic groups in other cities—New York, Chicago, Philadelphia— took up the cause in a fight against poverty and neglect that was also meant to influence the education and socialization of children and teenagers. In 1890, Charles B. Stover (1861–1929), who was active in the Settlement House Movement of philanthropic social reformers, began a campaign for the creation of playgrounds on both public and private empty lots in New York.[4] The playgrounds were so successful that in 1903 the Parks Department opened the first playground financed by the city itself, Seward Park on the Lower East Side. New York now took the lead among American cities in playgrounds and recreational facilities, establishing them both in parks and on school grounds. At the same time, the playground movement was also developing into a network of local associations that met regularly at national congresses.[5]

In the 1930s, inexpensive, solid, and indestructible steel structures ordered from

N. Y. Playground, 1910 / 1915

5

Rings and Poles, Bronx Park, New York, 1911

6

15

8   Robinsonspielplatz und Gemeinschaftszentrum / Robinson Crusoe playground and community center, Wipkingen, Zürich / Zurich, c. 1960

9   „Spiel-Dörfli" auf dem Robinsonspielplatz / Hamlet of play-houses in the Robinson Crusoe playground, c. 1955

10   Doppelseite aus / Spread from Arvid Bengtsson, *Environmental Planning for Children's Play*, Praeger, New York 1970, p. 142–143.

4

2

5

3

6

18

2 Table tennis area sheltered by a wooden
   wall
3 Work tables outside the playground building
4 The central area
5 Play hut
6 The asphalt-surfaced hill is popular for
   cycling and cart riding
7 Circular bank for rope games
8 From the top of the hill you can run your
   cart right into the sand — furthest wins

7

8

143

Zu seinen schärfsten Kritikern gehörte die Journalistin Jane Jacobs (1916–2006), deren Analyse der amerikanischen Stadtplanungspolitik (*The Death and Life of Great American Cities*, 1961) für Furore sorgte.[7]

2. Auf der Suche nach dem kreativen Spiel

Parallel zu den Bemühungen der Sozialreformer Ende des 19. Jahrhunderts gewann die Reformpädagogik, die eine kindergerechtere Erziehung verlangte, stetig an Anhängern. Zahlreiche Arbeiten zur Kinder- und Jugendpsychologie aus den ersten Jahrzehnten des 20. Jahrhunderts stützen ihre Forderungen auch aus wissenschaftlicher Sicht.[8] Forschern wie etwa dem Schweizer Entwicklungspsychologen Jean Piaget (1896–1980) gelangen wichtige Beweise, dass die Kindheit in der Menschwerdung ein zentraler Moment ist. In verständlicher Sprache geschriebene Bücher und Artikel machten die Ergebnisse einem breiten Publikum zugänglich, so beispielsweise ab den 1930er Jahren in Dänemark oder nach dem Zweiten Weltkrieg in den USA. Der Kinderarzt und Psychologe Arnold Gesell (1880–1961) veröffentlichte dort den Erziehungsratgeber *Infant and Child in the Culture of Today* (1943) und der Kinderarzt und Psychiater Benjamin Spock (1903–1998) seinen Bestseller *Baby and Child Care* (1946).[9] Aufbauend auf diesen Erkenntnissen und getragen von der Aufbruchstimmung in Kunst, Architektur und Landschaftsarchitektur testeten Schweden, Dänemark und Holland in der Zwischen- und Nachkriegszeit neue Spielplatzkonzepte und gaben international die stärksten Impulse. Im Unterschied zum Spielplatz der Sozialreformer stand nun das freie Spiel als Urbedürfnis des Kindes im Zentrum.

Kaum ein anderes modernes Konzept hat einen tiefgreifenderen und nachhaltigeren Einfluss ausgeübt als der Skrammellegeplads. Unterstützt durch den dänischen Lehrer Hans Dragehjelm (1875–1948) war Carl Theodor Sørensen (s. S. 185) davon überzeugt, dass das natürliche Spiel für das Kind das Beste sei. Dragehjelm hatte bereits 1908 eine Studienreise nach Deutschland unternommen, um mehr über das dort bereits verbreitete Spielen im Sand zu erfahren.[10] Seine dabei gesammelten Erkenntnisse publizierte er 1909 auf dänisch und deutsch und beschrieb unter anderem, wie das Spielen mit Sand, Wasser und Erde die Gesundheit, aber auch die Phantasie fördere: „Sand, der grösste Pädagoge […], spornt das spielende Kind an, Idee an Idee zu reihen."[11] Dragehjelm richtete Kopenhagens ersten Sandplatz ein, worauf die Idee sehr populär wurde. Für Sørensen war der Sandplatz zusammen mit einem Planschbecken fester Bestandteil seiner Spielplätze für Siedlungen. Im Skrammellegeplads, wie er ihn 1943 in Emdrup erstmals realisierte, gab Sørensen dem kreativen Moment noch mehr Raum: Das Kind erhielt Material und Werkzeug, um sich seine eigene Welt zu bauen.

Zur gleichen Zeit ging auch das Nachbarland Schweden im Bereich Landschafts- und Spielplatzplanung neue Wege, um die schlechte Lebensqualität in der Hauptstadt zu verbessern und der Bevölkerung mehr Grün- und Spielräume anzubieten. Als Teil dieses Programms wurde 1949 im Stockholmer Volkspark erstmals eine abstrakte Spielskulptur in einem Sandbecken aufgestellt. *Tufsen*, geheimnisvolle Rutsche und Kletterberg in einem, weckte die kindliche Phantasie und Neugier. Die vom schwedisch-dänischen Künstler Egon Møller-

catalogues began to replace the individually built equipment used until then. In addition, local governments began to lose interest in paying for playground supervisors.[6]

After the political scientist and politician Robert Moses (1888–1981) was named Parks Commissioner by New York Mayor Fiorello La Guardia in 1934, Moses changed New York City at least as much as anyone else ever has, building streets, bridges, and public parks, as well as facilities for sports, recreation, and play. He standardized the design of playgrounds and established play areas all over the city, with 20 new playgrounds in Central Park alone. But what the children were given were prison-like "pipe frame exercise units": playgrounds separated by age and gender with standardized steel equipment on asphalt foundations. Moses kept developing such facilities until his retirement in 1960, even though he was increasingly criticized by playground experts and city planners, as well as by the journalist Jane Jacobs (1916–2006) in her vehement 1961 critique of American urban-planning policy, *The Death and Life of Great American Cities*.[7]

2. In Search of Creative Play

At the end of the 19th century, alongside the efforts of social reformers, the idea of progressive education steadily gained more supporters; its goal was to make education more appropriate for children. Numerous early 20th-century works on the psychology of children and teenagers offer a scientific perspective as the basis for their claims.[8] Researchers like the Swiss developmental psychologist Jean Piaget (1896–1980) convincingly demonstrated how important childhood is to becoming human. Books and articles for a popular audience made such results available to a broader public, in Denmark in the 1930s, for example, and then in the United States after the Second World War. In 1943, the American pediatrician and psychologist Arnold Gesell (1880–1961) published the educational advice book *Infant and Child in the Culture of Today*, and in 1946, Benjamin Spock (1903–1998), another American pediatrician and psychiatrist, followed with his bestseller *Baby and Child Care*.[9] In this period, the strongest international impulses for playgrounds came from Sweden, Denmark, and Holland before and after the war, where new playground concepts emerged that were based on psychological research, and encouraged by the latest developments in art, architecture, and landscape architecture. Unlike the playground of the social reformers, the focus was now on free play as one of children's fundamental needs.

Hardly any other modern concept had a more far-reaching and enduring influence than the Skrammellegeplads. Inspired by the

Nielsen (s. S. 139) geschaffene Plastik war weder Monument noch Inszenierung einer Ideologie. Vielmehr verband sie erstmals abstrakte Kunst mit Spiel im öffentlichen Raum und war Ausdruck eines anti-elitären Kunstverständnisses. Dieser neue Ansatz löste ab den 1950er Jahren einen Boom von Spielskulpturen aus.

Ein dritter Entwicklungsstrang nahm in Amsterdam unter der Leitung des städtischen Planungsamtes seinen Anfang. Bereits vor dem Zweiten Weltkrieg hatte die Stadt begonnen, ein neues Konzept für mehr öffentliche Spielflächen zu entwickeln. Einer ihrer jungen Angestellten, der Architekt Aldo van Eyck (s. S. 89), setzte das Vorhaben konsequent um: 1947 entwarf er für die vom Krieg gezeichnete Innenstadt einen grossen Sandplatz mit elementaren Klettergerüsten, jedoch ohne diesen von der unmittelbaren Stadtumgebung zu trennen (Abb. 7). Es gelang van Eyck, einen durchlässigen Ort für Spiel und Begegnung zu schaffen. Damit unterlief er die gängige Praxis des Congrès Internationaux d'Architecture Moderne (CIAM), der mit einer Politik der grossen Würfe Zwischenräume überging. Stattdessen verhalf van Eyck ebendiesen zu Aufmerksamkeit und gab ihnen eine neue Bedeutung.[12]

In New York entwarf der amerikanisch-japanische Künstler Isamu Noguchi (s. S. 155) Anfang der 1930er Jahre zum ersten Mal überhaupt Spiellandschaften. Diese kamen ohne jegliche Spielgeräte aus und setzten dagegen Erdmodellierungen, Sand und Wasser ein. Zwischen 1933 und 1966 entwarf Noguchi mehrere Projekte für Parks in New York, die jedoch alle scheiterten. Als Modelle wurden sie im Museum of Modern Art in New York ausgestellt, wo sie Gestalter wie M. Paul Friedberg (s. S. 99) und Richard Dattner (s. S. 79) inspirierten. Ihre Spiellandschaften lösten ab Mitte der 1960er Jahre in New York die sogenannte „Spielplatzrevolution" aus.

Diese verschiedenen neuen Spielkonzepte gelangten erst nach dem Zweiten Weltkrieg ins Bewusstsein breiter Kreise. Eine entscheidende Rolle kam dabei gut vernetzten „Spielplatzadvokaten" zu: Allen voran der Engländerin Marjory Allen (s. S. 51), die den Skrammellegeplads nach England brachte und seine Verbreitung unter der Bezeichnung „Adventure Playground" (Abenteuerspielplatz) förderte. Der Spielplatz-Lobbyist Alfred Ledermann (s. S. 109) brachte das Konzept in die Schweiz und engagierte sich international für kindergerechte Spielplätze. In Schweden verhalf Arvid Bengtsson (1916–1993) als Direktor des Gartenbauamtes ab 1951 in Helsingborg und ab 1962 in Göteborg dem Abenteuerspielplatz und dem Spiel im öffentlichen Raum zum Durchbruch (Abb. 10).

In Dänemark bildete sich um den Psychologen, Pädagogen und Kinderbuchautor Jens Sigsgaard (1910–1991), den Architekten Max Siegumfeldt und Carl Theodor Sørensen eine starke Spielplatz-Lobby: 1959 gründeten sie die Dansk Legeplads Selskab (Dänische Spielplatzvereinigung), und 1961, zusammen mit Marjory Allen, die bis heute bestehende International Play Association (IPA). Progressive Zeitschriften wie *Architectural Record*, *Progressive Architecture* und *Landscape Architecture* in den USA, *Architecture d'Aujourd'hui* in Frankreich, *Casabella* und *Domus* in Italien und *Werk* in der Schweiz dienten als Plattformen für die Diskussionen neuer Projekte. Kunstausstellungen wie die *Biennale di Venezia*, die *Triennale di Milano* oder die *Biennale de Paris* sowie Institutionen wie das Centre de Création Industrielle in Paris, das Moderna Museet in Stockholm, das

Danish teacher Hans Dragehjelm (1875–1948), Carl Theodor Sørensen (see p. 185) was convinced that natural play was best for children. In 1908 Dragehjelm undertook a trip to Germany to study playing in sand, which was widespread there.[10] He published the findings from his trip in 1909 in Danish and German and described among other things how playing with sand, water, and earth fostered health and encouraged the imagination: "Sand, the greatest teacher [...] spurs the playing child to generate idea after idea."[11] Dragehjelm set up Copenhagen's first sand playground, which helped popularize the idea. For Sørensen, the sand playground, along with a wading pool, was an essential part of his playgrounds for housing developments. In the Skrammellegeplads as he first realized it in Emdrup in 1943, Sørensen made even more room for the creative moment: the children were given materials and tools to build their own worlds.

At the same time, Denmark's neighbor Sweden also began to pursue new approaches in landscape architecture and playground planning in order to improve the poor quality of life in the capital and offer the population more parks and play areas. In 1949, as part of this program, an abstract sculpture for playing was set up in a sandbox in the People's Park in Stockholm. *Tufsen*, a curious construction for both sliding and climbing, piqued the imagination and curiosity of children. The sculpture by Swedish-Danish artist Egon Møller-Nielsen (see p. 139) was neither a monument nor the expression of an ideology, but the first work of anti-elitist art to connect abstract art and play in a public space. This new approach generated a boom in playground sculptures from the 1950s on.

A third line of playground development originated in Amsterdam in the city's urban planning office. Before the Second World War, the city had already begun to develop new plans for more public playgrounds. The plan was first really put into practice in 1947 by a young architect working for the city, Aldo van Eyck (see p. 89). His huge sand playground with simple jungle gyms was not separated from its immediate urban surroundings, a city center still scarred by the war (ill. 7). As an open public space for children to play and people to meet, this design ran counter to the prevailing practice of the Congrès Internationaux d'Architecture Moderne (CIAM), which focused on large projects and overlooked the spaces between them. Van Eyck drew attention to such intermediate spaces and gave them new significance.[12]

In New York at the beginning of the 1930s, the Japanese-American artist Isamu Noguchi (see p. 155) was the first to design landscapes for play. Doing completely without playground equipment, his designs focused on

MoMA in New York oder das Institute of Contemporary Arts in London boten Künstlern Raum, ihre Spielprojekte einem breiten Publikum zu präsentieren.

Die neuen Ideen fanden nicht zuletzt deshalb immer grösseren Anklang, weil mit der Entwicklung der Freizeitgesellschaft auch neue Spielkonzepte gefragt waren. Durch freie Samstage, mehr Ferien und zunehmenden Wohlstand standen mehr Zeit und Geld zu Verfügung. Neue Unterhaltungsmedien wie Film, Fernsehen und Comics gelangten in Reichweite der jungen Generation, was „rechtschaffenen" Bürgern ein Dorn im Auge war. Nach ihrer Ansicht sollten sich Kinder und Jugendliche nicht der passiven Unterhaltung hingeben, sondern etwas „Sinnvolles" machen. Staatliche und parastaatliche Organisationen nahmen sich dieses „Freizeitproblems" an, so beispielsweise die 1912 gegründete Schweizer Jugendstiftung Pro Juventute. Eine wichtige Plattform war der 1953 von ihr organisierte V. Internationale Kongress für Schulbaufragen und Freilufterziehung in Zürich. Alfred Ledermann, Zentralsekretär der Pro Juventute, gelang es, dem Thema Spielplatz auf dem Kongress einen wichtigen Platz einzuräumen und die Vernetzung auf nationaler und internationaler Ebene zu fördern. Nach dänischem Vorbild setzte Ledermann mit Unterstützung des neugegründeten Zürcher Kreises der Spielplatzfreunde das Konzept des Skrammellegeplads um. 1954 wurde an der Limmat der erste dieser Plätze eröffnet, die in der Schweiz den Namen „Robinsonspielplatz" erhielten. Zu einer anfänglich leeren Wiese mit Baumaterialien und Werkzeug, einem alten Tram als Wetterschutz und einem Spielplatzleiter als Betreuer kamen später ein „Spiel-Dörfli", ein Bauplatz, ein Kleinkinderspielbereich und 1957 Zürichs erstes Gemeinschaftszentrum dazu. Letzteres bot musische und handwerkliche Aktivitäten für die ganze Bevölkerung an, diente der Begegnung und ist bis heute der Ort, wo die Fäden des Quartiers zusammenlaufen (Abb. 8–9). „Wenn die Jungen ausfliegen und auf Abenteuer ausgehen wollen, dann sollen die Eltern beruhigt sein, der Robinsonspielplatz wird in ihrem Wohnquartier die ‚Strasse als Spielplatz' ersetzten, er wird ganz allgemein die Freude am aktiven Spiel fördern und wertvolle Anregungen für Arbeiten am Familientisch vermitteln."[13]

Der visionär-paternalistische Migros-Gründer Gottlieb Duttweiler (1888–1962) nahm die Idee auf und liess zur gleichen Zeit in Rüschlikon in dem von ihm der Öffentlichkeit geschenkten Park im Grüene einen Robinsonspielplatz einrichten (Abb. 11–12). Auf diese Weise engagierte sich das Bürgertum mit Begeisterung und Entschlossenheit in Kinder- und Jugendfragen und machte seinen Einfluss geltend.

Bei der Verbreitung der abstrakten Spielskulptur beteiligten sich dagegen Firmen und kulturelle Institutionen wie Museen. In den USA spielte dabei Creative Playthings[14], eine 1951 in Princeton (New Jersey) gegründete Firma für Spielgeräte, eine bedeutende Rolle. Ihr Mitbegründer Frank Caplan reiste 1953 nach Europa, um dortige Entwicklungen kennenzulernen und verschiedene Künstler unter Vertrag zu nehmen, unter anderem den Schweizer Holz-Plastiker Nino Vitali und den Dänen Egon Møller-Nielsen.[15] Von nun an waren Spielplastiken ab Katalog bestellbar (Abb. 13). Caplan pflegte auch engen Kontakt mit dem MoMA in New York und gemeinsam schrieben sie 1954 die Play Sculpture Competition aus, einen Wettbewerb für Spielskulptur.

sand, water, and landscaping. Between 1933 and 1966, Noguchi worked on a number of projects for parks in New York; however, not a single one of them was ever realized. Still, they were displayed as models at The Museum of Modern Art in New York, where they inspired other designers, such as M. Paul Friedberg (see p. 99) and Richard Dattner (see p. 79). Starting in the mid-1960s, their playground designs led to a "playground revolution" in New York.

This wide variety of new playground concepts only became known to a wider public after the Second World War. An important role in this growing awareness was played by an international network of "playground advocates," above all Marjory Allen in England (see p. 51). Allen introduced the Skrammellegeplads to England and promoted the idea as "Adventure Playground." The playground lobbyist Alfred Ledermann (see p. 109) introduced them in Switzerland and campaigned internationally for playgrounds that were appropriate for children. In Sweden, Arvid Bengtsson (1916–1993) helped popularize the adventure playground and the idea of play in public space as the director of the parks office in Helsingborg from 1961 to 1962, and then in the same role in Göteborg from 1962 on (ill. 10). In Denmark, a strong playground lobby formed around Carl Theodor Sørensen, the architect Max Siegumfeldt, and the psychologist, teacher, and children's book author Jens Sigsgaard (1910–1991): in 1959, they founded the Dansk Legeplads Selskab (the Danish Playground Association), and in 1961 Marjory Allen joined with them to establish the International Play Association (the IPA, which still exists today). Progressive magazines like Architecture d'Aujourd'hui in France, Werk in Switzerland, Casabella and Domus in Italy, and Architectural Record, Progressive Architecture, and Landscape Architecture in the United States created opportunities to discuss new projects. Art exhibitions like the Biennale di Venezia, the Triennale di Milano, and the Biennale de Paris, as well as such institutions as the Centre de Création Industrielle in Paris, the Moderna Museet in Stockholm, MoMA in New York, and the Institute of Contemporary Arts in London, provided space for artists to present their playground projects to a wider public.

These ideas caught on in part because the growth of leisure society encouraged new concepts of play. With more vacation, increasing prosperity, and many adults no longer working on Saturdays, people had more time and money. New entertainment technology like movies, television, and comics was becoming accessible to the younger generation. This irritated many "upright" citizens, who thought that children and teenagers should not indulge in passive entertainment, but instead do something

11 Park im Grüene, Robinsonspielplatz / Robinson Crusoe playground, Rüschlikon, c. 1954 / 1955

12 Park im Grüene, Robinsonspielplatz / Robinson Crusoe playground, Ballonwettbewerb / Balloon competition, Rüschlikon, 1955

23

P2 SPIRAL SLIDE©

Polished cast stone with marble aggregate, steel reinforced. Galvanized steel ladder of 1½" I.D. pipe. Four pre-finished sections are assembled on site, steel studs are welded to form continuous structure; joints are grouted, entire unit polished and waxed. Price includes assembly and finishing. Height 9'4". Diameter at base 11'0" wide. 5'6" outside diameter. Footing inside opening 3'6".
8 tons

F.O.B. Yonkers, N.Y., $3600.00

spirals *and* he

enter a cave . . . scale a l

climb to top of a mountain . . .

slide down the slippe

Tobogganing with proved safety, activ
saving, free form with boldness and
both of these unique slides the feature
every playground.

10

"meaningful." The "problem of free time" was taken up by governmental and para-governmental organizations such as Pro Juventute, a Swiss foundation for children and teenagers that was founded in 1912. An important platform was the Fifth International Congress on School Construction and Open-Air Education organized in Zurich in 1953. Alfred Ledermann, the General Secretary of Pro Juventute, made playgrounds a central theme of the congress and encouraged national and international cooperation. With the support of the newly founded Zurich Circle of Playground Friends, Ledermann then took up the Danish model of the Skrammellegeplads and opened the first "Robinson Crusoe playground" on the Limmat in 1954 (as they came to be called in Switzerland). At

Robert W. Crawford (1906–1995), Freizeit-Beauftragter der Stadt Philadelphia, gab in der landesweiten Diskussion um Freizeitplanung und Gestaltung von Spielplätzen wichtige Impulse. Er machte Philadelphia zum Mekka für neue Spielskulpturen und liess Møller-Nielsens *Saddle Slide* (1954) oder die „eigensinnigen" Spielgeräte von Joseph Brown (s. S. 59) installieren (Abb. 14). Die abstrakten Spielskulpturen entsprachen dem Zeitgeist, der die Kreativität im Kind fördern wollte. Das Angebot wuchs und bald gehörte es für städtische Ämter zum guten Ton, Spielskulpturen einzusetzen. Die zunehmende Massenproduktion brachte jedoch eine Banalisierung des Designs mit sich.

Einen vergleichbaren Boom erlebte die Spielskulptur Ende der 1950er Jahre in Wien. Auch hier war Møller-Nielsens Werk ausschlaggebend. Zudem ist van Eycks Konzept des nahtlosen Übergangs zwischen Spielskulptur und Stadt erkennbar. Das Wiener Stadtgartenamt beabsichtigte, individuell gestaltete Spielräume in Reichweite der Kinder anzubieten, wofür zahlreiche Künstler Aufträge erhielten. Im Gegensatz zu den USA handelte es sich hier immer um aufwendige Einzelanfertigungen, die versuchten, den Status als Kunst und die Funktion als Spielobjekt in Balance zu halten. Einer der herausragenden Vertreter war der Plastiker Josef Schagerl (s. S. 165).

In der Schweiz blieb die Entwicklung bei Spielskulpturen in Form von Tieren stehen. Erst in den 1960er Jahren wagten Künstler Experimente im öffentlichen Raum, durchbrachen überholte Vorstellungen und gaben sich der Lust zum waghalsigen Spiel hin. Frühe Beispiele sind Bernhard Luginbühls (1929–2011) *Zyklop* und Michael Grosserts (1927–2014) Spielhof für die Primarschule Aumatten in Reinach bei Basel, beide aus dem Jahr 1967 (Abb. 15–17). Eine Erfolgsgeschichte der besonderen Art begann 1972 mit der Spielplastik *Lozziwurm* des Zürcher Künstlers Yvan Pestalozzi (geb. 1937). Für einmal gelang es, ein bestechend einfaches Design mit hohem Spielwert in Serie zu produzieren und über hundert Mal im öffentlichen Raum aufzustellen (Abb. 21).

3. Selbstermächtigung in den 1960er Jahren

Die Ereignisse von 1968 wälzten neben Politik und Gesellschaft auch die Vorstellungen von Umwelt, Kindheit und Erziehung um. „Kreativität" und „Selbstbestimmung" wurden zu Zauberwörtern und die Pädagogik suchte nach neuen Wegen, um diese Fähigkeiten gerade auch beim Kind zu fördern. Der gemeinsame Nenner der heterogenen Bewegungen war die Infragestellung von Autoritäten, so auch in der Gestaltung von Spielplätzen. Diese sollte nicht mehr den Behörden überlassen werden, da der öffentliche nun als demokratischer Raum aufgefasst wurde. Das demokratische Feilschen um Lösungen durch alle Beteiligten wurde wichtiger Bestandteil der Gestaltung. Handschrift und Vormacht eines Einzelnen waren nicht mehr gefragt, vielmehr ging es darum, neuartige, anti-autoritäre und anti-institutionelle Spielkonzepte zu erproben. Eine wichtige Rolle spielten dabei Handbücher und selbstverlegte Pamphlete, die Ideen öffentlich machten und eine wichtige Grundlage zur Selbstermächtigung bildeten. Die DIY-Bewegung ermunterte die Leute, die verschiedensten Lebensbereiche selbst zu gestalten, so auch Spielplätze. Sie wurde in den USA zum ernstzunehmenden Akteur, denn sie brachte zahlreiche gemeinschaftlich erbaute Spielräume hervor.

to meet ever since (ill. 8–9). "When their children want to go out and have adventures, their parents will not have to worry about them at all. The Robinson Crusoe playground replaces the 'street as playground' in their neighborhood, and more generally, it fosters the children's enjoyment of active play and provides valuable ideas for things to do to the family table."[13]

At the same time, the founder of Migros, the visionary paternalist Gottlieb Duttweiler (1888–1962), took up the idea and opened a Robinson Crusoe playground in a park (the Park im Grüene) that he donated to the town of Rüschlikon (ill. 11–12). With enthusiasm and determination the bourgeoisie began to make their influence felt in children's and teenagers' issues.

The spread of abstract playground sculptures, though, was driven by companies and cultural institutions like museums. In the United States, a major role was played by Creative Playthings,[14] a playground equipment company founded in Princeton, New Jersey, in 1951. In 1953, its co-founder Frank Caplan traveled to Europe to see new developments there and to sign contracts with several artists, including the Swiss wood sculptor Nino Vitali and the Danish sculptor Egon Møller-Nielsen.[15] From then on, playground sculptures could be ordered from a catalogue (ill. 13). Caplan was also in close contact with MoMA in New York, and in 1954 the museum and Creative Playthings ran a Play Sculpture Competition for playground design.

Robert W. Crawford (1906–1995), Philadelphia's Commissioner of Recreation, contributed new impulses to the nationwide discussion of recreation planning and playground design. He made Philadelphia the capital of new playground sculptures and was responsible for the installation of Møller-Nielsen's *Saddle Slide* (1954) and Joseph Brown's idiosyncratic playground equipment (ill. 14; see p. 59). The abstract playground sculptures fit the mood of the age, which wanted to promote creativity in children. The supply grew, and soon it was good form for city governments to install playground sculptures, even if mass production led to more and more banal designs.

A comparable boom in playground sculptures took place in Vienna at the end of the 1950s. Møller-Nielsen's work was again important, as was van Eyck's concept of a seamless transition between playground sculptures and the city. Vienna's City Parks Office wanted to offer individually designed playgrounds in easy range of children, and numerous artists were given design commissions. Unlike in the United States, these were all expensive, custom-made works that tried to balance their status as art works and their function as playground installations. One of the

Planen und Bauen in Zusammenarbeit mit den zukünftigen Nutzern wurde in den Städten Amerikas zentral. An keinem anderen Ort wurde so viel Hoffnung in den „heilenden" Effekt des Spiels und dessen Verbreitung im öffentlichen Raum gesetzt. Nach dem Wirtschaftswunder der 1950er Jahre hatten die 1960er Jahre mit Rassenkrawallen und der Trennung zwischen weissen Suburbs und schwarzen Innenstädten grosse Ernüchterung gebracht. Bestimmte Innenstadtquartiere verkamen zu Slums, und Kriminalität machte sich breit. Unzählige Strategien sowie von Ämtern und privaten Gruppen getragene Initiativen versuchten diese Abwärtsspirale zu stoppen: In New York sollten Strassenfestivals, Feste in Parks und Kunsthappenings den öffentlichen Raum beleben und sicherer machen. Theater und Museen verliessen ihre Komfortzone, um ausserhalb der festen Mauern ihrem Publikum zu begegnen. Leere und vermüllte Parzellen wurden temporär in öffentliche Spielplätze, Gärten oder Plätze verwandelt. Der legendäre und bis heute bestehende Paley Park[16] in New Yorks Midtown von 1967 war der erste solche *Vest Pocket Park*, ein „Westentaschen-Park". Der Landschaftsarchitekt M. Paul Friedberg zählt zu den Pionieren, die solchen Resträumen vorübergehend eine neue Nutzung zuschrieben, er entwarf eine Reihe von Spielplatzmodulen, die flexibel und temporär eingesetzt werden konnten.

Der Ausdruck „to raise a barn" - das ab dem 18. Jahrhundert praktizierte, gemeinsame Errichten einer Scheune im ländlichen Nordamerika - ist ein treffendes Bild eines Gemeinschaftswerks, das mehr als die Summe einzelner Initiativen ist. Diese Vorgehensweise und Tradition lebt in den USA bis heute als sogenanntes „Advocacy Planning" weiter. Einer der Wegbereiter des Ansatzes war der in Deutschland geborene Landschaftsarchitekt Karl Linn (1923–2005). Nach seiner Emigration in die USA entwarf er Landschaftsgärten für reiche Vorstädter. Von der Kibbutz-Bewegung geprägt, vermisste Linn in den boomenden Vorstädten die öffentlichen Räume und das gemeinschaftliche Leben. 1959 nahm er einen Lehrauftrag im Departement für Landschaftsplanung und Architektur an der University of Pennsylvania in Philadelphia an. Er führte ein Community Design-and-Build Service Program ein, um die Landschaftsarchitektur gesellschaftlich relevanter zu machen. Statt nur Vorlesungen zu halten und trockene Übungen anzubieten, fuhr er mit seinen Studenten in vernachlässigte Innenstadtquartiere. Zuerst evaluierten sie, wie die Bewohner den öffentlichen Raum nutzen und ihn sich aneignen. Gestützt auf ihre Beobachtungen planten und bauten sie 1960 zusammen mit lokalen Organisationen auf Abbruchparzellen einen öffentlichen Spiel- und Begegnungsraum, die sogenannten „Melon Block Commons", deren Erfolg zu weiteren Anfragen aus anderen Städten führte. Leiter des Bauteams war der Zimmermann Paul Hogan (geb. 1927), der später im Auftrag von Pennsylvania das Programm Playgrounds for Free leitete, in dem zahlreiche Spielplätze aus Recycling-Materialien realisiert wurden. Von ihm stammte das wegweisende Buch *Playgrounds for Free*, das 1974 bei MIT Press erschien (Abb. 23–24).

Eine andere Initiative ging von Vereinigungen wie etwa The Architects' Renewal Committee (ARCH) in Harlem aus, die sich gegen die Zerstörung und Vernachlässigung von Quartieren und gegen die problematischen Slumsanierungen wandten. In ihren Lokalitäten entstand das erste Community Design Center, eine Einrichtung zur Ermächtigung der Bürger

outstanding contributors to these parks was the sculptor Josef Schagerl (see p. 165).

In Switzerland, playground sculptures first did not go beyond animal shapes. Only in the 1960s did artists begin to experiment in public space, break through outdated ideas, and explore the pleasures of reckless play. Early examples include *Zyklop*, by Bernhard Luginbühl (1929–2011), and the playground at the Aumatten primary school in Reinach, by Michael Grossert (1926–2014), both of which were erected in 1967 (ill. 15–17). A special kind of success story began in 1972 with the playground sculpture *Lozziwurm* by the Zurich artist Yvan Pestalozzi (b. 1937): for once, a strikingly simple design children loved to play on was mass produced and installed in more than a hundred public playgrounds (ill. 21).

3. Self-Empowerment in the 1960s

The events of 1968 revolutionized not only politics and society, but also ideas about the environment, childhood, and education. "Creativity" and "self-determination" became magic words, and pedagogy sought new ways to particularly promote these traits in children. The common denominator of the heterogeneous movements of the time was the questioning of authority, and playground design was no exception. Now that public space was also seen as a democratic space, playgrounds could no longer be left to government officials. Democratic negotiation of solutions by all those involved became an important element in design. It was no longer important to follow the style and authority of an individual designer; instead, new concepts of play that were anti-authoritarian and anti-institutional had to be tested. Handbooks and self-published pamphlets played an important role in this shift of emphasis; they made ideas public and laid the basis for self-empowerment. The DIY movement, which encouraged people to shape as many parts of their own lives as possible, including playgrounds, was taken quite seriously, especially in the United States, where it led to the building of numerous playgrounds as community efforts.

Planning and building in cooperation with future playground users became central in American cities. Nowhere else was so much invested in the "healing" effect of play and its diffusion in public spaces. After the economic boom of the 1950s, disenchantment set in in the 1960s, with race riots and the separation of white suburbs and black inner cities. Some inner-city neighborhoods deteriorated into slums, and crime spread. Countless plans and public and private initiatives tried to stop this downward spiral: in New York, street parties, festivals in parks, and art happenings were supposed to liven up public

in Planungsprozessen und zur Vermittlung von Architektur an Jugendliche.[17] Universitäten nahmen Service-Learning-Kurse in das Studium der Architektur, Landschaftsarchitektur und Stadtplanung auf: Ziel war eine pragmatische Ausbildung zum Dienst an der Gemeinschaft. Einige Professoren und Studenten brachten Nachbarschaftsgruppen technisches Wissen bei oder engagierten sich vor Ort für die Aufwertung des öffentlichen Raumes. 1965 wurde der britische Künstler Simon Nicholson (1934–1990), der Sohn der Bildhauerin Barbara Hepworth, als Dozent an die University of California in Berkeley berufen. Am College of Environmental Design bot er einen Kurs zum Thema Kinder, Spielplätze und Lernumgebungen an. Zuvor hatte er in Philadelphia unterrichtet, wo er mit grosser Wahrscheinlichkeit mit der Arbeit von Karl Linn in Berührung gekommen war. 1969 präsentierte er an einem Kongress das vielzitierte Pamphlet *How NOT to Cheat Children. Theory of Loose Parts*[18], worin er den Einbezug der Gemeinschaft in den Gestaltungs- und Planungsprozess von Spielplätzen forderte. Besonders Kindern aus benachteiligten Gebieten sollten dabei die Grundlagen des Planens vermittelt werden: „Es ist Design durch den Mitein-bezug der Gemeinschaft, aber in der gesamten Gemeinschaft sind die Kinder am wichtigsten."[19]

Während in den USA der Niedergang der Stadt, die zunehmende Suburbanisierung sowie die Rassenkonflikte nach pragmatischen Lösungen verlangten, lagen die Prioritä-ten in Europa anders. Hier waren nach dem Zweiten Weltkrieg der Wiederaufbau, die Wohnungsnot und die Verstädterung entscheidende Katalysatoren. Darüber hinaus wurde in Europa pädagogischen Fragen eine grössere Wichtigkeit zugespro-chen. Es bildeten sich eine Vielzahl von länderspezifischen Einzelinitiativen, die den jeweiligen sprachlichen, politischen und geografischen Eigenheiten verpflichtet waren. Gemeinsam war ihnen das Interesse für den Abenteuerspielplatz, der eine neue Blüte erlebte. Dabei ging es weniger darum, selbst Hütten zu bauen, sondern einer zunehmend von Konsum und Technik beherrschten Umwelt einen selbstverwalteten Ort entgegen-zustellen. Dies entsprach dem Ideal eines freien gesellschaftli-chen Labors und einer „Universität der Strasse".

Mit der Hochkonjunktur und insbesondere ab den 1960er Jahren standen den europäischen Städten genügend finanzielle Mittel für neuartige Spielplatzprojekte, für Kunst am Bau und die Gestaltung des öffentlichen Raumes zur Verfü-gung. So erhielten viele Wohnsiedlungen und Schulhäuser von Künstlern gestaltete Aussenräume (Abb. 16–20, 22). Diese von der öffentlichen Hand finanzierten Projekte standen im Gegen-satz zu den privat initiierten und den DIY-Lösungen in den USA, wo sich der Staat im öffentlichen Raum kaum engagierte.

Zu den exemplarischen Engagements gehör-ten die Aktionen von Group Ludic in Frankreich (s. S. 119). Als Kollektiv 1967 gegründet, griff die Gruppe auf die unterschiedli-chen persönlichen und beruflichen Erfahrungen ihrer Mitglieder zurück, um auf komplexe urbane Situationen angemessen zu reagieren. Einer nicht-hierarchischen Struktur verpflichtet, ent-wickelte Group Ludic von Beginn an eine präzise Formenspra-che, die sie mit einem Set von Modulen und Vorgehensweisen koppelte: Kugeln, Segel und abstrakte Spielmodule, Spielani-mationen und Ateliers an Ort und Stelle sowie temporäre Akti-onen und Bauten aus Recyclingmaterial. Mit ihren Gegenwelten reagierte Group Ludic auf das in Frankreich gängige „Encad-

space and make it safer. Theaters and museums left their comfort zones to find their audience out-side their solid walls. Vacant lots filled with gar-bage were temporarily turned into playgrounds, gardens, or squares. The legendary Paley Park[16] in New York's Midtown was founded in 1967 and still exists today; it was the first such "Vest Pocket Park." The landscape architect M. Paul Friedberg was one of the pioneers in finding new, temporary uses for such abandoned spaces; he designed a series of temporary playground modules that were easy to adapt to each new setting.

The expression "to raise a barn," as in the rural North American practice of the communal building of a barn (a practice which dates back to the 18th century), is an apt one for community work that is more than the sum of individual initiatives. Such a traditional approach lives on in the United States today as "advocacy planning," one of whose pioneers was the German-American landscape architect Karl Linn (1923–2005). After he emigrated to the United States, he first designed garden landscapes in rich suburbs. Influenced by the kibbutz movement, Linn began to notice the lack of public spaces and communal life in the booming suburbs. In 1959, when he began teaching in the Department of Landscape Architecture at the University of Pennsylvania in Philadelphia, he set up a "commu-nity design-and-build service program" to make landscape architecture more socially relevant. Instead of just offering lectures and dry seminars, he took his students into neglected inner-city neighborhoods. First, they evaluated how the in-habitants used public space and made it their own. Then, in 1960, on the basis of their observations, they worked with local organizations to plan and build a public playground and meeting space on a vacant lot, Melon Block Commons, whose suc-cess attracted further commissions from other cities. The head of the construction team was the carpenter Paul Hogan (b. 1927), who later ran the Playground for Free program started by the state of Pennsylvania, making numerous playgrounds out of recycled materials. He also wrote the in-fluential book *Playgrounds for Free*, published by MIT Press in 1974 (ill. 23–24).

Other initiatives came from such as-sociations as the Architects' Renewal Committee in Harlem (ARCH); these groups focused on the destruction and neglect of neighborhoods and the problematic ways slums were redeveloped. ARCH founded the Community Design Center to empower citizens in the planning process, and to teach teenagers about architecture.[17] At the same time, as an approach to practical training, univer-sities began to incorporate community-service courses into curricula in architecture, landscape architecture, and urban planning. Professors and

14   Cornelia Hahn Oberlander, 18th and Bigler Street Playground, Philadelphia, 1954, Seite aus / Page from Alfred Ledermann and Alfred Trachsel (eds.), *Spielplatz und Gemeinschaftszentrum*, Gerd Hatje Verlag, Stuttgart 1959, p. 101.

2. Die halbkreisförmigen Stahlrohr-Kletterbögen mit verschiedenen Durchmessern wurden für diesen Platz entwickelt.
3. Spielplastik von Egon Møller Nielsen aus glattgeschliffenem Stahlbeton zum Klettern und Rutschen.
4. Über eine Rutschbahn kommen die Kinder in die Kleinkinderzone. Um die drei Sandflächen ist ein Hartbelaggürtel gelegt.
5. Das Spielgebirge aus Beton liegt abseits von den anderen Geräten in einer Grünzone und kann zum Springen, Sitzen und Theaterspielen benutzt werden.

2. Semi-circular climbing arches of tubular steel. They are arches of different radius which were specially developed for this playground.
3. Play sculpture by Egon Møller Nielsen made of polished reinforced concrete. It can be used for climbing and sliding.
4. By using a slide small children can enter their particular play zone. The three sand surfaces are surrounded by a hard-surface area.
5. The climbing hill of stepped concrete is on a grass area away from other equipment. It can be used for jumping, sitting and theatrical performances.

students taught technical knowledge and skills to neighborhood groups, or became involved on site in the renewal of public space. In 1965, the British artist Simon Nicholson (1934–1990), the son of the sculptor Barbara Hepworth, offered a course on children, playgrounds, and learning environments at the College of Environmental Design at the University of California at Berkeley. Previously he had taught in Philadelphia, where it is quite likely that he came into contact with the work of Karl Linn. At a conference in 1969, he presented his soon oft-cited pamphlet *How NOT to Cheat Children. Theory of Loose Parts*,[18] in which he called for the inclusion of the community in the designing and planning of playgrounds. Above all, children from neglected areas could thus be taught the foundations of planning: "This is design through community involvement, but in the total community children are the most important."[19]

In the United States, then, urban decline, the growth of the suburbs, and racial conflicts motivated the search for pragmatic solutions.

rement" (Beaufsichtigung) der Kinder durch die staatlichen Institutionen, aber auch auf die Lieblosigkeit der Wohnwüsten in den Vorstädten. Der Einbezug der Kinder war dabei ebenso radikal wie wegweisend. Group Ludic war Teil einer lebendigen französischen Spielplatzszene, deren Künstler, Designer, Architekten und Landschaftsarchitekten im Ausland viel Aufmerksamkeit genossen.

Italien gehörte auf dem Gebiet der Pädagogik und der Architektur zu den innovativsten Ländern. Der Architekt und Künstler Riccardo Dalisi (s. S. 69) war mit einem architektonisch-pädagogischen Projekt ein Exponent des *radical design* oder Anti-Designs, das Kreativität an die Stelle von Funktionalität und etabliertem Geschmack stellte. Zwischen 1971 und 1974 führte er mit seinen Architekturstudenten in einem vernachlässigten Quartier Neapels Seminare durch. Er interessierte sich dabei weniger für das Spiel, sondern es ging ihm vielmehr darum, den Kindern eine eigene Sprache zurückzugeben. Er und die Studenten nahmen jeweils Modelle sowie Werkmaterial mit und luden die Kinder ein, auf diese zu reagieren und mittels ephemeren Strukturen den abweisenden Raum selbständig zu besetzen, zu bauen oder eigene Ideen zu verwirklichen.

In Deutschland bildeten sich Bürgerinitiativen, die sich direkt in alle lebensrelevanten Bereiche wie Umwelt, Planung, Verkehr, aber auch in Kultur, Pädagogik und Bildung einmischten. Aktionsgruppen wie beispielsweise die KEKS (Kunst, Erziehung, Kybernetik, Soziologie) und die Pädagogische Aktion organisierten im Raum München und Nürnberg Aktionen auf Spielplätzen und in Museen. Ziel von KEKS war es, eine neue Kunstvermittlung in den Museen zu begründen. Zur 35. Biennale di Venezia 1968 entwarf die Gruppe in den Giardini einen Aktionsraum, in dem die Kinder mit einfachen Materialien wie Folien, Farben, Papier und Holz, aber auch mit technischen Medien wie Foto- und Videokameras, Kopiergeräten oder Diaprojektoren experimentieren konnten. Die Pädagogische Aktion betrieb die Aktion Spielbus, eine mobile Spielplatzbetreuung. Allen Unternehmungen gemein war, dem Kind in einer verplanten Umwelt Freiräume zu öffnen, die gleichzeitig als autonome Lernsituationen funktionierten.[20]

Der englische Abenteuerspielplatz hatte von Anfang an einen undogmatischen Charakter, weil verschiedene Gruppen und Initiativen involviert waren. 1961 veröffentlichte der Anarchist, Publizist und Architekt Colin Ward (1924–2010) im von ihm herausgegebenen Magazin *Anarchy* die Spezialnummer *Adventure Playground. A Parable of Anarchy*, worin er den Abenteuerspielplatz mit einer Mini-Gesellschaft verglich: „Warum behaupten wir, dass die Abenteuerspielplatz-Bewegung ein Experiment in Anarchie sei? Nun, wiederholen wir einmal mehr Kropotkins Definition einer anarchistischen Gesellschaft als eine, die die vollständigste Entwicklung der Individualität verbunden mit der höchsten Entwicklung des freiwilligen Zusammenschlusses in all seinen Aspekten sucht..."[21] 1978 beschrieb er in der einflussreichen Publikation *The Child and the City*[22] die Vielfalt von städtischen Erfahrungen, die er höher wertete als das Lernen im Klassenzimmer: „Selbst sehr junge Kinder sollten nicht auf den Spielplatz beschränkt werden, sondern aus dem Sandkasten heraus in die Stadt steigen."[23]

Der Künstler und Architekt Palle Nielsen (s. S. 147) setzte gleichzeitig auf das pädagogische und gesellschafts-

In contrast, Europeans had different priorities: after the Second World War, the decisive catalysts were the rebuilding of the cities, the housing shortage, and urbanization. Further, pedagogic issues were given greater weight in Europe. The numerous projects were separate and specific to the local contingencies of the language, politics, and geography of the countries they were planned in. What they all shared was a focus on the adventure playground, which thus had a new heyday. The point was not to build one's own sheds, but to create a self-administered space in an environment increasingly dominated by consumerism and technology. This was part of the ideal of a free, social laboratory, and a "university of the streets."

With the economic boom, and especially from the 1960s on, European cities had enough financial means for new kinds of playground projects, for the "percent for art" [*Kunst am Bau*], and for the design of public space. As a result, many housing developments and schoolhouses had outdoor spaces designed by artists (ill. 16–20, 22). These publicly financed projects stood in stark contrast to the private initiatives and DIY approaches in the United States, where the state played hardly any role in developing public space.

One of the exemplary initiatives in Europe was the Group Ludic in France (see p. 119). This collective, founded in 1967 with a commitment to non-hierarchical structure, profited from its members' wide-ranging personal and professional experiences as it tried to come up with appropriate responses to complex urban situations. From the beginning, the Group Ludic combined a precise language of forms with a set of modules and approaches: balls, sails, abstract play modules, projects stimulating play, and on-site workshops, as well as temporary events and structures made of recycled materials. With their counter-worlds, the Group Ludic responded to France's common practice of the *encadrement* of children by state institutions (supervision, that is, but in the form of surveillance), as well as to the coldness of the housing projects in the *banlieues*. The group's inclusion of children was as innovative as it was influential; it was part of a lively French playground scene whose artists, designers, architects, and landscape architects attracted a great deal of attention from abroad.

In pedagogy and architecture, Italy was one of the most innovative countries. The architect and artist Riccardo Dalisi (see p. 69) was an exponent of "radical design" or anti-design, which replaced functionality and established taste with creativity. Between 1971 and 1974, he combined architecture and pedagogy, teaching seminars with his architecture students in a neglected neighborhood in Naples. Dalisi was actually less interested

kritische Potential des Spielplatzes. In den 1960er Jahren forderte er mehr Freiräume für Kinder, indem er in und um Kopenhagen spontane Abenteuerspielplätze organisierte. 1968 erhielt er die Erlaubnis, mit einer Gruppe von politischen Aktivisten im respektablen und innovativen Moderna Museet in Stockholm einen wilden Abenteuerspielplatz einzurichten, den er als Modell einer „qualitativen" Gesellschaft verstand.

In der Schweiz war der meist von der Pro Juventute betriebene Robinsonspielplatz weit verbreitet. Im Verlauf der 1970er Jahre wurde das Konzept jedoch vereinzelt in Frage gestellt. Es war kaum noch möglich, in den Städten genügend und geeigneten Raum zu finden. Zudem wurde die Kritik laut, dass diese umzäunten Abenteuerspielplätze Ghettos gleichen und zu wenig Kinder erreichen würden. Als Reaktion entstanden mobile Spielanimationen wie beispielsweise Busse, die mit Spielmaterial die Quartiere besuchten. Zusammen mit pädagogisch geschulten Personen gründeten Eltern ungefragt temporäre Abenteuer-Aktionen. Spontan und billig, erregten diese viel Aufsehen und waren oft mit politischen Forderungen verbunden. Zeitungen und Fernsehen nahmen sich des Themas an und diskutierten öffentlich, was ein selbstbestimmtes Spiel ermöglichte und wie und wo Kinder in einer verbauten, motorisierten und durchreglementierten Welt spielen konnten (Abb. 25–26).

4. Rückzug

Zwischen 1949 und 1979 war der Spielplatz ein Ort im Umbruch und ein weit gefasstes Überlaufbecken für Ideen und Experimente aus Kunst, Architektur und Pädagogik. Mit dem Beginn der 1980er Jahre änderte sich die Situation jedoch grundlegend. Gepaart mit einer um sich greifenden Risikoaversion fand eine zunehmende Privatisierung und Kommerzialisierung statt, der sich die Kunst und Architektur einerseits nicht entziehen konnte, an der sie andererseits aber auch aktiv beteiligt war. In diesem Kontext verlor der Spielplatz an Bedeutung, da er weder Erfolg noch Prestige versprach, sondern Einengungen durch Sicherheitsauflagen mit sich brachte. 1976 wurden die sicherheitstechnischen Anforderungen an Spielplatzgeräte und -böden in Deutschland als DIN 7926 eingeführt und 1998 als DIN EN 1176 und 1177 zur Euronorm aktualisiert. 1981 publizierte die U.S. Consumer Product Safety Commission die erste Ausgabe der *Guidelines for Playground Safety*. Obwohl diese Normen rechtlich nicht bindend waren, wurden sie zum Massstab für Gartenbauämter und Spielgerätehersteller. Kam es zu einer Haftungsklage, wurden sie als Richtschnur herangezogen[24] und die Produzenten mussten diese Richtwerte einhalten, um eine Deckung allfälliger Schäden durch die Versicherung zu erreichen. Gestaltungen ausserhalb dieser Vorgaben wurden somit zum nicht mehr tragbaren Risiko.

Auch die Haltung und Erwartungen der Eltern veränderten sich. Aus Angst vor Entführungen und anderen vermeintlichen Gefahren schränkten sie den Aktionsradius ihrer Kinder erheblich ein und unterwarfen sie einer Dauerüberwachung. Unbeaufsichtigtes Spiel kommt besonders in den USA einer Verletzung der Aufsichtspflicht gleich. Der steigende Leistungsdruck ist für ein gefülltes Tagesprogramm der Kinder verantwortlich. Spielplätze werden daher fast nur noch von Vorschulkindern aufgesucht.

in play than in encouraging children to find their own language. He and his students always took models and materials along and invited children to be inspired by them to build things, to realize their own ideas, and to respond to the space that refused them by occupying it.

In Germany, newly formed local initiatives got directly involved in such relevant areas as planning, traffic, and the environment, as well as in culture and education. Action groups such as KEKS (Kunst, Erziehung, Kybernetik, Soziologie [Art, education, cybernetics, sociology]) and the Pädagogische Aktion (Pedagogical Action) organized projects on playgrounds and in museums in and around Munich and Nuremberg. KEKS aimed to establish a new kind of art education in museums. At the 35th Biennale di Venezia in 1968, the group turned part of the Giardini park into a space where children could experiment with simple materials like paint, paper, wood, and transparencies, as well as with such technologies as cameras (photography and video), copy machines, and slide projectors. Pedagogical Action ran a Spielbus [Play Bus] that offered mobile playground support.[20] The common goal of all such projects was to give children in an over-planned environment a kind of free space that simultaneously enabled autonomous learning.

From the beginning, the adventure playground movement in England involved a wide range of groups and initiatives; this gave it an undogmatic quality. In 1961, the journalist and architect Colin Ward (1924–2010), the editor of *Anarchy*, published a special issue of the magazine, *Adventure Playground: A Parable of Anarchy*, and compared the adventure playground to a miniature society: "Why do we claim the adventure playground movement as an experiment in anarchy? Well, let us repeat yet again, Kropotkin's definition of an anarchist society as one that seeks the most complete development of individuality combined with the highest development of voluntary association in all its aspects."[21] In 1978, in his influential book *The Child and the City*,[22] Ward described the many urban experiences he considered more important than learning in classrooms: "Even very young children should not be confined to the playground, but should climb out of the sandbox into the city."[23]

The artist and architect Palle Nielsen (see p. 147) saw the playground's pedagogical and social-critical potential as connected. In the 1960s, he called for more space to be available for children by organizing spontaneous adventure playgrounds in and around Copenhagen. In 1968, Stockholm's respectable but innovative Moderna Museet gave Nielsen and a group of political activists permission to turn part of the museum into a wild adventure playground that Nielsen saw as a model for a "qualitative" society.

30

Gleichzeitig hielt ein neues Konzept von Kindheit Einzug. 1982 provozierte der amerikanische Medienwissenschaftler Neil Postman (1931–2003) mit dem Buch *The Disappearance of Childhood*, in dem er den Einfluss der Massenmedien und des Konsums auf die Kinder und das Konzept Kindheit darlegte.

5. Ausblick

Erst zu Beginn des 21. Jahrhunderts zeichnete sich eine Wendung ab. 2005 veröffentlichte die Architekturhistorikerin Susan G. Solomon ihr Buch und Manifest *American Playgrounds. Revitalizing Community Space*[25]. Während ihrer Recherchen zum amerikanischen Architekten Louis I. Kahn war sie zufällig auf Unterlagen zu den Entwürfen von Isamu Noguchis Spiellandschaften gestossen. Von dieser Entdeckung ausgehend rollte sie die Geschichte des Spielplatzes in den USA auf und stellte neue Projekte zur Wiederbelebung des öffentlichen Raumes vor. 2006 prägte der amerikanische Autor Richard Louv in seinem Buch *Last Child in the Woods*[26] den Begriff „Nature deficit disorder". Darin macht er klar, dass Kinder, die fernab von Natur und Risiko aufwachsen, kein gesundes Selbstvertrauen aufbauen. Will ein Kind sich selbst einschätzen und kennenlernen, muss es etwas wagen und ausprobieren dürfen. Eine Balance zu finden zwischen Sicherheitsnormen und kreativem Spiel gehört daher zur grossen Herausforderung, der sich Gartenbauämter heute zu stellen haben. Oftmals bieten Brachen, Wohn- und Spielstrassen, Spielaktionen oder einfach nur ein Fussballplatz mehr Freiheiten als teure Spielplätze.

Eine Wiederbelebung könnte von einem erneuten Interesse von Seiten der Künstler ausgehen: Vom Markt eingeengt und gelangweilt, kehren sie in den öffentlichen Raum zurück. Unter dem Label „Kunst" ist noch immer mehr möglich, kann ein grösseres Risiko eingegangen werden und findet vieles mehr Akzeptanz bei Behörden, Institutionen und nicht zuletzt auch beim Publikum. Ein gutes Beispiel dafür ist der belgische Künstler Carsten Höller (geb. 1961), der in seinen Arbeiten die Kindheit immer wieder prekären Momenten aussetzt. Am bekanntesten sind seine spektakulären spiralförmigen Rutschen wie *Test Site* (2006), die in der Turbinenhalle der Tate Modern in London installiert wurde und Erwachsene im Spiel zu Kindern werden liess, während sich Kinder als Kinder begeistern konnten. Von Höller stammen eine Reihe weiterer Spielskulpturen, manche für den öffentlichen Raum, andere für wohlhabende Sammler.

Der polnische Künstler und Aktivist Paweł Althamer (geb. 1963) erneuerte 2003 auf Anregung von Kindern einen Spielplatz in einer Grosssiedlung im Quartier Bródno in Warschau. Eingeladen zu einer Ausstellung in der Nationalgalerie Zachęta nutzte er das ihm zur Verfügung stehende Budget für die Sanierung des Spielplatzes. Er strich die bestehenden Geräte aus Stahlrohr weiss, fügte neue hinzu und änderte die Form des Sandplatzes.[27]

Die japanische Textilkünstlerin Toshiko Horiuchi MacAdam (geb. 1940) und Tezuka Architects schufen 2009 für das Hakone Open-Air-Museum[28] *Woods of Nets*, eine Kletterlandschaft aus farbigen Netzen in einem aus Holzbalken konstruierten, lichten Kokon. Das Werk wurde zum Publikumsrenner. Takaharu und Yui Tezuka, die in ihren Arbeiten immer wieder versuchen, Gebäude für Kinder neu zu denken, wurden vor allem

In Switzerland, Robinson Crusoe playgrounds, mostly run by Pro Juventute, were quite popular. Yet the concept was occasionally called into question during the 1970s: it was increasingly difficult to find enough appropriate space in the cities, and the fenced adventure playgrounds seemed too much like ghettoes and failed to reach enough children. These criticisms led to the development of mobile play vehicles, such as buses, that went into neighborhoods and offered opportunities and materials for play. Parents worked with people with pedagogical training to start temporary adventure projects on their own initiative. These spontaneous and inexpensive projects, which were often connected with political demands, attracted a lot of attention. Newspapers and television picked up the topic and engaged in public discussions of the promise of autonomous play and of how and where children could play in a motorized, overdeveloped, and overregulated world (ill. 25–26).

4. Regression

Between 1949 and 1979, the playground was the focus of many new ideas and experiments in art, architecture, and pedagogy. The beginning of the 1980s, though, marked a fundamental change. Alongside a growing aversion to risk, privatization and commercialization were on the increase; not only could art and architecture not escape them, they even played an active role in the process. As it promised neither success nor prestige, the playground lost its significance, while also facing new restrictions in the form of safety requirements. In 1976 Germany introduced DIN 7926, a set of safety standards for playgrounds and their equipment; in 1998, they were updated as Eurocodes DIN EN 1176 and 1177. In 1981, the US Consumer Product Safety Commission published the first edition of *Guidelines for Playground Safety*. These norms were not legally binding, but they became standards for parks departments and equipment companies. Once they began to be used as guidelines in liability cases,[24] companies had to follow them if they wanted any damages to be covered by insurance. As a result, designs outside the specifications became an unacceptable risk.

Parental attitudes and expectations changed as well. Fearing kidnappings and other reputed dangers, parents kept their children under constant supervision and significantly reduced the time children were left to themselves. Especially in the United States, unsupervised play began to be seen as a breach of parental responsibility. At the same time, as the pressure on children to perform well in school has grown, their daily schedules have been filled with activities. Mostly, then, only preschoolers still go to playgrounds.

durch den 2007 eingeweihten Fuji-Kindergarten berühmt, der auf vorbildliche Weise Architektur, Spiel und Lernen verbindet.

Die 2001 im Umfeld der Madrid School of Architecture gegründete Künstlergruppe basurama („basura" bedeutet „Abfall" auf Spanisch) begann ihre Zusammenarbeit mit kleinen Recycling-Aktionen. 2010, mitten in der Finanzkrise, kuratierten sie das Stadtfestival *La Noche en blanco* in Madrid. Mit dem bestehenden, bescheidenen Budget gelang es ihnen, ein riesiges Festival zu organisieren und die Stadt in einen grossen Spielplatz zu verwandeln. Neben zahlreichen Aktionen auf vier Kontinenten realisierten sie auch Spielplätze in Adis Abeba, Lima, Malabo (Äquatorialguinea) oder Niamey (Niger). Design, Planung und Durchführung geschahen jeweils mit den Menschen vor Ort unter Verwendung von Abfallmaterialien wie Holzpaletten, Getränkekisten, Pneus, etc.[29]

In letzter Zeit entdeckten auch vermehrt Architekten den Spielplatz wieder als kreativen Freiraum. 2014 realisierte das englische Architektenkollektiv Assemble den Baltic Adventure Playground in Glasgow.[30] Da die 2014 Commonwealth Games den benachteiligten Stadtteil Dalmarnock in eine unwirtliche Baustelle verwandelt und die spärlichen Freiflächen eingenommen hatten, entstand als partielle Wiedergutmachung der Abenteuerspielplatz an der Baltic Street: „Als Antwort auf das Chaos wollten wir einen Raum kreieren, den die Kinder kontrollieren konnten – ein Ort, wo sie Dinge für sich tun konnten."[31] Zuerst musste die Parzelle von Müll und einer alten Kohleschicht befreit werden, bevor Tonnen frischer Erde und Lehm angeliefert werden konnten. Dann bauten sie Spielhügel und -tunnels, ein Wasserspiel, einen Garten, richteten ein Lagerfeuer zum Kochen einer warmen Mahlzeit ein und brachten Werkzeug und Material zum Bauen. Ein Sozialarbeiter betreut die Kinder.

Die vielleicht vielversprechendsten Ansätze stammen aus der Weiterentwicklung und Anpassung des Advocacy Planing, also von Gemeinschaftsprojekten, wie sie insbesondere in den 1960er Jahren mit viel Idealismus und gleichzeitigem Pragmatismus erprobt wurden. Sie zeichnen sich dadurch aus, dass sie sich konkret auf einen Ort beziehen und sich direkt mit ihm auseinandersetzen, aber aufgrund des gemeinschaftlichen Ansatzes nicht zu Prestigeobjekten einzelner Gestalter oder Firmen werden. Als Beispiel kann Rural Studio genannt werden, ein Ausbildungslehrgang (Off-Campus Design-Build Program) der School of Architecture an der Auburn University, Alabama. 1994 von D. K. Ruth und Samuel Mockbee ins Leben gerufen, beabsichtigte dieses Programm, den Bürgern und Gemeinden in der wirtschaftlichen Randregion von Alabamas Hale County Wohnraum und Gemeinschaftseinrichtungen zu bauen. Seither haben die Studierenden 150 Projekte verschiedenster Art realisiert: Wohnhäuser, Studentenwohnungen, Kinder- und Jugendzentren, ein Bauernmarkt, eine Kapelle, ein Feuerwehrhaus, ein Museum, ein Baseballfeld, die sogenannten 20K Houses (Fertighäuser für 20'000 USD) aber auch Spielplätze (Abb. 27). Hale County kennt kein Baureglement und setzt keinen Bauinspektor ein, das machte es zum architektonischen Labor, wo dem Einfallsreichtum keine Grenzen gesetzt waren.[32] Die mehrheitlich weissen Studenten und Lehrkräfte wurden nach und nach von den Behörden und der überwiegend schwarzen Bevölkerung akzeptiert. „In einer Zeit, in der die Welt der Architektur auf glänzende städtische Megapro-

At the same time, a new understanding of childhood began to emerge. In 1982, the American media theorist Neil Postman (1931–2003) published his provocative book *The Disappearance of Childhood*, in which he discussed the influence of consumption and the mass media on children and the concept of childhood.

5. Outlook

Only at the beginning of the 21st century did a shift begin to take place. In 2005, the architectural historian Susan G. Solomon published her book and manifesto *American Playgrounds. Revitalizing Community Space*.[25] While doing research on the American architect Louis I. Kahn, she had come across material about Isamu Noguchi's playground designs. From this starting point, she explored the history of the playground in the United States and outlined new projects to "revitalize community space." In his 2006 book *Last Child in the Woods*,[26] the American author Richard Louv coined the term "nature deficit disorder": children who grow up far from nature and risks cannot develop healthy self-confidence. For children to judge and get to know themselves, they must be allowed to take chances and try things out. Finding a balance between security norms and creative play is thus part of the great challenge parks departments face today. Often empty lots, residential and play streets, temporary projects, or even just a football field offer more freedom than expensive playgrounds.

Renewed interest in public space on the part of artists bored and constrained by the market could also contribute to its revitalization. The concept of "art" can still make things happen: greater risks can be taken, and acceptance from authorities, institutions, and not least the public is more likely. A good example of this is the Belgian artist Carsten Höller (b. 1961), who constantly exposes childhood to precarious moments in his work. The best known are his spectacular spiral slides such as *Test Site* (2006), which was installed in the Turbine Hall at the Tate Modern in London, allowing adults to play like children, and children to just be excited. Höller has made a whole series of play sculptures, some for public space, others for wealthy collectors.

In 2003, the Polish artist and activist Paweł Althamer (b. 1963) was asked by children from a large development in Warsaw's Bródno neighborhood to renovate a playground. With the budget he was given for an exhibition at the Zachęta National Gallery, he painted the existing steel equipment white, added several new elements, and changed the shape of the sandbox.[27]

15

In 2009, at the Hakone Open Air Museum,[28] the Japanese textile artist Toshiko Horiuchi MacAdam (b. 1940) and Tezuka Architects created the extremely popular *Woods of Nets*, a climbing pavilion with colorful nets in a bright wooden structure made of very large beams. Takaharu and Yui Tezuka have always tried to rethink buildings for children in their work, above all in the well-known Fuji kindergarten opened in 2007, which combines architecture, play, and learning in an exemplary fashion.

Basurama, a group of artists formed in 2001 at the Madrid School of Architecture, began with small recycling projects ("basura" means "garbage" in Spanish). In 2010, in the middle of the financial crisis, they curated the Madrid festival *La Noche en blanco*. With the modest budget they were given, they organized a huge festival and turned the city into a giant playground. Along with numerous other projects on four continents, they have also built playgrounds in Addis Ababa, Lima, Malabo (in Equatorial Guinea), and Niamey (in Niger). The design, planning, and construction are all done with local residents, and the playgrounds are made of waste materials—for example, wooden pallets, crates for drinks, or old tires.[29]

Recently, architects have also begun to rediscover the playground as a space of creative freedom. In 2014, the English architectural

jekte und feudale Privathäuser blickt, bietet Rural Studio eine gehaltvolle Alternative. Rural Studio ist nicht nur ein Sozial-hilfe-Projekt, sondern auch ein erzieherisches Experiment und eine Aufforderung an die Architektenzunft, nach bestem Wissen und Gewissen zu handeln."[33]

Ein weiteres Beispiel von zeitgenössischem Advocacy Planing ist das Projekt *The Park* der Vereinigung Ankur[34] und der indischen Künstlerin Sreejata Roy im Dakshinpuri-Quartier in Neu-Dehli (s. S. 217). Es zeigt auf, dass der Ansatz gemeinschaftlicher Arbeit nichts an Aktualität eingebüsst hat und dass es ein effizienter, wenn auch arbeitsintensiver Weg ist, im öffentlichen Raum zu intervenieren und dabei eine gesell-schaftliche Funktion auszuüben. Mit unglaublich bescheidenen Ressourcen konnten Ankur und Roy Perspektiven und Lebens-qualität des Quartiers verbessern.

Wie Marjory Allen 1946 die Möglichkeiten des Gerümpelspielplatzes von Carl Theodor Sørensen bewunder-te, schauen wir heute mit Staunen auf die lebendigen Szenen in Maputo, Neu-Delhi oder Greensboro, Alabama, – während Eltern in New York darüber streiten, ob ein Spielplatz stolper-frei sein sollte oder nicht. Die hohen Sicherheitsstandards in der westlichen Welt haben aus unseren öffentlichen Räumen goldene Käfige gemacht. Aber die Geschichte des Spielplatzes lehrt uns, dass gerade Krisen neue Lösungen erzwingen.

„In einer Zeit des Wandels und der Krise sind die Leute der wichtigste Faktor. Daher glaube ich, dass alle kultu-rellen Aktivitäten zu Eigeninitiative und Verantwortungs-bewusstsein führen sollten und so in den Menschen ein Gefühl für Würde, Selbstrespekt und Gemeinschaftssinn wecken. Ich bin überzeugt, dass kulturelle Aktivitäten auf Partizipation beruhen und die Bewohner in ihrer unmittelbaren Umgebung einbeziehen sollten."[35] (Robert Rauschenberg, 1968)

Gabriela Burkhalter ist Politologin und Raum-planerin, sie lebt in Basel. Seit 2008 baut sie ein umfassendes Online-Archiv zur Geschichte des Spielplatzes auf: www.architekturfuerkinder.ch. Sie kuratierte *The Playground Project* im Rahmen der *2013 Carnegie International*, Carnegie Museum of Art, Pittsburgh und 2014 die Ausstellung *Archi-tektur für Kinder – Zürichs Spielplätze* für gta exhibitions, ETH Zürich. 2014 übertrug ihr Group Ludic ihr Archiv zur Bewahrung und Aufarbeitung. 2015 erhielt das Projekt *Group Ludic's Visionary Urban Landscapes, 1968-1979* ein Stipendium der Graham Foundation Chicago.

Anmerkungen:

1   Marjory Allen und Mary Nicholson, *Memoirs of an Uneducated Lady. Lady Allen of Hurtwood*, Thames and Hudson, London 1975, S. 196.
2   Hans Dragehjelm, *Das Spielen der Kinder im Sande. Praktische Ratschläge und Winke zur Förderung des Sandspielens für Haus, Schule, Spielplatz und Behörde*, zusammengestellt auf Grundlage amtlicher und anderer Berichte aus den verschiedenen Ländern, autorisierte Übers. aus dem Dänischen von Alf. Dietrich, Tillge, Kopenhagen 1909, S. 85–86.

collective Assemble built the Baltic Adventure Playground in Glasgow.[30] As the 2014 Common-wealth Games had turned the neglected district of Dalmarnock into a barren construction site and taken over the few open spaces there had been, the adventure playground on Baltic Street was created as partial compensation: "In response to the chaos, we wanted to create a space that children could take control of—somewhere they could do things for themselves."[31] After the land was freed of garbage and an old layer of coal, tons of new earth and clay could be delivered. Then Assemble built a garden, hills to play on, and tunnels and a fountain to play in, set up a space for a campfire to cook hot meals, and brought tools and materials for building. A social worker takes care of the children.

Perhaps the most promising ap-proaches come from the further development and adaptation of advocacy planning, that is, from community projects like those tried out in the 1960s with a great deal of idealism as well as pragmatism. Their primary focus is always one particular place and its concrete conditions, but as they are com-munity organized, they do not become sources of prestige for individual designers or companies. One example is the Rural Studio, a training program (Off-Campus Design-Build Program) at the School of Architecture at Auburn University in Alabama. Founded in 1994 by D. K. Ruth and Samuel Mockbee, this program aims to provide residences and com-munity centers for people and communities in the economically disadvantaged region of Alabama's Hale County. Since 1994, students have realized 150 quite varied projects: playgrounds, of course (ill. 27) —but also apartment buildings, dormitories, centers for children and teenagers, a farmers' market, a chapel, a firehouse, a museum, a baseball field, and the so-called 20K houses (prefabricated houses for $20,000). Hale County has no construction laws, and there is no building inspector, so the project has turned into an architectural laboratory with no limits on the imagination.[32] The primarily white students and teachers have been gradually accept-ed by the authorities and the predominantly black population. "In a time when architectural attention focuses on large, glossy urban projects and palatial homes, the Rural Studio provides an alternative of substance. In addition to being a social welfare venture, the Rural Studio is also an educational ex-periment and a prod to the architectural profession to act on its best instincts."[33]

Another example of contempo-rary advocacy planning is *The Park* Project run by Ankur[34] and the Indian artist Sreejata Roy in the Dakshinpuri neighborhood in New Delhi (see p. 217). As this project shows, the community approach is as timely as ever; it is an effective, if labor-intensive, way to intervene in public space

3   Richard F. Knapp, „The National Recreation Association, 1906–1950, Part II From Ideas to Association: Founding and Early Years", in: *Parks and Recreation*, Ashburn, Oktober 1972, S. 20.

4   1898 wurde die Outdoor Recreation League in New York City gegründet. Siehe: http://www.nycgovparks.org / about / history / timeline / playgrounds-public-recreation (zuletzt aufgerufen am 1. Oktober 2015).

5   Die Playground Association of America wurde 1906 gegründet.

6   Galen Cranz, *The Politics of Park Design. A History of Urban Parks in America*, MIT Press, Cambridge, Massachusetts 1982, S. 131.

7   „Neighborhood Playgrounds and Parks", in: Hilary Ballon und Kenneth T. Jackson (Hg.), *Robert Moses and the Modern City. The Transformation of New York*, W.W. Norton and Company Inc., New York 2007, S. 174.

8   Wolfgang Keim und Ulrich Schwerdt (Hg.), *Handbuch der Reformpädagogik in Deutschland (1890–1933). Teil 1: Gesellschaftliche Kontexte, Leitideen und Diskurse*, Peter Lang, Frankfurt a. Main 2013, S. 365.

9   Amy F. Ogata, *Designing the Creative Child. Playthings and Places in Midcentury America*, University of Minnesota Press, Minneapolis 2013, S. 3 und 77.

10   Kaiserin Augusta (1811–1890) regte das Anlegen von Sandspielplätzen im Berliner Tiergarten an, nachdem sie solche in Londoner Parkanalagen gesehen hatte. (Dragehjelm, *Das Spielen der Kinder im Sande* (s. Anm. 2), S. 57)

11   Ebd., S. 18.

12   Liane Lefaivre und Alexander Tzotis, *Aldo van Eyck, Humanist Rebel. Inbetweening in a Postwar World*, 010 Publishers, Rotterdam 1999, S. 17.

13   Alfred Trachsel, „Spielplätze und Gemeinschaftszentren", in: *Bauen und Wohnen 11*, Städteheft Zürich, November 1957, S. 401.

14   Frank und Theresa Caplan gründeten die Vorgängerfirma Playhouse 1945 in New York. 1951 gründeten Bernard Barenholtz und Caplan Creative Playthings, Inc. 1953 kam die Abteilung Play Sculptures dazu. (Ogata, *Designing the Creative Child* (s. Anm. 9), S. 57–60)

15   Susan G. Solomon, *American Playgrounds. Revitalizing Community Space*, University Press of New England, Hanover 2005, S. 27.

16   Ungefähre Grösse: 390 m², Entwurf: Zion and Breene Associates für William S. Paley Foundation.

17   Brian Goldstein, *A City within a City. Community Development and the Struggle Over Harlem, 1961–2001*, Ph.D. Harvard University Thesis, Cambridge, Massachusetts 2012, S. 4.

18   Veröffentlicht in: *Landscape Architecture*, Washington, Oktober 1971.

19   Simon Nicholson, „The Theory of Loose Parts", in: Ebd., S. 33.

20   Siehe: Hans Mayrhofer und Wolfgang Zacharias, *Aktion Spielbus*, Belz Verlag, Weinheim und Basel 1973.

21   Colin Ward, „Adventure Playground. A Parable of Anarchy" (zugleich Titel der Sondernummer), in: *Anarchy. A Journal of Anarchist Ideas*, London, Nr. 7, September 1961, S. 200.

and have a social purpose while doing so. With incredibly modest resources, Ankur and Roy were able to improve the quality of life in Dakshinpuri and offer its residents new perspectives.

Just as Allen admired the potential of Carl Theodor Sørensen's Skrammellegeplads in 1946, we can now be astonished by the lively scenes in Maputo, New Delhi, or Greensboro, Alabama—while parents in New York argue about whether a playground should be free of tripping risks or not. The high security standards in the Western world have made our public spaces into golden cages. But as the history of the playground shows, it is crises that force people to find new solutions.

"In time of change and crisis, the most important element is the people themselves. Therefore, I believe that all cultural activities should be designed to encourage the personal initiative and sense of reponsability in each individual, thereby creating and inspiring a sense of personal dignity, self-respect, and community spirit. All cultural activities should, I believe, be dependent on pariticipation and involvement by the inhabitants in their specific localized environment."[35] (Robert Rauschenberg, 1968)

Gabriela Burkhalter is a Swiss political scientist and urban planner based in Basel. She has documented the history of playgrounds on www.architekturfuerkinder.ch since 2008. She was a guest curator of *The Playground Project* at the *2013 Carnegie International*, Carnegie Museum of Art, Pittsburgh, and in 2014 for *Architectures for Children—Zurich's playgrounds* at gta exhibitions, ETH Zurich. In the same year Group Ludic assigned their archives to her for preservation and research. In 2015 the project *Group Ludic's Visionary Urban Landscapes, 1968–1979* received a grant from the Graham Foundation Chicago.

Notes:

1   Marjory Allen and Mary Nicholson, *Memoirs of an Uneducated Lady*, Thames and Hudson, London 1975, p. 196.

2   Hans Dragehjelm, *Das Spielen der Kinder im Sande*, Tillge, Copenhagen 1909, p. 85–86.

3   Richard F. Knapp, "The National Recreation Association, 1906–1950, Part II From Ideas to Association: Founding and Early Years," in *Parks and Recreation*, Ashburn, October 1972, p. 20.

4   The Outdoor Recreation League was founded in New York City in 1898.

22   Colin Ward, *The Child in the City*, Pantheon, New York 1979.

23   zitiert nach: Ken Worpole, „On the street where you live. Colin Ward and environmental education", in: Catherine Burke und Ken Jones (Hg.), *Education, Childhood and Anarchism. Talking Colin Ward*, Routledge, London 2014, S. 50.

24   Hanna Rosin, „The Overprotected Kid", in: *The Atlantic*, Washington, April 2014, http://www.theatlantic.com/magazine/archive/2014/04/hey-parents-leave-those-kids-alone/358631/ (zuletzt aufgerufen am 1. Oktober 2015).

25   Solomon, *American Playgrounds* (s. Anm. 15).

26   Richard Louv, *Last Child in the Woods. Saving Our Children From Nature-Deficit Disorder*, Algonquin Books, Chapel Hill 2006.

27   Bonnefantenmuseum, Maastricht (Hg.), *Paweł Althamer. The Vincent Award 2004*, Hatje Cantz, Ostfildern 2004, S. 186–187.

28   1969 eröffneter Skulpturenpark südwestlich von Tokyo

29   Für weitere Informationen siehe http://www.basurama.org (zuletzt aufgerufen am 1. Oktober 2015).

30   Siehe: http://www.assemblestudio.co.uk (zuletzt aufgerufen am 1. Oktober 2015). Gefördert als zentrales Kunstprojekt der 2014 Commonwealth Games.

31   „Glasgow kids rediscover adventure in shadow of the Commonwealth Games", in: *The Guardian*, London, 25. Juli 2014, http://www.theguardian.com/cities/scotland-blog/2014/jul/25/glasgow-kids-rediscover-adventure-shadow-commonwealth-games (zuletzt aufgerufen am 1. Oktober 2015).

32   Andrea Oppenheimer Dean und Timothy Hursley, *Rural Studio. Samuel Mockbee and an Architecture of Decency*, Princeton Architectural Press, New York 2002, S. 7.

33   in: Ebd., Klappentext.

34   Ankur-Society for Alternatives in Education: „Für über zwei Jahrzehnte hat Ankur nun im Feld der experimentellen Pädagogik mit Kindern, jungen Menschen, Frauen und der Gemeinschaft unterversorgter Arbeitersiedlungen in Delhi gearbeitet.", auf: http://www.ankureducation.net/about_us.html (zuletzt aufgerufen am 1. Oktober 2015)

35   Robert Rauschenberg, „Proposal for Public Parks", präsentiert an einem Treffen der New York City Cultural Commission im Frühjahr 1968, publiziert in: *TECHNE 1*, New York, Nr. 1, 14. April 1969.

See http://www.nycgovparks.org/about/history/timeline/playgrounds-public-recreation (last accessed November, 2015).

5   The Playground Association of America was founded in 1906.

6   Galen Cranz, *The Politics of Park Design: A History of Urban Parks in America*, MIT Press Cambridge, Massachusetts 1982, p. 131.

7   "Neighborhood Playgrounds and Parks," in Hilary Ballon and Kenneth T. Jackson (eds.), *Robert Moses and the Modern City. The Transformation of New York*, W.W. Norton and Company Inc., New York 2007, p. 174.

8   Wolfgang Keim and Ulrich Schwerdt (eds.), *Handbuch der Reformpädagogik in Deutschland (1890–1933). Teil 1: Gesellschaftliche Kontexte, Leidideen und Diskurse*, Peter Lang, Frankfurt a. Main 2013, p. 365.

9   Amy F. Ogata, *Designing the Creative Child. Playthings and Places in Midcentury America*, University of Minnesota Press, Minneapolis 2013, p. 3 and 77.

10   Kaiserin Augusta (1811–1890) encouraged the building of sand playgrounds in Berlin's Tiergarten after she had seen them in London's parks. Dragehjelm, *Das Spielen der Kinder im Sande* (see note 2), p. 57.

11   Ibid., p. 18.

12   Liane Lefaivre and Alexander Tzotis, *Aldo van Eyck, Humanist Rebel. Inbetweening in a Post-war World*, 010 Publishers, Rotterdam 1999, p. 17.

13   Alfred Trachsel, "Spielplätze und Gemeinschaftszentern," in: *Bauen und Wohnen 11*, Städteheft Zürich, November 1957, p. 401.

14   Frank and Theresa Caplan founded the company's predecessor Playhouse in 1945 in New York. In 1951 Bernard Barenholtz and Frank Caplan founded Creative Playthings, Inc. In 1953, they added a department for "Play Sculptures." Ogata, *Designing the Creative Child* (see note 9), p. 57–60.

15   Susan G. Solomon, *American Playgrounds. Revitalizing Community Space*, University Press of New England, Hanover 2005, p. 27.

16   Approximate size: 390m². Design: Zion and Breene Associates for the William S. Paley Foundation.

17   Brian Goldstein, *A City within a City. Community Development and the Struggle Over Harlem, 1961–2001*, Ph.D. Harvard University Thesis, Cambridge, Massachusetts 2012, p. 4.

18   Published in *Landscape Architeture*, Washington, October 1971.

19   Simon Nicholson, "The Theory of Loose Parts," in ibid., p. 33.

20   See Hans Mayrhofer and Wolfgang Zacharias, *Aktion Spielbus*, Belz Verlag, Weinheim and Basel 1973.

16 Michael Grossert, Spiellandschaft nach der Restaurierung / playscape after renovation, Primarschule / Primary school Aumatten, Reinach, 2008

21 Colin Ward, "Adventure Playground. A Parable of Anarchy" (also title of the issue), in *Anarchy. A Journal of Anarchist Ideas*, London, no. 7, September 1961, p. 200.

22 Colin Ward, *The Child in the City*, Pantheon, New York 1979.

23 Cited in Ken Worpole, "On the street where you live. Colin Ward and environmental education," in Catherine Burke and Ken Jones (eds.), *Education, Childhood and Anarchism. Talking Colin Ward*, Routledge, London 2014, p. 50.

24 Hanna Rosin, "The Overprotected Kid," in *The Atlantic*, Washington, April 2014.

25 Solomon, *American Playgrounds* (see note 15).

26 Richard Louv, *Last Child in the Woods. Saving Our Children From Nature-Deficit Disorder*, Algonquin Books, Chapel Hill 2006.

27 Bonnefantenmuseum, Maastricht (ed.), *Paweł Althamer. The Vincent Award 2004*, Hatje Cantz, Ostfildern 2004, p. 186–187.

28 A sculpture park southwest of Tokyo that opened in 1969.

29 For more information, see http://basurama.org (last accessed October, 2015).

30 Funded as the lead public art commission for the 2014 Commonwealth Games. See http://assemblestudio.co.uk (last accessed October, 2015).

17 Michael Grossert, Spiellandschaft / Playscape, Primarschule / primary school Aumatten, Reinach, 1967

31   "Glasgow kids rediscover adventure in shadow of the Commonwealth Games," in *The Guardian*, London, July 25.

32   Andrea Oppenheimer Dean and Timothy Hursley, *Rural Studio. Samuel Mockbee and an Architecture of Decency*, Princeton Architectural Press, New York 2002, p. 7.

33   In ibid., cover blurb.

34   Ankur–Society for Alternatives in Education: "For over two decades now Ankur has been working in the field of experimental pedagogy with children, young people, women and the community in underserved worker settlements in Delhi." See http://www.ankureducation.net/about_us.html (last accessed November, 2015)

35   In Robert Rauschenberg, "Proposal for Public Parks," presented at a meeting of the New York City Cultural Commission in Spring 1968, published in *TECHNE 1*, New York, no. 1, April 14, 1969.

Ueli Berger, *Stufenpyramide*, Schulhaus / School Wiesenthal, Baar, 1970

18

Ueli Berger, Spielplastik / play sculpture, Schulhaus / School Melchenbühl, Muri, 1970

19

20   Michael Grossert, Kletterskulptur / Climbing sculpture,
Siedlung / Housing estate Moosjurtenstrasse Muttenz bei Basel (1971 / 1972),
2010

21   Yvan Pestalozzi, *Lozziwurm* (1972), *2013 Carnegie
International*, Carnegie Museum of Art, Pittsburgh, 2013

22 Ralph Bänziger, farbige Betonschleifen / Ribbons in colored
concrete, Schulhaus / School Grünau, Zürich-Altstetten, 1977

To my knowledge, this was the first merry-go-round built from a cable reel. It was put together in Melon Park, Philadelphia, in the early sixties. Now there are ones like it all over Pennsylvania.

Plans for a cable reel merry-go-round. The size of the reel to be used depends upon the size of the children that the merry-go-round is installed for.

MERRY-GO-ROUND

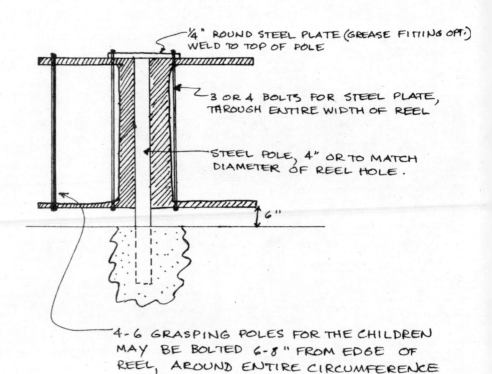

¼" ROUND STEEL PLATE (GREASE FITTING OPT.) WELD TO TOP OF POLE

3 OR 4 BOLTS FOR STEEL PLATE, THROUGH ENTIRE WIDTH OF REEL

STEEL POLE, 4" OR TO MATCH DIAMETER OF REEL HOLE.

6"

4-6 GRASPING POLES FOR THE CHILDREN MAY BE BOLTED 6-8" FROM EDGE OF REEL, AROUND ENTIRE CIRCUMFERENCE

Plans for the cable reel seesaw. I've made some seesaws by taking a slat out of the core of the reel and moving three or four slats so that I have two narrow slots. By inserting the board and bolting down, you have a very neat-looking seesaw.

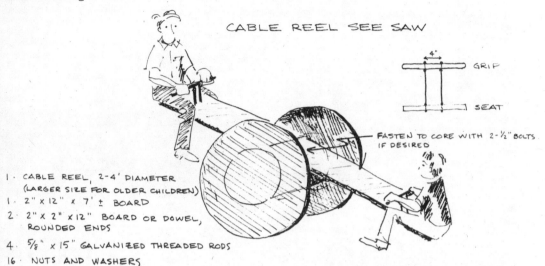

CABLE REEL SEE SAW

GRIP

SEAT

FASTEN TO CORE WITH 2-½" BOLTS IF DESIRED

1 · CABLE REEL, 2-4' DIAMETER
(LARGER SIZE FOR OLDER CHILDREN)
1 · 2" x 12" x 7' ± BOARD
2 · 2" x 2" x 12" BOARD OR DOWEL,
ROUNDED ENDS
4 · ⅝" x 15" GALVANIZED THREADED RODS
16 · NUTS AND WASHERS

The children of Casey Park, the Wilkes-Barre flood disaster trailer site, called this assembly "Mushroom City." The park was built by VISTA volunteers, working with the author and the Pennsylvania Department of Community Affairs. The ladder is made from several pallets bolted together. In fact, all the materials were bolted for stability and hence safety. The Park was bulldozed to make a baseball field in 1973.

The high point of Melon Commons just before the vandals took over. The marble amphitheater was built from steps salvaged from homes destroyed by urban renewal

nborhood

Renewal
Comes

45

25-26   Wohnspielaktion in einem Abbruchhaus (Flyer und spielende
Kinder) / Play activities on a demolition site (flyer and playing children),
Robi-Spiel-Aktionen, Basel, 1981

Einen schönen Teil des Lebens verbringt der Mensch
in seiner Behausung. Darum ist es nicht ganz unwich-
tig <u>wo er wohnt</u> und <u>wie er wohnt</u>. Besonders für Familien die mit Kindern in Städten leben wird sich
die Wohnsituation entscheidend auf die Lebensqualität auswirken.

Spiel und Bewegung gehören zu den wichtigsten Vor-
aussetzungen für die gesunde Entwicklung der Kinder.

Dies sollten Eltern und andere Erwachsene immer
der bedenken, wenn es um die Gestaltung und Möb-
rung von Wohnräumen geht.
Die Einrichtungen sollten vor allem den Bedürfn
der täglichen Benützer und nicht denen von gele
lichen Besuchern entsprechen. Das heisst, das S
der Kinder sollte eigentlich höher eingestuft w
als der Wert des Spannteppichs und der Wohnwand

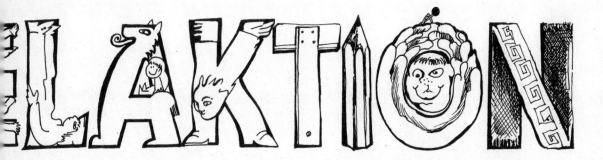

erer Wohnspielaktion möchten wir aufzeigen,
der und Erwachsene auch in einfachen Wohnver-
sen besser wohnen, besser spielen, besser le-
nen.

r von diesen Ideen haben wir hier aufgezeich-
sind Anregungen, die ohne grossen Kostenauf-
d ohne "Fachmann" ausgeführt werden können.

Wir wissen, dass sich nicht alles in jeder Wohnung
realisieren lässt und wir wissen auch, dass damit
die städtischen Wohnprobleme noch nicht gelöst sind.
Wir meinen aber, dass auch durch kleine Verbesserungen oder Veränderungen da und dort ein Kind oder
ein Erwachsener ein wenig besser wohnen könnte.

Pro Juventute Basel, Quartierspielplätze

Rural Studio, Lions Park Playscape, Greensboro, 2010

27

48

Marjory Allen (Lady Allen of Hurtwood) 1897–1976

Landschaftsarchitektin,
London

Marjory Allen (-Gill) stammt aus einfachen Verhältnissen. Nach einer Ausbildung zur Baumschulgärtnerin nimmt sie Aufträge als Landschaftsarchitektin an. In den 1930er Jahren entwirft sie einen Dachgarten für eine Kinderkrippe in London und beobachtet, wie die Kinder dort so ausgelassen wie Landkinder spielen. Dies ist der Anfang ihres lebenslangen Engagements für die Kleinkindererziehung und eine bessere Umwelt für Kinder. Sie ist bestrebt, die Fähigkeiten jedes Kindes zu fördern und ihm Freiheit zuzutrauen.

Während des Zweiten Weltkrieges engagiert sich die Pazifistin Allen für das Wohl der Kinder. So hilft sie mit, Kinder aus London zu evakuieren oder organisiert Workshops, in denen Soldaten aus Material von zerbombten Grundstücken Spielsachen für die Kindergärten und -krippen anfertigen. Bei allen Bemühungen von Allen geht es darum, Kinderkrippen zu fröhlicheren, kindgerechten Orten zu machen.

Unmittelbar nach dem Krieg folgt sie einer Einladung des Zürcher Psychiaters Oscar Forel, an einer Konferenz zum Thema Kinder als Kriegsopfer teilzunehmen. Von dort reist sie weiter nach Oslo und Kopenhagen, wo sie auch den ersten Gerümpelspielplatz in Emdrup besucht (s. S. 185). Sie ist so sehr von diesem Konzept fasziniert, dass sie zu dessen engagiertester Förderin wird. Ihre volle Aufmerksamkeit gilt jedoch der Bildung einer internationalen Dachorganisation für die Berufe der Frühkindererziehung (OMEP–World Council for Early Childhood Education, 1948). Auch auf politischer Ebene lobbyiert sie für die Rechte der Kinder, etwa für den Children Act 1948, der die Kinder- und Jugendfürsorge unter staatliche Obhut stellt und Kinder besser vor Willkür schützen soll.

Ihr Artikel über den Gerümpelspielplatz für *Picture Post*[1] stösst 1946 auf grosses Interesse und der National Under Fourteen's Council, ein Gremium zur Förderung von Jugendkultur und -freizeit, nimmt die Idee auf. Auf einem leeren Grundstück in Camberwell, London wird 1948 der erste Spielplatz nach diesem Konzept eröffnet, er bleibt drei Jahre bestehen. Allen wird nun selbst auch eine aktive Kämpferin für einen Platz auf einem zerbombten Grundstück: Trotz Problemen und Widerstand wird 1952 an der Clydesdale Road ein Abenteuerspielplatz eröffnet. Viel Lobbyarbeit ist nötig, um dem „experimentellen Spielplatz" in London zum Durchbruch zu verhelfen und die Aktivisten an einen Tisch zu bringen. Die bereits etablierte National Playing Field Association (NPFA) bietet sich dabei als Plattform an. Die Einführung der Bezeichnung „Abenteuerspielplatz" erfolgt im gemeinsam erarbeiteten Pamphlet von 1953, das grossen Enthusiasmus auslöst. Zusammen mit Ruth Littlewood und Mary Nicholson gründet Allen eine neue Untergruppe – „the ladies" – im männerdominierten Vorstand

Landscape architect,
London

Marjory Allen (née Gill) came from humble origins. After obtaining a diploma in horticulture, she worked as a landscape architect. In the 1930s she designed a roof garden for a nursery school in London and noticed that when the city children played there, they were as rambunctious as children in the country. This was the beginning of her lifelong commitment to the education of small children and to the environments they live in. She strove to encourage the individual abilities of all children and to let them be free.

During the Second World War Allen, who was a pacifist, campaigned for children's welfare. She helped evacuate children from London and organized workshops in which toys for kindergartens and nurseries were made by soldiers from material taken from bomb sites. In all of Allen's work, she focused on making nurseries into happier places that were appropriate for children's needs.

Immediately after the war, she was invited by the Zurich psychiatrist Oscar Forel to a conference on children as victims of war. She then traveled to Oslo and Copenhagen, where she visited the first adventure playground in Emdrup (see p. 185). The concept fascinated her so much that she became its most vocal advocate. But her primary focus was on establishing an international umbrella organization, the OMEP–The World Council for Early Childhood Education, which was founded in 1948. She also lobbied the government for children's rights, for example, for the Children Act of 1948, which placed childcare under the supervision of the local authorities and aimed to provide better protection for children from arbitrary authority.

Her 1946 *Picture Post* article on the adventure playground[1] attracted a great deal of attention, and the idea was taken up by the National Under Fourteen's Council, a group promoting youth culture and recreation. In 1948 the first adventure playground in Britain was opened on an empty lot in Camberwell in London; it existed for three years. Allen herself then became an active campaigner for a playground on a bombsite; despite many obstacles and significant resistance, an adventure playground was finally opened on Clydesdale Road in 1952. It took a huge amount of lobbying to realize the idea of the "experimental playground" in London, but the already established National Playing Field Association (NPFA) provided a platform for activists to work together on the project. The expression "adventure playground" was introduced in 1953 in a joint pamphlet publication that generated a great deal of enthusiasm for the subject. Along with Ruth Littlewood

51

der NPFA, deren finanzielle Mittel nun neue Perspektiven in der Schaffung zusätzlicher Abenteuerspielplätze und für die Bezahlung von Spielplatzbetreuern eröffnen. Bald darauf werden Abenteuerspielplätze in Crawley und Lollard in Lambeth (1955) eingerichtet. Andere Städte in England sind ebenfalls an einem Spielplatzkonzept interessiert, das weiter geht als das Modell „Schaukel auf Asphalt". Die grösste Schwierigkeit jedoch ist, einen geeigneten Spielplatzleiter und genügend Baumaterial zu finden. Allen fördert die Idee des freien Spiels und des Abenteuerspielplatzes weit über England hinaus und bewirkt dessen Verbreitung in den USA und Europa.

Bei einem Besuch in Stockholm 1954 lernt Lady Allen die betreuten Spielparks kennen und führt diese auch in London ein. Sie kritisiert zudem die beschränkten Spielmöglichkeiten von jungen Kindern in Hochhäusern, die ihr – ebenso wie behinderte Kinder – besonders am Herzen liegen. Stärker noch als die Abenteuerspielplatz-Bewegung auf dem Festland betont Lady Allen den Aspekt der Freiheit und sogar der Anarchie an diesen Orten.

In Allens Aktivität sind die Abenteuerspielplätze ein Nebenschauplatz, denn sie ist voll mit der Arbeit für die OMEP und UNICEF beschäftigt. Sie kann jedoch durch ihre zahlreichen Kontakte im In- und Ausland, die unzähligen Vorträge, Pamphlete und Bücher der Abenteuerspielplatz-Bewegung zum Durchbruch verhelfen – nicht zuletzt in dem Land, wo er erfunden wurde: „Seitdem ich in Kopenhagen das magische Potential von Abenteuerspielplätzen begriffen habe, habe ich viel Zeit und Anstrengungen aufgewendet, dass sie in diesem Land auch akzeptiert werden."[2] GB

Anmerkungen:

1   Lady Allen of Hurtwood, „Why Not Use Our Bomb Sites Like This?", in: *Picture Post*, London, 16. November 1946, S. 26–27.
2   Marjory Allen und Mary Nicholson, *Memoirs of an Uneducated Lady. Lady Allen of Hurtwood*, Thames and Hudson, London 1975, S. 249.

and Mary Nicholson, Allen founded a new sub group—"the ladies"—on the male-dominated board of the NPFA, and the organization's considerable financial means made it possible not only to create more adventure playgrounds, but even to pay playground leaders. As a result, further adventure playgrounds could be opened in 1955 in Crawley and on Lollard Street in Lambeth. Other cities in England were also interested in a playground concept that was more than swings on asphalt. The greatest difficulty, though, was finding a suitable playground leader and enough building materials. Allen also promoted the idea of free play and the adventure playground outside of England, especially in Europe and the United States.

On a visit to Stockholm in 1954, Lady Allen saw supervised play parks, which she then introduced in London, too. She also regretted the limited opportunities young children living in high-rises had for play; she especially took such children to heart, along with handicapped children. In such living conditions, even more than with the adventure playground movement, Lady Allen emphasized the need for freedom, and even anarchy.

In Allen's work, adventure playgrounds were actually a sideline, for she was quite busy with her work for the OMEP and UNICEF. Through her numerous contacts at home and abroad, as well as her countless lectures, pamphlets, and books, she made a huge contribution to the success of the adventure playground—and not only in the country where it was invented: "Since I first grasped in Copenhagen, the magic potential of adventure playgrounds, I have spent much time and effort getting them accepted in this country."[2] GB

Notes:

1   Lady Allen of Hurtwood, "Why Not Use Our Bomb Sites Like This?" in *Picture Post*, London, November 16, 1946, p. 26–27.
2   Marjory Allen and Mary Nicholson, *Memoirs of an Uneducated Lady. Lady Allen of Hurtwood*, Thames and Hudson, London 1975, p. 249.

29   Lagerfeuer auf dem Abenteuerspielplatz / Bonfire on the
adventure playground, Clydesdale Road, London, c. 1958

32   Abenteuerspielplatz / Adventure playground World's End,
London, 1972

33   Abenteuerspielplatz / Adventure playground, Clydesdale
Road, London, c. 1956

*The secret of a successful adventure playground
is in its continual development,
it is never complete, never developed.
It is a sort of 'terrain vague'
that can be many things to many children.*

JACK LAMBERT, *Leader*

Adventure playgrounds are places where children of all ages can develop their own ideas of play. Most young people, at one time or another, have a deep urge to experiment with earth, fire, water and timber, to work with real tools without fear of undue criticism or censure. In these playgrounds their love of freedom to take calculated risks is recognized and can be enjoyed under tolerant and sympathetic guidance.

It is to be hoped that the now old-fashioned playgrounds of fixed equipment on a sea of asphalt will soon be relics of the past. They are condemned because children quickly tire of the inflexible ironmongery. Static objects have a place in the total play picture, but alone they are not enough. Playground designers advanced a small step forward when they turned away from ironmongery and instead used piles of equally static logs, climbing-frames and expensive play sculpture of abstract shapes. As these failed to sustain the children's interest, there was a resort to concrete boats, traction engines, lorries and broken-down cars. But, to the exasperation of authority, the children soon tired of these novelties too and went back to their more exciting play in the streets, or found more creative amusement on waste land. Here at least they could move things around to their liking, build houses with old bricks and timber, and (when the policeman was not looking) light a fire or channel muddy ditch water into rivulets and pools. Nowadays such precious waste land is becoming scarce, the streams are hidden in the sewers, hills and mounds are levelled and buried under concrete, and the trees are not for climbing.

The inspiration for adventure playgrounds came from Denmark where the Emdrup playground was opened in 1943, during the German occupation.

Professor C. Th. Sørensen, the famous landscape architect, had designed many beautiful playgrounds in Copenhagen, but was impressed by the fact that children seemed to prefer messing about in junk yards and building sites, and developing their own brand of play with the waste objects they found there. With great perception and courage, he started the Emdrup waste material playground in a new housing estate outside Copenhagen. He and the children were fortunate in its first understanding leader. John Bertelsen was a trained nursery school teacher and an ex-seaman; he was, therefore, well equipped to tackle this experiment. From that beginning, Emdrup has inspired the world.

Writing in 1947, Professor Sørensen stressed his convictions:

When contemplating an adventure playground it is opportune to warn against too much supervision and too many arrangements for the children. It is my opinion that children ought to be free and by themselves to the greatest possible extent. A certain supervision and guidance will, of course, be necessary but I am firmly convinced that one ought to be exceedingly careful when interfering in the lives and activities of children. The object must be to give the children of the city a substitute for the rich possibilities for play which children in the country possess.[23]

The Skrammelegeplade of Denmark, the Robinson playgrounds in Switzerland and the adventure playgrounds in the United Kingdom and other countries are all descendants of Emdrup. They are all, however, significantly different from one another, for waste material playgrounds are influenced by the country, the nature of the site, the wishes of the children, the imagination of the

◄ *The two most important human needs are experience and control over one's own experience.*

R. Laing, *Politics of Experience*

Joseph Brown 1909–1985

Boxer und Bildhauer,
Princeton

1937 wird der ehemalige Profiboxer Joseph Brown an der School of Architecture der Princeton University als Boxcoach angestellt. Als aktiver Künstler und Bildhauer schlägt er vor, die Architekturstudenten auch in Skulptur zu unterrichten, und wird Assistenzprofessor. Als er Spielplatzprojekte seiner Studenten als langweilig kritisiert, fordern ihn diese heraus. Er geht in die Offensive und beginnt mit herumliegenden Metallschnipseln zu experimentieren. Es entsteht das Modell für ein spinnenartiges Gebilde, auf dem Kinder balancieren und springen können – der spätere *Jiggle Rail* ist geboren. Spiel beinhaltet für Brown Gleichgewicht, ein zentrales Element für ihn als Boxer, und ist immer auch eine Förderung der Reaktions- und Teamfähigkeit. Zudem soll es den Faktor „Überraschung" enthalten, das heisst, es darf nicht repetitiv sein, sondern es sollen stets neue Situationen entstehen. Deshalb haben Browns Geräte bewegliche Teile wie Seile (wie beim *Jiggle Ring* und *Swing Ring*) oder federnde Metallbänder (wie beim *Jiggle Rail*).

  Brown erhält die Erlaubnis, die Prototypen vor der School of Architecture aufzubauen. Die Installation wird zum Riesenerfolg und 1954 kann Brown seine Modelle vor dem National Recreation Congress präsentieren. In Zeitungen erscheinen Artikel, Brown startet eine eigene Radiosendung zu Spiel und Freizeit und beginnt, selbst zum Thema zu publizieren. Plötzlich weht eine frische Brise durch die langweiligen Spielplätze Amerikas. Die Nachfrage nach seinen Geräten ist gross, so dass Brown erste Kleinstserien produziert und versucht, sie über einen Produzenten seriell herzustellen. In Philadelphia und einigen Städten New Jerseys werden erste Geräte installiert, Spielplätze in Tokyo und London erhalten je einen *Jiggle Rail* geschenkt und 1957 ist Browns *Whale* aus Fiberglas Teil des Spielplatzes des legendären All-Weather Drive-In in Copiague, New York.

  Brown gibt jedoch die Versuche auf, seine Spielgeräte in Massen herzustellen, obschon er weiterhin Anfragen erhält, u.a. vom Architekten Walter Gropius: „Wären Sie so freundlich mich wissen zu lassen, ob diese entzückende Vorrichtung [Zappelnetz / *Jiggle Ring*] in diesem Land erhältlich ist und wer es produziert."[1] Ein Partner aus Marcel Breuers Büro schreibt: „Ich glaube, dass diese Instrumente herrlich einfach, sympathisch und dynamisch sind und es schaffen, erstklassige skulpturale Objekte zu sein."[2] Paradoxerweise gehört Browns *Swing Ring* (Abb. 35) heute zu den beliebtesten Spielgeräten überhaupt. Damals entsprechen sie nicht den Vorstellungen einer modernen, abstrakten Spielskulptur und stellen zudem hohe technische Anforderungen an den Produzenten, um nur zwei der Gründe zu nennen, wieso Browns Entwürfe weder in die Kataloge der „modernen" noch in jene der herkömmlichen Gerätefabrikanten aufgenommen werden.

  Obwohl Brown die Massenproduktion seiner Erfindungen nicht gelingt, bleibt er in der Folge als Experte

Boxer and sculptor,
Princeton

In 1937, the former professional boxer Joseph Brown was hired as a boxing coach at the Princeton University School of Architecture. An active artist and sculptor, he also began to teach sculpture courses for the architecture students. When he told his students their playground projects were boring, he took up their challenge to do better and began experimenting with metal shavings that were lying around. He came up with a spider-like structure children could balance and jump around on—thus the future *Jiggle Rail* was born. For Brown, play was a matter of balance, which was central to him as a boxer, and play also always challenged children to react to things and be part of a team. But play should also contain an element of surprise. To avoid being too repetitive, playground equipment always had to allow new situations to come up. Brown's playground equipment thus includes mobile parts like ropes (as in the *Jiggle Ring* and the *Swing Ring*) or metal springs (as in the *Jiggle Rail*).

  Brown was given permission to set up his prototypes in front of the School of Architecture, where they proved very popular, and he went on to give a presentation at the National Recreation Congress in 1954. With reports appearing in newspapers, Brown started his own radio show about play and recreation and began to publish on the subject himself. Suddenly America's boring playgrounds took on new life. The demand for his equipment was so high that Brown first produced very small sets of them and then tried to produce them in series. His products were first installed in Philadelphia and several cities in New Jersey, and playgrounds in Tokyo and London received *Jiggle Rails* as gifts. Then, in 1957, Brown's fiberglass *Whale* became part of the playground at the legendary All-Weather Drive-In in Copiague, New York.

  Brown gave up the goal of mass production of his equipment, even though he continued to receive offers, including one from the architect Walter Gropius: "Would you be kind enough to let me know whether this lovely contraption [*Jiggle Ring*] is available in this country and who manufactures it."[1] A partner from the offices of Marcel Breuer wrote: "These are I believe magnificently simple, sympathetic, and dynamic instruments and succeed in being first rate sculpted objects."[2] Paradoxically, Brown's *Swing Ring* (ill. 35) is now one of the most popular pieces of playground equipment in the world. Back then, Brown's equipment did not live up to the current ideas about modern, abstract playground sculptures, while also being quite technically challenging to produce. These were but two of the reasons

und Gestalter von Spielplätzen aktiv. „Ich denke noch immer, dass das Spiel der wichtigste Bereich der Erziehung in unserem Land heute ist und dass seine Bedeutung leider nicht geschätzt wird."[3] GB

Anmerkungen:

1   Brief von Walter Gropius, Cambridge, Massachusetts, an Joseph Brown, 19. März 1960, enthalten in: Joseph Brown Papers, MS.3287. University of Tennessee Libraries, Knoxville, Special Collections, Inv. Nr. MS-1884, Box 22, Folder 12.
2   Brief von Marcel Breuer and Associates, New York (unbekannter Autor) an Joseph Brown, 31. März 1964, enthalten in: Joseph Brown Papers, MS.3287. University of Tennessee Libraries, Knoxville, Special Collections, Inv. Nr. MS-1884, Box 22, Folder 13.
3   Brief von Joseph Brown an Mr. John E. Hill, Creative Parks and Playground Inc., Quincy Mass., 15. März 1965, enthalten in: Joseph Brown Papers, MS.3287. University of Tennessee Libraries, Knoxville, Special Collections, Inv. Nr. MS-1884, Box 22, Folder 13.

Brown's designs did not become part of the catalogues either of "modern art" or of traditional playground equipment manufacturers.
        Although mass production of Brown's inventions did not succeed, he continued to be active as an expert on and a designer of playgrounds. "I still think that play is the most important area of education in our country today and that its importance is sadly unappreciated."[3] GB

Notes:

1   Letter from Walter Gropius, Cambridge, Massachusetts, to Joseph Brown, March 19, 1960, in Joseph Brown Papers, MS.3287. University of Tennessee Libraries, Knoxville, Special Collections, Inv. no. MS-1884, box 22, folder 12.
2   Letter from Marcel Breuer and Associates, New York (unknown author), to Joseph Brown, March 31, 1964, in Joseph Brown Papers, MS.3287. University of Tennessee Libraries, Knoxville, Special Collections, Inv. no. MS-1884, box 22, folder 13.
3   Letter from Joseph Brown to Mr. John E. Hill, Creative Parks and Playground Inc., Quincy Mass., March 15, 1965, in Joseph Brown Papers, MS.3287. University of Tennessee Libraries, Knoxville, Special Collections, Inv. no. MS-1884, box 22, folder 13.

Joseph Brown, *Whale*, c. 1955

Joseph Brown, *Whale*, c. 1955

36

39　　Joseph Brown, Zappel-Struktur / Jiggle structure, "Design-in,"
Central Park New York, 1967, gesponsert von / funded by the School of Arts
of New York University, the New York Chapter of the Industrial Designers
Society of America and Department of Parks

40　　Joseph Brown, *Jiggle Rail*, c. 1953

63

Joseph Brown, *Jiggle Rail*, c. 1953

42

Jeux d'enfants

Le professeur Joseph Brown, de l'Université Princeton (U.S.A.), qui est le créateur des d'enfants que nous présentons ci-contre, d ainsi le jeu :

« Le jeu ne doit pas être seulement cons comme un moyen de se débarrasser des en ou de les développer physiquement, ou de apprendre à s'amuser ensemble. Il doit les pr rer aux luttes qu'ils auront à soutenir lorsc seront des adultes... Le jeu est un système d cation universel qui doit permettre à l'enfan découvrir ses droits et ses limitations naturell

Les enfants doivent pouvoir utiliser spon ment les jeux grâce auxquels ils mesureront forces et leurs possibilités en prenant en m temps conscience de la présence des autres.

1   2   3

4

5

6

7

1. 2. 3. Système de cordage autour d'un mât fixe et que peuvent faire tourner les enfants. Facilite tous les exercices de grimper.

4. Jeu de cordages horizontaux.

5. 6. 7. Le « Jiggle Rail » : trois bandes métalliques minces de 6,10 m de long se croisent à 0,60 m du sol. Quand une pression se fait sentir sur l'un quelconque des points, la structure toute entière se met à bouger. Le mouvement créé par un enfant en atteint un autre et le créateur de ce jeu pense qu'il peut ainsi permettre une excellente expérience sociale et « apprendre à l'enfant, pour la première fois, qu'un S.O.S. est lancé dans le monde, mais qu'il est parfois difficile de savoir où ». C'est le sens même de la vie en société et de l'interdépendance des hommes les uns par rapport aux autres que ce jeu peut inculquer.

Photos Harriet Arnold.

Riccardo Dalisi
*1931

Architekt, Designer und Künstler,
Neapel

Architect, designer, and artist,
Naples

Als Riccardo Dalisi Ende der 1960er Jahre einen (nie realisierten) Kindergarten für das periphere Neubauviertel Rione Traiano entwirft, kommt er zum ersten Mal in Kontakt mit diesem neuen Stadtteil Neapels. Seit 1957 waren dort in desolater Umgebung für 24'000 Einwohner Sozial- und Notwohnungen entstanden. Im Herbst 1971 geht Dalisi, seit 1969 freier Dozent an der Facoltà di Architettura dell'Ateneo Federiciano in Neapel, erstmals mit seinen Architekturstudenten in dieses Quartier, in welchem die Kinder teilweise der Schule fernbleiben und sich selbst überlassen sind. Mit einfachen, aus Holz und Schnur angefertigten Modellen erscheinen sie vor Ort und kommen mit den Kindern in Kontakt. Inmitten einer chaotischen Atmosphäre beginnen einige von ihnen zu zeichnen. Dalisi bemüht sich stets von neuem, ihnen einen kreativen Raum ausserhalb der Wände und Zwänge der Institutionen zu öffnen. Während drei Jahren bringen er und seine Mitarbeiter immer wieder neue Objekte, Material oder Werkzeuge nach Traiano und veranstalten Workshops. Dalisi entdeckt dabei das reiche, abstrakte oder figürliche Formenvokabular, das einige Kinder fernab jedes Wissens über modernes Design oder Kunst hervorbringen. In einem Tagebuch, das er 1974 unter dem Titel *Architettura d'animazione* veröffentlicht, notiert er die Vorgänge und ergänzt sie mit Zeichnungen und Fotos. „Mich fasziniert ihre ursprüngliche Welt, frei von jeglichen Konventionen, ihre herausprudelnden Worte; es wäre unverzeihlich, sie zur Konzentration zu zwingen und sie in ihrem Verhalten zu beengen."[1] Meistens finden diese Workshops draussen in den steinigen Zwischenräumen zwischen den Wohnblöcken statt, manchmal in einem Keller. Gute Tage wechseln mit schlechten ab, manchmal zerstören die Kinder und Jugendlichen das Geschaffene, sind den Eindringlingen feindlich gesinnt, während im Quartier Feuer brennen. Im Lauf der Jahre stösst Dalisi immer wieder an seine Grenzen, einige Studenten steigen aus, andere zeigen sich resistent. Viele Kinder lassen sich jedoch mitreissen, arbeiten in Gruppen, und die Studenten, Dalisi und die Kinder inspirieren sich gegenseitig. Erwachsene werden neugierig. „Sie hämmerten in Zweier- oder Dreiergruppen, fügten räumliche Objekte zusammen, indem sie die Verarbeitungsweise, die sie bei den Studenten gesehen hatten, frei anwendeten: Sie behandelten die Masten, Bolzen und Schrauben gemäss einer Logik, die ich nicht für möglich hielt."[2] Eigeninitiativen wie das Anlegen von Pflanzbeeten überraschen Dalisi. „Dass es gelungen ist, die beiden Landstücke urbar zu machen und sie in experimentelle Beete zu verwandeln, ist, als ob das Misstrauen der Bewohner ins Gegenteil gekehrt worden wäre. Sie fragen nun mit grossem Interesse: ‚Werdet ihr mit diesen Beeten weitermachen?' Es ist eine Veränderung des kollektiven Bewusstseins (vom passiven Abwarten, dass die Gemeinde…) zur Tat hin."[3] Nach drei Jahren, Ende 1973, wirft die Verwaltungsbehörde Dalisi aus den beanspruchten Kellerräumen hinaus, womit Anfang 1974 das Experiment ein Ende findet.

At the end of the 1960s, Riccardo Dalisi designed a kindergarten for the newly built suburb of Rione Traiano on the outskirts of Naples. Though the design was never built, this was his first contact with this new part of Naples, where public housing and emergency housing for 24,000 people had been built in a desolate setting; construction had begun in 1957. After Dalisi began teaching at the Facoltà di Architettura dell'Ateneo Federiciano in Naples in 1969, he went to Traiano for the first time with his architecture students in the fall of 1971 with simple models made of wood and string, and quickly made contact with many children who did not go to school, and were often left to their own devices. The atmosphere was chaotic, but several of them began to draw. For three years Dalisi tried to provide a creative space for them outside the walls and restrictions of institutions; he and his team brought new objects, materials, and tools to Traiano for workshops. Through his interactions with the children Dalisi discovered the rich vocabulary of forms (whether abstract, figural or both) that some children produce far from the worlds of modern design and art. In a diary he published in 1974 titled *Architettura d'animazione*, he talked about their work and included drawings and pictures: "I am fascinated by how original their world is, how free of all convention, and by how their words pour out of them; it would be inexcusable to force them to concentrate or to restrict their behavior at all."[1] Dalisi's workshops mostly took place outside in the rocky areas between the apartment buildings, but sometimes they were held in a basement. Some days were good, some bad; sometimes, while fires burned in Traiano, the young participants destroyed what they had just made and saw the interlopers as enemies. Over the years, Dalisi repeatedly confronted the limits of what he could do; some students dropped out, while others resisted his ideas. But many children found the project very exciting and formed their own groups to work in. They inspired the students and Dalisi, and were inspired by them in turn, which made other adults curious. "They hammered in groups of two or three and fitted things together by creatively copying what they had seen the students do, using rods, bolts, and screws according to a logic I would not have thought possible."[2] Individual initiatives like the creation of gardens surprised Dalisi. "With the success of making two plots of land arable and turning them into experimental gardens, it is as if the suspicions of the residents have been turned into their opposite. Now they're really interested: 'Are you going to keep these gardens going?' It is a change in collective consciousness (from passive

Ziel von Dalisi und seiner Gruppe ist es, den untersten Schichten der Bevölkerung die Werkzeuge und das Selbstvertrauen zu geben, um mittels einer „tecnica povera" (billigem Material wie Papier, Schnur, Holz, Stoff, Papiermaschee) ihre Umgebung zu gestalten und in Selbstermächtigung Design zu schaffen. Die soziale Komponente der Architektur und die Notwendigkeit, diese für die Allgemeinheit nutzbar zu machen, stehen dabei im Zentrum. Seine pädagogischen Experimente und Konzepte macht Dalisi ab 1967 in Publikationen zugänglich. Grosses Aufsehen erregt zwischen 1972 und 1973 die fünfteilige Serie in der renommierten italienischen Architekturzeitschrift *Casabella*. Die einzelnen Beiträge sind programmatisch überschrieben mit „Die kreative Zusammenarbeit ist möglich", „Technik von unten", „Die kindliche Aneignung in städtischen Ruinen", „Technik von unten und hoffnungslose Produktivität".[4]

1973 gehört Dalisi zu den Gründungsmitgliedern von Global Tools[5], einem Netzwerk von italienischen Designern, Künstlern, Architekten und Kunsthistorikern zur Verbreitung einer radikalen anti-institutionellen Pädagogik. In den folgenden Jahrzehnten ist Dalisi neben seiner Tätigkeit als Dozent an der Architekturfakultät als Designer, Künstler, Forscher und Architekt tätig. Er ist Autor zahlreicher Publikationen und lebt noch heute in Neapel. GB

Anmerkungen:

1 „Mi affascina comunque il loro mondo, originario e senza alcuna convenzione, la fertile sorgente di linguaggi che essi posseggono, lo sforzo per renderli capaci di concentrarsi non deve convenzionalizzarli, sarebbe imperdonabile." Riccardo Dalisi, *Architettura d'animazione. Cultura di proletariato e lavoro di quartiere a Napoli*, B. Carucci, Assisi 1974, S. 34.
2 „A gruppi di 2 o 3 martellavano, componevano oggetti spaziali usando liberamente i modi di elaborazione che avevano visto tra gli studenti: hanno tratato le aste, le balestre, i tiranti secondo un logica che non osavo immaginare potesse sgorgare così facilmente." Ebd., S. 73.
3 „Esser riusciti a dissodare i due lembi di terra ed a trasformarli in aiuole sperimentali è come capovolgere la sfiducia rassegnata degli abitanti che, interessatissimi, chiedono: ‚le continuerete queste aiuole?'; è un capovolgimento della coscienza collettiva (da passiva attesa che il Comune…) all'azione." Ebd., S. 96.
4 Die italienischen Originaltitel lauten: „La partecipazione creativa è possibile", „Tecnica povera", „L'usucapione infantile negli scheletri urbani", „Tecnica povera e produttività disperata"
5 In den Redaktionsräumen der von Alessandro Mendini geleiteten Architekturzeitschrift *Casabella* gegründet. Dazu gehörten Ettore Sottsass Jr., Alessandro Mendini, Andrea Branzi, Riccardo Dalisi, Remo Buti, Ugo La Pietra, Franco Raggi, Davide Mosconi, Franco Vaccari, Giuseppe Chiari, Luciano Fabro und Germano Celant, Mitglieder von Archizoom, 9999, Superstudio, UFO und Zziggurat. Das Netzwerk bestand bis 1975.

waiting for the municipality to …) to action."[3] After three years, at the end of 1973, officials threw Dalisi out of the cellar rooms he had been using, so the project ended at the beginning of 1974.

The goal of Dalisi and his group was to give the lowest classes of people the tools and the self-confidence to be their own self-empowered designers and shape their environment with a "tecnica povera" (inexpensive materials like paper, string, wood, cloth, papier-mâché). The focus was on the social components of architecture and the need to make it useful for the community. Dalisi began publishing reports about his pedagogical experiments and ideas in 1967, most prominently in a well-received five-part series in the prestigious Italian architecture journal *Casabella* in 1972 and 1973, with its clearly programmatic titles: "Creative Cooperation Is Possible"; "Technology from Below"; "The Child's Appropriation of Urban Ruins"; "Technology from Below and Hopeless Productivity."[4]

In 1973, Dalisi was one of the founders of Global Tools,[5] a network of Italian designers, artists, architects, and art historians promoting a radical, anti-institutional pedagogy. In the ensuing decades, Dalisi has continued teaching architecture while also working as a designer, artist, researcher, and architect. The author of countless publications, he still lives in Naples. GB

Notes:

1 "Mi affascina comunque il loro mondo, originario e senza alcuna convenzione, la fertile sorgente di linguaggi che essi posseggono, lo sforzo per renderli capaci di concentrarsi non deve convenzionalizzarli, sarebbe imperdonabile." Riccardo Dalisi, *Architettura d'animazione. Cultura di proletariato e lavoro di quartiere a Napoli*, B. Carucci, Assisi 1974, p. 34.
2 "A gruppi di 2 o 3 martellavano, componevano oggetti spaziali usando liberamente i modi di elaborazione che avevano visto tra gli studenti: hanno tratato le aste, le balestre, i tiranti secondo un logica che non osavo immaginare potesse sgorgare così facilmente." Ibid., p. 73.
3 "Esser riusciti a dissodare i due lembi di terra ed a trasformarli in aiuole sperimentali è come capovolgere la sfiducia rassegnata degli abitanti che, interessatissimi, chiedono: 'le continuerete queste aiuole?'; è un capovolgimento della coscienza collettiva (da passiva attesa che il Comune…) all'azione." Ibid., p. 96.
4 The original Italian titles are "La partecipazione creativa è possibile," "Tecnica povera," "L'usucapione infantile negli scheletri urbani," "Tecnica povera e produttività disperata."
5 The network was founded in the offices of Alesandro Mendini's architecture journal

45 Experimente mit Röhren und Anlegen von Gartenbeeten /
Experiments with steel pipes and gardening, Rione Traiano, Neapel /
Naples, 1972

Casabella. The members included Alessandro
Mendini, Ettore Sottsass Jr., Andrea Branzi,
Riccardo Dalisi, Remo Buti, Ugo La Pietra, Franco
Raggi, Davide Mosconi, Franco Vaccari, Giuseppe
Chiari, Luciano Fabro, and Germano Celant,
as well as members of Archizoom, 9999,
Superstudio, UFO, and Zziggurat. The network
existed until 1975.

47-48 Raumstrukturen und -objekte, Modelle / Spatial structures
and objects, models, Rione Traiano, Neapel / Naples, 1971/1973

46 Experimente mit Röhren / Experiments with steel pipes,
Rione Traiano, Neapel / Naples, 1972

73

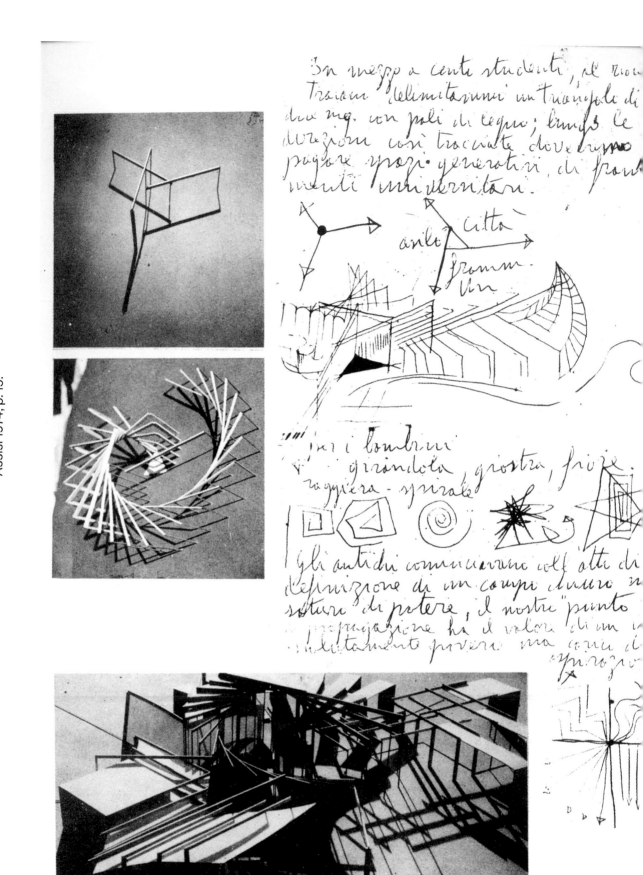

50   Riccardo Dalisi, Modell für einen Kindergarten / Model for a
kindergarten, Rione Traiano, Neapel / Naples, c. 1958 / 1959

55   Richard Dattner, Heckscher Playground, Central Park,
New York, 1972

Richard Dattner
*1937

Architekt,
New York

Während seiner Studienzeit 1957 bis 1958 an der Architectural Association School of Architecture in London wird Richard Dattner vom damals viel diskutierten Brutalismus geprägt. Gleichzeitig lernt er die populären Abenteuerspielplätze kennen, in denen er Orte des ungezwungenen Spiels erkennt.[1] Nach New York zurückgekehrt, gründet er 1964 sein eigenes Büro. Hier ist die Entwicklung der Spielplätze lahmgelegt (s. S. 14), beziehungsweise wird sie vom allmächtigen Parks Commissioner Robert Moses verhindert. Unter John Lindsay, dem 1966 gewählten demokratischen Stadtpräsidenten, übernimmt Thomas Hoving, späterer Direktor des Metropolitan Museum of Art, das Amt des Stadtgärtners. Er zeigt sich offen für neue Lösungen, die den öffentlichen Raum attraktiver und sicherer machen sollen. Mit der Wirtschaftskrise und dem Wegzug der weissen Mittelschicht verarmt die Stadt, und die Parks verwahrlosen zusehends. So unterstützt Hoving das Anliegen des Mother's Committee, einer Gruppe von Eltern, einen desolaten Spielplatz im Central Park zu sanieren. Die Finanzierung übernimmt die Estée and Joseph Lauder Foundation, die bereits seit einiger Zeit einen Ort gesucht hatte, um einen Abenteuerspielplatz nach europäischem Vorbild zu realisieren. Richard Dattner erhält den Auftrag, ein Projekt auszuarbeiten: Der Adventure Playground (West 67th Street) wird der erste von sieben Spielplätzen, die Dattner für den Central Park gestaltet.

Neben dem europäischen Abenteuerspielplatz ist Isamu Noguchis und Louis I. Kahns gemeinsames Projekt für eine Spiellandschaft in New Yorks Riverside Park (in der Nähe der 103rd Street) die wichtigste Inspirationsquelle. Die Planung des Adele R. Levy Playground (1961–1966) an einem bis anhin vernachlässigten Standort führt zu einem jahrelangen Streit zwischen Anwohnern, Auftraggebern und Parkverwaltung. Schlussendlich scheitert sie am Widerstand der Nachbarschaft.[2] Wiederholt berichten die Medien über das kontroverse Projekt, das Kunst, Architektur und Landschaftsarchitektur vereint hätte. Es steht am Anfang einer neuen Idee von Spielraumgestaltung, wie sie Dattner und M. Paul Friedberg weiterführen und umsetzen.

In Vorbereitung für seine Projekte beobachtet Dattner spielende Kinder in New Yorks Strassen und vertieft sich in die philosophischen, psychologischen und sozialen Aspekte des kindlichen Spiels. Seine Erkenntnisse macht er 1969 im Buch *Design for Play* zugänglich. Für den Adventure Playground geht Dattner auf die konkreten Bedürfnisse der Benutzer ein. Erste Skizzen werden mit dem Mother's Committee diskutiert, das begeistert ist von der Alternative zur üblichen Einöde aus Schaukel, Rutsche und Schwinge auf Asphalt. Das Komitee willigt ein, gemeinsam aktiv Geld zu sammeln, damit ein Spielplatzleiter angestellt werden kann. Während der betreuten Zeit stehen sogenannte „play panels" (farbige Bauelemente aus Holz) sowie anderes Material zum Bauen und Malen

Architect,
New York

While he was a student at the Architectural Association School of Architecture in London in 1957 and 1958, Richard Dattner was influenced by Brutalism, which was then quite influential. He also came across the popular adventure playgrounds, which he saw as places of unrestricted play.[1] Back in New York, he founded his own firm in 1964. But the development of playgrounds was paralyzed there (see p. 20), or at least blocked by the power of Parks Commissioner Robert Moses. With the election of the Democrat John Lindsay as mayor in 1966, Moses' position was filled by Thomas Hoving, later director of the Metropolitan Museum of Art. Hoving was open to new ideas about how to make public space safer and more attractive. The city was growing poorer due to the economic crisis and the exodus of the white middle class, and its parks were increasingly neglected, so Hoving gave his support to the Mother's Committee, a group of parents who wanted to renovate an abandoned playground in Central Park. The project was sponsored by the Estée and Joseph Lauder Foundation, which had been looking for a place to build an European-style adventure playground. Dattner was commissioned to develop such a playground at West 67th Street, which became the first of seven playgrounds he designed for Central Park.

Dattner was inspired not only by the European adventure playground but also by Isamu Noguchi and Louis I. Kahn's joint project for a playground in New York's Riverside Park (near 103rd Street). The planning of the Adele R. Levy Playground (1961–1966) on a previously abandoned site had taken years because of conflict between local residents, sponsors, and park administrators; the project was finally called off due to neighborhood resistance.[2] But the media reported again and again on the controversial design, which would have combined art, architecture, and landscape architecture, and this failed project laid the foundations for new concepts of how to design space for play that were developed further by Dattner and M. Paul Friedberg and finally put into practice.

Dattner prepared for his projects by watching children playing on the streets of New York and by doing extensive research into the philosophy, psychology, and sociology of children's play. He published his ideas in his book *Design for Play* in 1969. For his first adventure playground, Dattner took the concrete needs of its users into account. His first designs were discussed with the Mother's Committee, which was excited about the alternative to the usual wasteland of swings and slides. The committee agreed to collect money

bereit. Betonpyramiden, -kegel und -tunnels sowie Kletter-strukturen aus Holz schaffen vielfältige Bewegungsräume, die durch verschiedene Bodentexturen bereichert werden: der südliche Teil ist mit Sand ausgelegt, der nördliche mit Kies oder einem stabilem Bodenbelag und Wasser. Der innere Spielbe-reich ist von Sitzgelegenheiten und einer asphaltierten Fahr-bahn für Kindervelos durch eine spielerisch gegliederte Mauer getrennt, um Eltern und Kindern je eigene Räume zu geben.

Bisher wurden fünf von Dattners Spielplätzen im Central Park renoviert. Bei der Anpassung an heutige Sicher-heitsstandards verlor das Design jedoch viel von seiner ursprünglichen Eigenheit, so wurde beispielsweise taktiler Sand durch weichen Gummiboden ersetzt.

In den 1980er Jahren beendet Dattner seine Karriere als Spielplatzdesigner, da das Risiko von Haftungs-klagen bei Unfällen zu hoch wurde. GB

Liste der Spielplätze von Richard Dattner im Central Park, New York

• Adventure Playground, 1967, finanziert durch Estée and Joseph Lauder Foundation; 1997 und 2015 saniert
• Tots Playgound (Nähe Adventure Playground), 1968; 1987 ersetzt
• East 72nd Street Playground, 1970, finanziert durch Louis and Bessie Adler Foundation; 2001 und 2015 saniert
• West 81st Street Playground, 1969; 1987 durch den Diana Ross Playground ersetzt
• Ancient Playground (East 85th Street), 1972, finan-ziert durch Estée and Joseph Lauder Foundation; 2009 saniert
• Heckscher Playground (7th Ave and Central Park South): Kleinkinderspielplatz, 1969 und Water Playground, 1972; 2005 saniert vom Central Park Conservancy
• Wild West Playground (West 93rd Street), 1989; 2014–2015 saniert

Anmerkungen:

1 „Als ich von 1957–58 an der Architectural Associa-tion war, wurde ich von meiner Fakultät beeinflusst – von James Sterling, James Gowan, Peter und Allison Smithson, Michael Killick und anderen. Was den ‚Brutalismus' in der Nachkriegszeit charakterisierte, war die Notwendigkeit, mit ehrlichen, billigen Materialien – Sichtbeton, Profilstahl, Ziegelsteine – zu arbeiten. Diese Palette war auch eine Reaktion auf die ‚schöne' Architek-tur, die in den USA damals *en vogue* war – Yamasaki, Edward Durrell Stone, etc.

Beim Spiel war die entsprechende Situation die Allgegenwärtigkeit von Nachkriegs-Trümmern und die Entdek-kung, dass Kinder aus solchen ihre eigenen Spielumgebungen bauten. Lady Allen of Hurtwood hat über dieses Phänomen geschrieben und war sicherlich eine Beeinflussung. Ich hatte in den 1960er Jahren die Gelegenheit, sie zu treffen." Korrespon-denz mit Richard Dattner, 8. September 2015.
2 Susan G. Solomon, *American Playgrounds. Revi-talizing Community Space*, University Press of New England, Lebanon 2005, S. 44–53.

to hire a playground supervisor. Whenever a super-visor was present, "play panels" (colorful wooden construction elements) were available, as well as other materials for building and painting. Concrete structures—pyramids, spheres, and tunnels—as well as wooden jungle gyms created complex spaces to move around in. These spaces were enriched by a variety of surfaces for the ground: sand to the south; to the north, gravel or a robust surface, and water. The inner play area was separated from a seating area and there was an asphalt track for children's bicycles next to a playfully designed wall that gave children and parents their own spaces.

Five of Dattner's playgrounds in Central Park have been renovated in recent years. However, the designs lost much of their original idiosyncrasy when they were adapted to meet contemporary security standards; for example, tactile sand was replaced by a soft plastic surface.

In the 1980s Dattner ended his ca-reer as a playground designer, because the risk of liability suits after accidents had become too high. GB

List of Richard Dattner's Playgrounds in Central Park, New York

• Adventure Playground, 1967, sponsored by the Estée and Joseph Lauder Foundation; renovated in 1997 and 2015
• Tots Playgound (close to Adventure Playground), 1968; replaced in 1987
• East 72nd Street Playground, 1970, sponsored by the Louis and Bessie Adler Foundation; renovated in 2001 and 2015
• West 81st Street Playground, 1969; replaced by the Diana Ross Playground in 1987
• Ancient Playground (East 85th Street), 1972, sponsored by the Estée and Joseph Lauder Foundation; renovated in 2009
• Heckscher Playground (7th Ave and Central Park South): toddler playground, 1969, and Water Playground, 1972; renovated in 2005 by the Central Park Conservancy
• Wild West Playground (West 93rd Street), 1989; renovated in 2014–2015

Notes:

1 "I was influenced by my Architectural Association faculty when there in 1957–1958—James Sterling, James Gowan, Peter and Allison Smithson, Michael Killick, others. What has been characterized as 'brutalism' was the necessity in that postwar period of working with honest, inexpensive materials—exposed concrete, steel sections, brick. This palette was

Richard Dattner, Heckscher Playground, Central Park, New York, 1972

56

also somewhat of a reaction to the 'pretty' architecture then in vogue in the US—Yamasaki, Edward Durrell Stone, etc.

"The corresponding situation with play was the ubiquity of postwar rubble, and the discovery that children would use such materials to craft their own play environments. Lady Allen of Hurtwood wrote about this phenomenon, and was certainly an influence—I had the opportunity of meeting her in the 1960s." Correspondence with Richard Dattner, September 8, 2015.

2   Susan G. Solomon, *American Playgrounds. Revitalizing Community Space*, University Press of New England, Lebanon 2005, p. 44–53.

59   Spielmodule / Play panels Adventure Playground, Central Park, New York, 1967

60   West 81st Street Playground, Central Park, New York, 1969 (ersetzt / replaced)

61–62
Doppelseiten aus / Spreads from Richard Dattner AIA,
Design for Play, Van Nostrand Reinhold Company, New York 1969,
p. 58–59, 84–85.

Beer cans are round and shiny and make a fine clatter
when kicked into the street. Many discarded products of
our industrial society make excellent play materials.

Junk

A little boy is standing in a filthy street, which
apparently is not on the maps of the Department of Sanitation. He carefully selects an
armful of shiny, empty beer cans and proceeds
to line them up on the sidewalk. He works with
great patience, getting the cans to line up
exactly, until everything is the way he wants it.
Then he stands behind the cans and kicks
them noisily, one by one, into the street. When
they are all in the street, he begins again with
as much care as before.

Across the street, another boy is pushing a
discarded milk carton around and around, like
a driver on a miniature racecourse. He is completely absorbed. It is not possible for an adult
watching him ever to know what the milk
carton has become in his imagination.

The same little boy who was kicking the cans
now takes them across the street to the steps
of a church. There he finds a box that once
contained soft-drink bottles, and he turns it on
its side. Starting from one corner, he puts a
beer can in every slot, from left to right in each
row, until all the slots are filled.

Cartons and crates come in an endless variety of sizes. They can be stacked, pushed, and sat in, and they are probably the most sought-after junk for play.

The concentric mounds, or crater. In the background is the tunnel leading from the interior of the volcano. The beginning of the ramp around the volcano can also be seen.

Modular toys are stored inside the pyramid and distributed by the playground supervisor. The panels are made of plywood notched to fit together. For toddlers there are small wood blocks, nesting boxes, and a smaller version of the modular panels (opposite page, below).

The path around the playground, lined with benches, is used by parents, children, and passers-by.

tunnel and ladder leading to the summit); along a gently inclined ramp circling the mound; or directly up the sides, where recessed cobblestones serve as hand- and footholds. Recessed steps rather than projecting ones were used because they allow for a harmless slide to the sand below in the event someone does slip or fall. (At the rear of the volcano, where there is asphalt paving, the ramp forms an intermediate level to break falls.) For those who reach the top, there is a safe vantage point, protected by a handrail, from which children can look around or descend via a medium-sized slide or any other route they wish.

The tunnel (14) underneath the volcano and the shaft that leads to the summit are great favorites. The first rung of the ladder is high enough to prevent the youngest children from making the six-foot climb, and the area under the ladder is padded with rubber safety surfacing. All the entrances to the tunnel (there are two at each end, plus the one at the top) are big enough for an adult to use if necessary, but the effort required effectively keeps most parents out. The tunnel floor is pitched to prevent water accumulation when it rains, and there

are no blind corners to encourage use of the tunnel as a toilet.

At the south end of the playground are the concentric mounds (15), often called the "crater." Like the other structures, this is used in different ways by children of different ages. The youngest play in the sand between the inclined cobblestone walls and make their way to the center mound by way of small openings. Older children climb up and over the walls to reach the center, and the most intrepid leap from wall to wall.

We thus complete our circuit of the playground and its facilities. Two portions of the playground remain to be mentioned: the open central space and the area between the main structures and the outer fence. The first is full of children running from place to place — or just running — and others playing in the sand or building with construction materials. The second, paved with asphalt, is used by adults and children both. It provides a hard-surfaced path for baby carriages and tricycles and other wheeled toys, as well as a promenade for parents and passers-by. This traffic does not interfere with the children playing in the cen-

63   Aldo van Eyck, Zeedijk, Amsterdam (1956), 1958; Wandmalerei
von / Mural by Joost van Roojen

Aldo van Eyck
1918–1999

Architekt,
Amsterdam

Während des Zweiten Weltkrieges studiert Aldo van Eyck an der ETH Zürich Architektur. Im Haus der Kunsthistorikerin, Autorin und Kuratorin Carola Giedion-Welcker lernt er zahlreiche Exponenten der europäischen Kunst-Avantgarde kennen, die ihn tief beeindrucken. Nach Kriegsende zieht er nach Amsterdam, wo er eine Anstellung beim städtischen Planungsamt findet. Dessen Vorsteher, Cor van Eesteren, ist Präsident des Congrès Internationaux d'Architecture Moderne (CIAM) und führt van Eyck in De 8 en Opbouw ein, die lokale CIAM-Gruppe. 1947 reist van Eyck als Delegierter an den sechsten Internationalen CIAM-Kongress nach Bridgewater, wo er sich gegen die Vorherrschaft des Rationalen auflehnt und sich gegen die Dominanz der Vernunft über die Imagination wehrt. 1953 spaltet sich eine Gruppe um van Eyck ab; sie gründen das Team X[1]. Anstelle eines kalten, die Menschen trennenden Funktionalismus wollen sie Umgebungen schaffen, die Menschen verbinden.[2] In seiner Arbeit setzt van Eyck diese Maximen tagtäglich um, angefangen bei der Planung von Spielplätzen, seinem ersten Betätigungsfeld.

Bis zum Zweiten Weltkrieg gibt es in Amsterdam nur halböffentliche Spielgärten, die von Vereinen mit verschiedener politischer Ausrichtung verwaltet werden. Die Wirtschaftskrise der 1930er Jahre verlangt nach neuen, kostengünstigen Konzepten anstatt der betreuten „Spielgärten"[3], und mit der Erarbeitung des Stadterweiterungsplans 1934 sucht die Stadt nach öffentlichem Grund für Spielorte. Nach der Kriegszäsur verfolgt die neue sozialdemokratische Regierung das Projekt der Schaffung von Spielplätzen weiter, da mit dem Babyboom das Problem immer dringlicher wird. Van Eycks Chefin, die Ingenieurin und Planerin Jakoba Mulder, beauftragt 1947 den jungen Architekten mit der Ausarbeitung eines ersten Spielplatzes, dem Bertelmanplein. Van Eyck schafft einen Sandplatz mit Springsteinen aus Beton als Zentrum, erweitert durch Kletterbögen und Turnstangen aus Stahlrohr. Diese klare Komposition wird zu seinem Markenzeichen. Nicht nur überzeugt das innovative und bestechend einfache Design, sondern auch die niedrigen Kosten und die grosse Flexibilität, denn die Spielplätze müssen sich in der dicht bebauten Innenstadt in knappe Räume einpassen oder oftmals bereits nach wenigen Jahren Neubauten weichen. Hunderte von Spielplätzen, die van Eyck in den folgenden dreissig Jahren in den alten und neuen Quartieren Amsterdams realisiert, werden zur beispiellosen Erfolgsgeschichte. Das Echo in Bevölkerung und Fachpresse ist positiv und van Eyck wird bis heute für die sorgfältig geplanten, charismatischen und offenen Orte verehrt. Es gelingt ihm, die Spielräume nicht gegen den Stadtraum abzugrenzen, was beweist, dass diese nicht zwingend Ghettos sein müssen.

Van Eyck ist von der Idee beseelt, dass Kinder Teil der Stadt sein müssen, wie auch ihr Spiel in all seinen Formen darin integriert werden muss. Als keine grossen Flächen mehr

Architect,
Amsterdam

Aldo van Eyck studied architecture at the ETH in Zurich during the Second World War. He met and was deeply impressed by numerous artists of the European avant-garde at the house of the art historian, curator, and writer Carola Giedion-Welcker. When the war ended he moved to Amsterdam, where he found a job with the city's urban planning office. Its director, Cor van Eesteren, was President of the Congrès Internationaux d'Architecture Moderne (CIAM), and introduced van Eyck to De 8 en Opbouw, the local CIAM group. In 1947 van Eyck was a delegate to the sixth International CIAM Congress in Bridgewater, where he rejected the dominance of the rational, and resisted the priority given to reason over the imagination. In 1953 van Eyck was the center of a group that split with CIAM to found Team X.[1] Instead of a cold functionalism that separates people, they sought to create environments that connect people.[2] Van Eyck practiced such maxims everyday in his work, starting with the planning of playgrounds, the first field he worked in.

Until the Second World War, Amsterdam had only had semiprivate "play gardens" administered by clubs of various political stripes. The economic crisis of the 1930s created a demand for new, cost-effective concepts instead of such supervised spaces,[3] and with the drafting of the city's development plans in 1934, Amsterdam began to look for public space for playgrounds. After the interruption caused by the war, the new Social Democratic government again took up the creation of playgrounds, just as the issue was becoming more urgent with the baby boom. In 1947 van Eyck's boss, the engineer and urban planner Jakoba Mulder, assigned him the project of designing the first playground, the Bertelmanplein. Van Eyck designed a sandy playground with concrete stepping stones as well as arches to climb on and bars for gymnastics. Such clear composition became his trademark. It was not just the innovative and strikingly simple design that is so convincing, but also its low cost and extreme flexibility: van Eyck's playgrounds had to fit into tight spaces in the closely built city center and often had to give way to new buildings even just a few years later. He went on to build hundreds of playgrounds in the old and new districts of Amsterdam over the next 30 years—a success story like no other in the history of the field. The response from Amsterdam's residents and from the professional journals was positive, and van Eyck is still respected today for his carefully planned, charismatic, and open playgrounds. He was able to avoid isolating the play areas from the city, which showed that playgrounds did not have to be like ghettos.

frei sind, nutzt er kleine Bereiche als Inseln, die er mit einem einzigen Spielgerät, wie beispielsweise einer Turnstange, bestückt. So überzieht er die Stadt mit einem dichten Netz von Spielgelegenheiten. Dabei sollen diese *spots* nicht nur von Kindern, sondern von allen genutzt werden und sich ästhetisch in die Stadt einfügen.[4]

1951 gründet van Eyck sein eigenes Architektur-büro; im Auftrag der Stadtverwaltung realisierte er über 700 Spielplätze. Daneben entwirft er rund 30 Spielgeräte, die so elementar wie eine Bank oder ein Zeitungskiosk sein sollen. Als Architekt gelingt ihm mit dem Amsterdamer Waisenhaus (1955–1960) der internationale Durchbruch. Er ist zudem als Dozent, Verleger und Autor tätig.[5] GB

Anmerkungen:

1   Bestehend aus Georges Candilis, Jaap Bakema, Aldo van Eyck, Rolf Gutman, Alison und Peter Smithson, Bill Howell sowie John Voelcker.
2   Vincent Ligtelijn und Francis Strauven (Hg.), *Aldo van Eyck. Collected articles and other writings 1947–1998*, SUN, Amsterdam 2008, S. 180.
3   Lianne Verstrate und Lia Karsten, „The Creation of Play Spaces in Twentieth-Century Amsterdam. From an Intervention of Civil Actors to a Public Policy", in: *Landscape Research*, Oxford, Jg. 36, Nr. 1, Januar 2011, S. 19.
4   „On the Design of Play Equipment and the Arran-gement of Playgrounds," in: Ligtelijn / Strauven, *Aldo van Eyck* (s. Anm. 2), S. 112–119.
5   Kurzbiografie, in: Ebd., S. 650–651.

Van Eyck was driven by the idea that children are part of the city, as are all the forms of their play. When no big open spaces were left, he used smaller areas as islands with one piece of equipment, such as a bar for gymnastics. He thus wove play opportunities into the fabric of the city. All these spots, while also fitting the city's aesthet-ics, were not only for children, but for everyone.[4]

In 1951 van Eyck started his own archi-tectural office; over the years, Amsterdam com-missioned him to build over 700 playgrounds. At the same time he designed around 30 types of playground equipment, which he tried to make as elementary as benches or newspaper kiosks. The Amsterdam Orphanage (1955–1960) provided him with his international breakthrough as an architect, and he was also active as a teacher, publisher, and author.[5] GB

Notes:

1   The members of the group were Georges Candilis, Jaap Bakema, Aldo van Eyck, Rolf Gutman, Alison and Peter Smithson, Bill Howell, and John Voelcker.
2   Vincent Ligtelijn and Francis Strauven (eds.), *Aldo van Eyck. Collected articles and other writings 1947–1998*, SUN, Amsterdam 2008, p. 180.
3   Lianne Verstrate and Lia Karsten, "The Creation of Play Spaces in Twentieth-Century Amsterdam. From an Intervention of Civil Actors to a Public Policy," in *Landscape Research*, Oxford, vol. 36, no. 1, January 2011, p. 19.
4   "On the Design of Play Equipment and the Arrangement of Playgrounds," in Ligtelijn / Strauven, *Aldo van Eyck* (see note 2), p. 112–119.
5   Biographical note, in ibid., p. 650–651.

Aldo van Eyck, Gordijnensteeg, Amsterdam

64

Aldo van Eyck, Zandstraat, Amsterdam, 1965

67

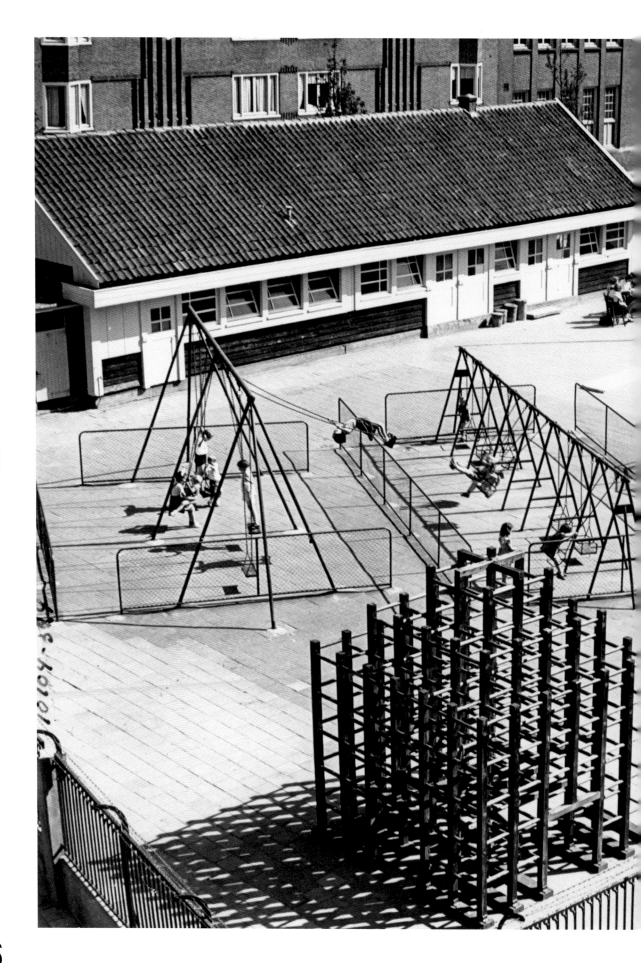

M. Paul Friedberg, Pausenhof der / Buchanan High School
schoolyard, Washington, 1966

69

M. Paul Friedberg, Riis Plaza, Jacob Riis Houses, New York, 1965

70

98

M. Paul Friedberg
*1931

Landschaftsarchitekt,
New York

M. Paul Friedberg kommt als junger Baumschulgärtner[1] nach New York, wo er 1958 sein eigenes Büro eröffnet. Auf dem Gebiet der Landschaftsarchitektur noch unerfahren, kann er jedoch erste Aufträge der New York Housing Authority, der Behörde für gemeinnützigen Wohnungsbau, akquirieren. Die strengen Reglemente erlauben dabei kaum Gestaltungsfreiheit. Es gelingt Friedberg jedoch eine Bresche zu finden: Anstelle der geforderten Statue bei den Nathan Straus Houses schafft er einen kleinen öffentlichen Platz und beauftragt zudem kurzerhand einen befreundeten Künstler, statt der Büste eine Skulptur zu entwerfen, auf der Kinder spielen können. „Die Tatsache, dass ich das System herausgefordert hatte und damit erfolgreich war, gab mir den Anreiz, mit einer erweiterten Perspektive an künftige Arbeiten heranzugehen. Dieses Spiel der Genugtuung durch die Austestung traditioneller Grenzen, des ‚Status quo'."[2]

In *The Death and Life of Great American Cities* (1961), dem meistdiskutierten Werk zur Stadtplanung, kritisiert die Journalistin und Aktivistin Jane Jacobs die städtische Behörde, die Slums saniert, indem sie deren Bewohner in riesige Sozialwohnungssiedlungen umquartiert. Betroffen vom Befund des Buches wendet sich die visionäre Philanthropin und Präsidentin der Vincent Astor Foundation, Brooke Astor, an die Housing Authority. Brooke ist bemüht, der Stiftung ein neues philanthropisches Profil zu verleihen und bietet Unterstützung an, die ghettoartige Situation der Wohnblocks zu verbessern. Ihr Idealbild sind „grüne Aussenräume", die als Treffpunkte für verschiedene Gruppen von Bewohnern wie Kinder, Jugendliche und Senioren fungieren. Friedberg gewinnt den Wettbewerb für das erste Projekt, die Gestaltung einer besseren Umgebung für die Carver Houses in Spanish Harlem, Manhattan. Dabei hat er vollkommene Gestaltungsfreiheit. Er projektiert eine Spiellandschaft, in der die Topografie das zentrale Spielmoment bildet. Er wagt jedoch noch nicht, das Konzept radikal zu Ende zu führen und bestückt die Landschaft zusätzlich mit vorgefertigten Spielgeräten. Erst beim nächsten Entwurf für die Jacob Riis Houses im East Village vertraut er voll dem Potential der Topografie: Es entsteht eine Art Berglandschaft aus Pflastersteinen, Beton- und Holzskulpturen, einem Amphitheater und zahlreichen Sitzgelegenheiten. Friedberg nennt sein Vorgehen, das er 1970 in der Publikation *Play and Interplay* vorstellt, „Linked Play": „Wir begannen den Wert vom sogenannten ‚Linked Play' zu erkennen. Der Spielplatz wurde zur Umgebung und alles auf dem Spielplatz war Teil dieser Umgebung... aber er hatte nicht das, was ein Spielplatz normalerweise haben sollte: lose Elemente, die die Kinder selber kontrollieren."[3]

Die Neugestaltung des Aussenraumes der Riis Houses erregt grosse Aufmerksamkeit und Friedberg erhält zahlreiche Auszeichnungen. Wie für Richard Dattner sind auch für Friedberg die Abenteuerspielplätze Londons und die nie

Landscape architect,
New York

M. Paul Friedberg arrived in New York in 1958 to set up shop as a young nursery gardener.[1] Although he had no experience in landscape architecture, he still managed to win his first commissions from the New York Housing Authority, which was responsible for building public housing. The strict regulations offered hardly any room for creative design. Yet Friedberg managed to find a gap in them: instead of the statue planned for the Nathan Straus Houses, he designed a small public square; then, at short notice, he even asked an artist friend to make a sculpture for children to play on instead of a bust. "The fact that I had challenged the system, and been successful, gave me an incentive to approach future work with a broader perspective. The satisfaction came from pressing the limits of traditional boundaries, the 'status quo.'"[2]

In *The Death and Life of Great American Cities* (1961), the most controversial book on urban planning, the journalist and activist Jane Jacobs criticized urban authorities for renovating slums by relocating their residents to giant public housing projects. Brooke Astor, a visionary philanthropist who was president of the Vincent Astor Foundation, was so struck by the book's claims that she turned to the Housing Authority. In what was also an attempt to give the foundation a new philanthropic profile, she offered to help improve the ghetto-like situation in the projects. Her ideal image was "green outdoor spaces" that could serve as meeting places for a wide range of residents, from children and teenagers to seniors. Friedberg won the first competition to design a better environment for the Carver Houses in Spanish Harlem in Manhattan, and was given complete freedom for the project. He came up with a landscape whose topography was the main feature to play in and with; however, he did not make the project that radical after all and ended up equipping the landscape with prefabricated playground equipment. Only with his next design, for the Jacob Riis Houses in the East Village, did he fully trust the potential of topography and produce a kind of hilly landscape of paving stones, concrete and wooden sculptures, an amphitheater, and numerous places to sit. Friedberg called this approach "Linked Play," as he described it in his 1970 book *Play and Interplay*: "We began to see the value of something called linked play. The playground became an environment and everything in the playground was a part of that environment ... but it didn't have what a playground really should have: loose elements that kids control themselves."[3]

The new design of the outdoor spaces at Riis Houses attracted a great deal of attention, and Friedberg received numerous awards.

99

gebauten Spiellandschaften Isamu Noguchis wichtige Weg-weiser. Zentral ist zudem die unmittelbare Stadtumgebung, die Friedberg als vielfältige Inspirationsquelle dient. Als er beim Bau der New Yorker Subway vertikal in den Boden gerammte Holzpfosten sieht, übernimmt er die Idee. Es entstehen daraus Klettergerüste mit angehängten Schaukeln. Dazu entwirft er mobile Spielplatzmodule, mit denen leere Grundstücke vorüber-gehend in Spielplätze – zu *Vest Pocket Parks* – umgewandelt werden. Die dazu benötigten Holzpfosten werden aus Portland angeliefert. Als die Nachfrage nach dieser Art von einfacher Gestaltung zunimmt, gründet Friedberg zusammen mit Ron Greene, dem Grafiker der Holzfirma in Portland, die Firma Tim-berform. Zusammen entwerfen sie Modelle für Holzspielplätze, die je nach Ort und Budget einfach realisiert werden können: Ein Set von Holzpfosten kann bestellt und dann selbst zusam-mengebaut werden, sei es nach einer mitgelieferten Vorlage oder nach eigenen Vorstellungen. So entstehen zahlreiche Spielplätze in den ganzen USA.

Friedberg führt seine Karriere als Landschafts-architekt fort und entwirft bis in die 1980er Jahre gelegentlich noch Spielplätze. Anstelle von „reinen" Spielräumen für Kinder schafft er Stadtlandschaften, die Spiel, Raum- und Sinnes-wahrnehmungen einbeziehen. GB

Liste der Projekte (Auswahl):

• Nathan Straus Houses, New York City Housing Authority, New York
• Quincy Street (zusammen mit dem Pratt Institute), New York
• Carver Houses, New York City Housing Authority, New York, 1963, finanziert durch die Astor Foundation
• Leffert Place Brooklyn, Vest Pocket Park, New York, 1964, finanziert durch die Rockefeller Foundation
• Jacob Riis Plaza an der Lower East Side, New York, 1965, finanziert durch die Astor Foundation
• Buchanan School, Washington, 1966, finanziert durch die Astor Foundation für Lady Bird Johnson's Beautify America Program
• P.S. 166 an der West 89th Street, New York, 1967; 2000 saniert, besteht noch in Teilen
• Zehn Vest Pocket Parks 1967–1968: Bedford Stuy-vesant (Brooklyn), Mulberry Street Park, 29th Street, New York
• Housing and Urban Development Demonstration Grant (Grant from the Department of Housing and Develop-ment; Beautification Act), 1968
• Spielplatz für soziale Wohnbausiedlung, Pruitt-Igoe, St. Louis (Timberform, Oregon), 1968
• Wohn- und Spielstrasse, Superblock Bedford-Stuyvesant, New York, 1969
• Gottesman Plaza Playground, West 94th Street, New York, 1970
• Spielplatz für Fort Lincoln New Town, Washington, 1972
• Billy Johnson Playground, East 67th Street, Central Park, New York, 1985; bestehend

For Friedberg, like Richard Dattner, the adventure playgrounds in London, and Isamu Noguchi's unrealized playground designs for New York were important inspirations. In addition, the immediate urban environment was central; it served Friedberg as a versatile source of ideas. When he saw wood-en posts hammered vertically into the ground at a subway construction site, he adapted the idea and created jungle gyms with swings hung on them. He also designed mobile playground modules that could turn vacant lots into temporary play-grounds: "Vest Pocket Parks." The wooden posts needed for these were delivered from Portland. As the demand for this kind of simple design grew, Friedberg and Ron Greene, the graphic designer at the lumber company in Portland, founded Timberform. Together, they designed models for playgrounds made of wood that were easy to adapt to a playground's site and budget: you could order a set of wooden posts and then install them yourself, according to either the company's plans or your own ideas. Numerous playgrounds thus sprang up all over the United States. Friedberg continued his career as a landscape architect and even occasionally built playgrounds in the 1980s. Instead of "pure" play spaces for children, he created urban landscapes that incor-porated play, space, and the senses. GB

Selected List of Projects:

• Nathan Straus Houses, New York City Housing Authority, New York
• Quincy Street (with the Pratt Institute), New York
• Carver Houses, New York City Housing Authority, New York, 1963, sponsored by the Astor Foundation
• Leffert Place Brooklyn, Vest Pocket Park, New York, 1964, sponsored by the Rockefeller Foundation
• Jacob Riis Plaza on the Lower East Side, New York, 1965, sponsored by the Astor Foundation
• Buchanan School, Washington, 1966, sponsored by the Astor Foundation for Lady Bird Johnson's Beautify America Program
• P.S. 166 on West 89th Street, New York, 1967; renovated in 2000, still existant in part
• Ten Vest Pocket Parks 1967–1968: Bedford Stuyvesant (Brooklyn), Mulberry Street Park, 29th Street, New York
• Housing and Urban Development Demonstration Grant (Grant from the Department of Housing and Development; Beautification Act), 1968
• Playground for Housing Project Pruitt-Igoe, St. Louis (Timberform, Oregon), 1968

Anmerkungen:

1   Studium des Ziergartenbaus an der School of Agriculture, Cornell University, Ithaca, New York

2   M. Paul Friedberg, „My design process", in: *Process: Architecture*, Tokyo, Nr. 82 (*M. Paul Friedberg. Landscape Design*), 1989, S. 21.

3   Zitiert nach: Daniel Jost, „Changing Places. Resurrecting the ‚Adventure-Style' Playground", in: *Landscape Architecture Magazine*, Washington, Nr. 3, März 2010, S. 63.

•   Residential and Play Street, Superblock Bedford-Stuyvesant, New York, 1969
•   Gottesman Plaza Playground, West 94th Street, New York, 1970
•   Playground for Fort Lincoln New Town, Washington, 1972
•   Billy Johnson Playground, East 67th Street, Central Park, New York, 1985; still existant

Notes:

1   He studied ornamental horticulture at the Cornell University School of Agriculture in Ithaca, New York.

2   M. Paul Friedberg, "My design process," in *Process: Architecture*, Tokyo, no. 82 (*M. Paul Friedberg. Landscape Design*), 1989, p. 21.

3   Cited in Daniel Jost, "Changing Places. Resurrecting the 'Adventure-Style' Playground," in *Landscape Architecture Magazine*, Washington, no. 3, March 2010, p. 63.

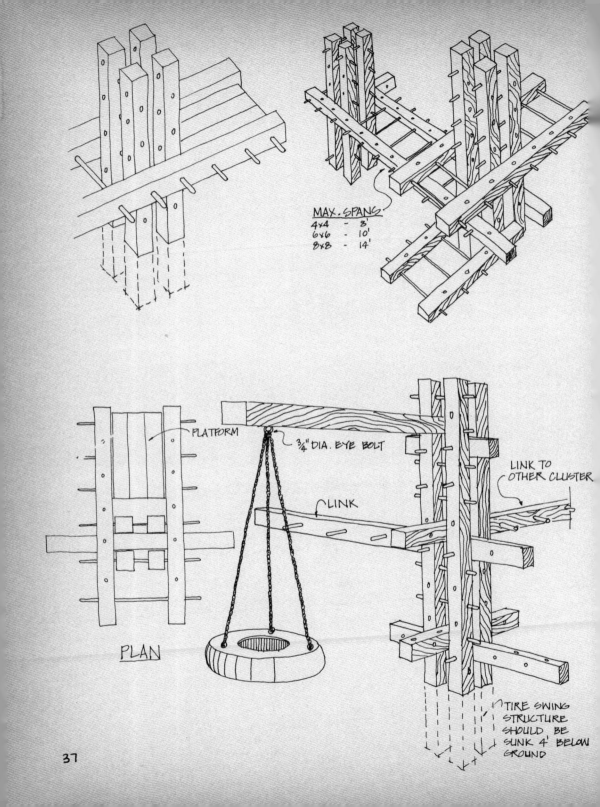

MAX. SPANS
4x4 - 8'
6x6 - 10'
8x8 - 14'

PLATFORM

3/4" DIA. EYE BOLT

LINK

LINK TO
OTHER CLUSTER

PLAN

TIRE SWING
STRUCTURE
SHOULD BE
SUNK 4' BELOW
GROUND

NOTES

BOTH THE SIDES AND TOPS OF ALL WOOD EDGES SHOULD BE CHAMFERED OR ROUNDED A MIN. OF $\frac{1}{4}$", AND SOMETIMES AS MUCH AS 1". SAND ALL ROUGH SPOTS AND ELIMINATE ALL LARGE SPLINTERED AREAS.

WOOD WILL CONTINUE TO CHECK AND SHRINK, BUT AS LONG AS THERE ARE NO MAJOR SPLINTER AREAS, CHILDREN WILL DEVELOP A SENSE OF DISCRETION AND USE CAUTION.

P.S. 166 transforms another dismal and inadequate schoolyard into a community facility. It is different from Buchanan, serving a more local population and a smaller age range (five to twelve). Also, large-scale facilities were not needed with Central Park nearby. The comfort station is below the slide mound to save space. Unfortunately, integration of the playground with the rest of the neighborhood was prevented by a fence, installed at the insistence of the school authorities.

Alfred Ledermann
*1919
Alfred Trachsel
1920–1995

Jurist, Zürich
und Architekt, Zürich

Lawyer, Zurich,
and architect, Zurich

Nach Abschluss des Jurastudiums 1944 in Basel sucht Alfred Ledermann eine Arbeit im Jugendbereich. Der Zweite Weltkrieg geht zu Ende und er hegt den Wunsch, sich in der Nachkriegshilfe zu engagieren. Während zwei Jahren hilft er im Ausland bei der Betreuung von kriegsgeschädigten Jugendlichen und im Wiederaufbau. Danach erhält er den Auftrag, eine Kinderhilfsaktion im Ruhrgebiet zu leiten: 7'000 Kleinkinder und 20'000 Schüler müssen täglich eine Mahlzeit erhalten. Er stellt fest, dass die Kinder geistige Nahrung ebenso wie Essen und Kleidung brauchen, und organisiert daher auch Feste und Spielaktionen. Die Erlebnisse im Deutschland der Nachkriegszeit prägen ihn ein Leben lang, insbesondere die Fähigkeit der Kinder, inmitten von Zerstörung ihre eigene kleine Spielwelt zu schaffen.

1948 wird Ledermann Mitarbeiter der Schweizer Jugendorganisation Pro Juventute. Von 1958 bis 1979 amtiert er als deren Zentralsekretär. Die Pro Juventute wurde 1912 gegründet, um die weit verbreitete Tuberkulose zu bekämpfen. Später übernimmt sie vielfältige soziale Aufgaben, bekämpft Armut, stärkt Familien und alleinerziehende Mütter und bietet seit den 1920er Jahren Freizeitangebote für Jugendliche an.[1]

Ledermann will als Zentralsekretär der Pro Juventute die Familie als Bezugsort für das Kind stärken und generationenübergreifende Angebote schaffen. Zusammen mit dem Architekten und Adjunkt im Zürcher Hochbauamt Alfred Trachsel ruft er 1954 den ersten Robinsonspielplatz in Zürich-Wipkingen ins Leben. Trachsel hatte zuvor nach dem Vorbild der progressiven Spielplätze Dänemarks einen ähnlichen Platz für seine Genossenschaftssiedlung geplant und gemeinsam mit anderen Familienvätern selber gebaut. Nachdem er für die städtische Siedlung Heiligfeld einen weiteren Spielplatz entworfen hatte, betraute ihn das Hochbauamt fortan mit dieser Aufgabe. Ledermann wird auf Trachsel und dessen Engagement aufmerksam. Anlässlich des V. Internationalen Kongresses für Schulbaufragen und Freilufterziehung in Zürich gründen sie zusammen mit anderen Persönlichkeiten den Kreis Zürcher Spielplatzfreunde, der bei der Eröffnung des ersten Robinsonspielplatzes die Patenschaft übernimmt. „Diesen umfassenden Spielplatz, der bis jetzt weder in Dänemark noch sonstwo verwirklicht werden konnte, haben wir ‚Robinsonspielplatz' getauft und Architekt Trachsel beschreibt ihn wie folgt: ‚Der Robinsonspielplatz ist der Bauplatz ohne Verbote und ohne Gefahren. Hier dürfen die Kinder etwas tun, ohne dass der Lehrer sagt wie, die Mutter wo und der Vater warum. Hier können ausgediente Fahrzeuge, die nun nicht mehr lebensgefährlich sind, zerlegt und erforscht

After receiving his law degree in Basel in 1944, Alfred Ledermann looked for work with children. The Second World War was coming to an end, and he wanted to get involved in postwar aid in some way. He went abroad for two years, working on rebuilding projects and helping to take care of children traumatized by the war. Then he found a job running an aid project for children in the Ruhr valley: 7,000 preschoolers and 20,000 schoolchildren needed to be given one meal a day. He noticed that the children needed not only food and clothing, but also nourishment for their minds, so he began to organize festivals and events where the children could play. These experiences in postwar Germany informed the rest of his life, especially in terms of how children were able to create their own little world of play in the middle of devastation.

In 1948 Ledermann began working for the Swiss youth organization Pro Juventute. From 1958 to 1979 he was the General Secretary. Pro Juventute was founded in 1912 to fight tuberculosis, which was still ubiquitous. Later it tackled a wide variety of social issues: it fought poverty, supported families and single mothers, and, beginning in the 1920s, ran recreational programs for children and teenagers.[1]

As the General Secretary of Pro Juventute, Ledermann wanted to offer transgenerational programs and support the family as the central part of children's lives. In 1954 he teamed up with the architect Alfred Trachsel, who worked for Zurich's Building Department, to build the first Robinson Crusoe playground in the Zurich neighborhood of Wipkingen. Before realizing this project, Trachsel had been inspired by the progressive playgrounds in Denmark to plan and build a similar playground with other fathers at the cooperative housing development he lived in. After he had designed a further playground in the new development of Heiligfeld, the Building Department assigned him to playground design permanently, and Ledermann heard about Trachsel and his projects. At the Fifth International Congress on School Construction and Open-Air Education in Zurich, they co-founded the Zurich Circle of Playground Friends to support the setup of the first Robinson Crusoe playground. "We called it the 'Robinson Crusoe playground,' this comprehensive type of playground that has not yet been realized anywhere else, even in Denmark, and the architect Trachsel describes it as follows: 'The Robinson Crusoe playground is a construction site without rules and without dangers. Here, the children are allowed to do things without having the teacher say how, the mother where, or the

werden, hier gibt es Material für Hoch- und Tiefbau, Werkzeug und Farben, Rüstzeug für Technik und Kunst, hier kann Demokratie und Anstand geübt werden, denn Nachbarprobleme und Materialbeschaffungssorgen können nur so befriedigend gelöst werden.'"[2]

In der Folge entwirft Trachsel im Auftrag der Pro Juventute zahlreiche Robinson- und andere Spielplätze für Schweizer Städte und beschreibt in Publikationen, Zeitschriften und Merkblättern, was einen guten Spielplatz ausmacht. Zudem lässt er seine Spielgeräte aus Stahlrohren patentieren und entwirft 1958 für die SAFFA[3] den Verkehrsgarten und die Eternit-Iglus.

Ledermann mit seinem politisch-institutionellen Rückhalt und Trachsel mit seinem planerischen Wissen und Tatendrang initiieren die sogenannten Gemeinschaftszentren in Zürich. Zwischen 1954 und 1979 entstehen 14 dieser bis heute funktionierenden Quartierzentren[4], meistens ergänzt mit einem Robinson- oder anderen Spielplatz. 1959 geben Ledermann und Trachsel auf Anfrage des international vernetzten Kunst- und Architekturverlags Gerd Hatje in Stuttgart ein Buch zur Planung von Spielplätzen heraus: *Spielplatz und Gemeinschaftszentrum* erscheint zweisprachig, wird nach wenigen Jahren in weitere Sprachen übersetzt und avanciert zum Standardwerk.

Für Ledermann sind Spielplätze Impulsgeber, um die soziokulturelle Stadtlandschaft neu zu gestalten. Seine Erfahrungen in Zürich sind im Ausland gefragt und er reist 1967 im Auftrag der UNO nach Jugoslawien, um das Land in Fragen zur Freizeit und Stadtentwicklung zu beraten. Zudem wirkt er bei der Gründung der European Leisure and Recreation Association (ELRA) mit. 1976 spricht er für den UNO-Weltkongress Habitat / Menschliche Siedlung Empfehlungen aus. 1979 tritt Ledermann vorzeitig in den Ruhestand, widmet sich aber weiterhin sozialen Aufgaben zum Wohl des Kindes. GB

Anmerkungen:

1   Ein schwarzes Kapitel der Pro Juventute beginnt 1926 mit dem Kinderhilfswerk Kinder der Landstrasse. Auf Anfrage der kommunalen und kantonalen Behörden übernimmt dieses die Vormundschaft für rund 600 Kinder von Fahrenden, um sie fremd zu platzieren. Diese skandalöse Praxis wird erst Anfang der 1970er Jahre thematisiert und führt zu grossem Imageschaden für die Stiftung. Weitere Informationen zur Stiftungsgeschichte der Pro Juventute auf: http://www.projuventute.ch / Geschichte.69.0.html (zuletzt aufgerufen am 1. Oktober 2015).
2   Alfred Ledermann, „Robinson kommt nach Zürich... Tagebuchnotizen von Dr. A. Ledermann", in: *Neue Zürcher Zeitung*, Zürich, 21. Mai 1954.
3   2. Schweizerische Ausstellung für Frauenarbeit auf der Landi-Wiese in Zürich, 17. Juli-15. September 1958
4   Zwischen 1954 und 1977 entstehen folgende Gemeinschaftszentren: Wipkingen, Heuried, Leimbach, Buchegg, Bachwiesen, Wollishofen, Neubühl, Neu-Affoltern, Altstadt, Heerenschürli, Lochergut, Seebach, Loogarten und Grünau. Danach entstehen noch Zentren in Affoltern, Witikon, Schindlergut und Oerlikon.

father why. Here, junk cars that are no longer life threatening can be taken apart and examined; here, there is material for building and digging, there are tools, paint, and whatever you need for technology and art; here, democracy and integrity can be put into practice, for only with them can problems with neighbors or with the acquisition of materials be satisfactorily solved.'"[2]

Trachsel continued to be commissioned by Pro Juventute to design numerous other Robinson Crusoe playgrounds for Swiss cities (as well as conventional playgrounds). In addition to writing about what made for a good playground in books, magazine articles, and flyers, he patented his playground equipment made of steel pipes, and designed a "traffic garden" and asbestos "igloos" for a 1958 fair.[3]

With Ledermann's political-institutional support and Trachsel's drive and planning skills, the two teamed up to establish community centers in Zurich. Between 1954 and 1979, 14 of these neighborhood centers[4] were built (all of which are still in use today), and most of them have a playground, whether a Robinson Crusoe playground or a conventional one. In 1959, Ledermann and Trachsel were asked by the internationally renowned art and architecture publisher Gerd Hatje in Stuttgart to write a book about the planning of playgrounds: *Spielplatz und Gemeinschaftszentrum* [*Creative Playgrounds and Recreation Centers*] was published bilingually and, with translations into more languages within a few years, eventually became a standard work.

For Ledermann, playgrounds provided impulses for a sociocultural redefinition of the urban landscape. His experiences in Zurich were in demand abroad, and in 1967 he was sent to Yugoslavia by the UN as an advisor on recreation and urban development. He also helped found the European Leisure and Recreation Association (ELRA) and, in 1976, came up with recommendations for the first United Nations Conference on Human Settlements (UN-Habitat). After taking early retirement in 1979, he continued to work on social projects for children's welfare. GB

Notes:

1   A dark chapter in the history of Pro Juventute began in 1926 with the founding of the organization *Kinder der Landstrasse* ["Highway Children"]. Local and cantonal authorities asked Pro Juventute to serve as the legal guardian of about 600 traveler children who were taken from their parents and sent to foster homes. This scandalous practice was only made public at the beginning of the 1970s; the foundation's image was seriously damaged. More information about the history of Pro Juventute is available on their

77   Alfred Trachsel, Spielplatz / Playground Bergwiesen, Siedlung / Housing estate Triemli, Albisrieden, Zürich / Zurich, 1951.
78   Alfred Trachsel, Kletterturm / Climbing tree, Robinsonspielplatz / Robinson Crusoe playground, Wipkingen, Zürich / Zurich.

website: http://www.projuventute.ch/Geschichte.69.0.html (last accessed November, 2015).
2   Alfred Ledermann, "Robinson kommt nach Zürich... Tagebuchnotizen von Dr. A. Ledermann," in *Neue Zürcher Zeitung*, Zurich, May 21, 1954.
3   The fair was the Second Swiss Fair for Women's Work (2. Schweizerische Ausstellung für Frauenarbeit) at the Landi park in Zurich, July 17–September 15, 1958. A "traffic garden" is a small park that gives children playful opportunities to learn traffic rules for pedestrians and cyclists.
4   Between 1954 and 1977, the following community centers were founded: Wipkingen, Heuried, Leimbach, Buchegg, Bachwiesen, Wollishofen, Neubühl, Neu-Affoltern, Altstadt, Heerenschürli, Lochergut, Seebach, Loogarten, and Grünau. Centers were also founded later in Affoltern, Witikon, Schindlergut, and Oerlikon.

81   Alfred Trachsel, Spielplatz / Playground Heiligfeld, Zürich /
      Zurich, 1955

82   Kinder spielen in Kriegstrümmern / Children playing in war
      rubble, Gelsenkirchen, c. 1946

83   Alfred Trachsel, Eternit-Iglus, Pro Juventute Kinderland,
2. Schweizerische Ausstellung für Frauenarbeit auf der Landi-Wiese /
Asbestos "igloos," Pro Juventute Children's Land, Second Swiss Fair for
Women's Work, Zürich / Zurich, 1958

84   Spielmodule bei der Freizeitanlage / Play modules near the
community center Bachwiesen, Albisrieden, Zürich / Zurich, c. 1961

Wasserspielplätze, Düsseldorf, Deutschland

Planung: Stadtgartenamt Düsseldorf (Ulrich Wolf)

Water playgrounds at Düsseldorf, Germany

Designed by the Municipal Gardens Department of Düsseldorf (Ulrich Wolf)

1. Lageplan: Wasserspielplatz mit Geräten (1), Abflußkanal (2), Spritzrohre (3), Kleinkinderbad (4), Unterstandhalle mit Wärter- und Geräteraum und Toiletten (5), Sandspielplatz (6), Liegewiesen (7).
2. Großes Klettergerüst aus Metallrohren mit Düsen in und unter den Ständern(Wasservorhang).

1. Site plan: water playground with equipment (1), drainage channel (2), spray pipes (3), paddling pool for small children (4), shelter with attendants' room, store and lavatories (5), sandpit (6), lawn (7).
2. Large climbing structure of tubular steel with jets inside and below the supports (water curtain).

Wasser übt eine starke Anziehungskraft auf Kinder aus: Duschen, Pfützen, Brunnen und Rasensprenger sind Anlaß zu immer neuer Begeisterung. Deshalb dürfte Wasser eigentlich auf keinem Kinderspielplatz fehlen. Da Planschbecken im allgemeinen rasch verschmutzen und zudem nur mit verhältnismäßig hohen Bau- und Unterhaltungskosten erstellt werden können, ging das Stadtgartenamt Düsseldorf neue Wege und entwickelte in den vergangenen vier Jahren verschiedene sogenannte Wasserspielplätze. Auf leicht geneigten, plattenbelegten Flächen werden Kletter- und Hüpfgeräte aufgestellt, die durch Spritzrohre, Düsen und Dreharme Wasser ausstoßen. Die aus verzinkten oder gestrichenen Metallrohren zusammengesetzten Geräte werden für jeden Platz neu kombiniert und auf die Spielbedürfnisse der verschiedenen Altersstufen abgestimmt. Bewegliche Spritzrohre am äußeren Rand und ein Abflußkanal an der tiefsten Stelle des Platzes sorgen für eine ständige Reinigung der Anlage.

Water has a great fascination for children: showers, paddling in dirty water, fountains and sprays arouse ever-fresh enthusiasm. That is why water should never be missing from any playground. As paddling pools generally get dirty quickly and as they can only be built and maintained at comparatively high cost, Düsseldorf Municipal Gardens Department made a new departure with its so-called water playgrounds, several of which have been installed during the last four years. Areas, paved on a slight incline, have climbing and hopping equipment which also discharges water by means of jets and revolving sprays. The plant, which consists of galvanised or painted steel tubes, is made up in different combinations for each playground and is modified according to the age-group for which it is intended. Movable sprays at the outer edge and a drainage channel at the lowest point of the paving keep the whole installation constantly clean.

2

3. Hangelgerät mit Düsen. Auf den Platten Trichterdüsen.
4. Eines der beweglichen Spritzrohre am Rande der Wasserfläche, mit denen die Platten »spielend« gereinigt werden.
5. Automatisches Kippgerät. Durch Wasserzulauf füllt sich die Schale, kippt um und kehrt wieder in die alte Lage zurück.
6. Stahlrohr-Spirale mit abwechselnd nach innen und außen gerichteten Düsen.

3. Curved horizontal bars with water jets. On the pavement are funnel jets.
4. One of the movable spray pipes at the edge of the water playground, with the help of which the paving slabs are kept clean by children having fun with the pipes.
5. Automatic splashing device. Water pouring into the bowl turns it over and returns it to its former position.
6. Circular pipe with jets directed to the outside and inside alternately.

3

5

6

86   Group Ludic, Hérouville Saint-Clair (in der Nähe von / near
Caen, Basse-Normandie), 1968

Group Ludic
Paris

Simon Koszel, *1939 (Warschau), Architekt, Fotograf, Filmer / David Roditi, *1937 (Manchester), Architekt, Designer / Xavier de la Salle, *1938 (Brest), Seemann, Bildhauer, Sozialwissenschaftler

Simon Koszel, David Roditi und Xavier de la Salle lernen sich in Paris im Umfeld der Ve Biennale de Paris 1967 kennen. Roditi stellt dort *Elément Plein de Jeu No. 1* aus, eine modulare farbige Skulptur aus Polyurethan und Polyester, welche die Kinder nach Gutdünken zusammenbauen dürfen. De la Salle arbeitet zu diesem Zeitpunkt ebenfalls an Spielskulpturen und so scheint es ihnen sinnvoll, die verschiedenen Ideen und Projekte zu verbinden.

Mit ihrem eigenständigen, interdisziplinären Vorgehen ecken sie an, zumal sie an keine Institution gebunden sind. In Frankreich liegt die Freizeitgestaltung der Kinder in den Händen des Staates und dem von ihm pädagogisch geschulten Personal. Group Ludic widersetzt sich diesem Zwang zur institutionalisierten Kindheit, sie wollen selbst in einer freien, nicht hierarchischen Art und Weise zusammenarbeiten. Der innovative und bisweilen chaotische Ansatz von Group Ludic irritiert, so dass sie nur zögerlich Aufträge erhalten. Zu dieser Zeit gibt es in Paris kaum interessante Spielmöglichkeiten und in den Stadtparks ist gar das Betreten des Rasens verboten, woraufhin sich Roditi beim Sportministerium über die mangelnden Spielgelegenheiten beschwert. Die Organisatoren der *Colonies de vacances* interessieren sich für neue Spielgeräte, weshalb sich Roditi mit de la Salle und Koszel, die er zu dieser Zeit kennenlernt, in die Produktion von Prototypen stürzt. Roditi wohnt auf einem auf der Seine verankerten Kahn und lässt die Prototypen auf dem Quai stehen. Die eignen und vorbeigehende Kinder und Erwachsene benutzen diese, was Group Ludic interessante Rückschlüsse für Verbesserungen ermöglicht. An einem Kongress der *Écoles maternelles* lernen sie Fernand Nathan, Eigentümer des Verlagshauses Nathan, kennen, der, inspiriert vom Children's Creative Center der *Expo 67* in Montreal, nach neuen Spielgeräten sucht. Fortan unterstützt er die Arbeit der drei Aktivisten und schafft mit der Firma Aires et Volumes einen Produktions- und Vertriebskanal für ihre Spielmodule.

1968 realisiert Group Ludic eine erste Spiellandschaft in einer Feriensiedlung in Royan an der Atlantikküste[1]. Es ist ein im Sand vergrabenes „U-Boot", in welches die Kinder wie in eine Höhle hinabsteigen oder rutschen können. Gebaut aus recycelten industriellen Materialien, wird es mit den neu entwickelten Spielmodulen ergänzt. Die Gruppe bleibt längere Zeit vor Ort, um die Gestaltung den Bedürfnissen der Kinder anzupassen. Im Anschluss erhalten sie weitere Anfragen, was zu Überlegungen führt, wie die Objekte industriell angefertigt werden können. Als billige Möglichkeit bieten sich Abfallprodukte der Industrie an, z.B. ehemalige Gussformen für Luftballons oder altes Armeematerial. Für die Satellitenstadt Hérouville Saint-Clair bei Caën[2] kommt dieses Vorgehen erstmals zum Tragen und sie bauen eine Art Kinderstadt mit

Simon Koszel, *1939 (Warsaw), architect, photographer, filmmaker / David Roditi, *1937 (Manchester), architect, designer / Xavier de la Salle, *1938 (Brest), sailor, sculptor, social scientist

Simon Koszel, David Roditi, and Xavier de la Salle first met during the Ve Biennale de Paris in 1967, which featured Roditi's *Elément Plein de Jeu No. 1*, a colorful, modular sculpture of polyurethane and polyester, which children could put together any way they liked. At that time, de la Salle was also working on play sculptures, so they decided to work together on their ideas and projects.

Their independent and interdisciplinary position was controversial, especially as they were not connected to any institution. In France, recreational opportunities for children were in the hands of the state and its own trained pedagogical personnel. Group Ludic resisted the pressure to institutionalize childhood; they wanted to cooperate freely, without hierarchy. Their innovative and at times chaotic approach was so irritating that they only gradually began to get any commissions. At the time, there were hardly any interesting places for children to play in Paris, and in the city's parks people were not even allowed to walk on the grass. So Roditi contacted the Sports Ministry to complain about the lack of opportunities to play. The organizers of the *Colonies de vacances* were interested in new playground equipment, so Roditi, de la Salle, and Koszel (who had now joined them) plunged into the production of prototypes. Roditi lived on a houseboat on the Seine and put the prototypes on the quay, where they were used by the children of the members of the group, as well as by children and adults who were passing by, which gave the designers feedback on what needed to be improved. At a congress for the *Écoles maternelles*, they met the publisher Fernand Nathan, who had been inspired by the Children's Creative Center at *Expo 67* in Montreal to look for new playground equipment. He began to support the work of the three activists, and founded the company Aires et Volumes to produce and distribute their playground modules.

In 1968, in a vacation development in Royan on the Atlantic coast, Group Ludic made their first playground,[1] a "submarine" buried in sand that the children could climb or slide down into, as if it were a cave. It was made of recycled industrial materials, and newly developed modules were added to it. The group stayed on site for a long time to adapt the design to the children's needs. Subsequently, they received enough inquiries about their playground equipment that they began to consider how to produce it industrially.

119

futuristisch anmutenden *Sphères*. Diese *Sphères* werden zum Wahrzeichen der Group Ludic. Zum ersten Mal müssen sie sich in den Satellitenstädten mit dem Problem des Vandalismus und dem harten Klima in den französischen *Villes Nouvelles* auseinandersetzen. Weitere Spielumgebungen entstehen in französischen Ferienorten wie La Grande Motte, Anglet, Lotzari / Korsika oder Biarritz.

1970 erhält Group Ludic vom Centre de Création Industrielle (CCI) in Paris den Auftrag, eine Spielumgebung in den Halles de Paris[3] zu entwerfen, bevor diese endgültig zerstört werden. Die Ausstellung *jouer aux halles*, welche die Kinder gratis besuchen können, ist während drei Monaten täglich geöffnet und zieht sehr viele Kinder an. Da die Aktion als Ausstellung angekündigt wird, kann sie sich dem Blick und der Kritik der Erziehungsautoritäten entziehen. *Jouer aux halles* wird von einem grossen Medienecho begleitet. Die Ausstellung ist ein willkommenes geschütztes Experimentierfeld für neue Spielgeräte, die Group Ludic danach in anderen Umgebungen weiterverwenden kann. Im gleichen Jahr realisiert Group Ludic auf Einladung des holländischen Warenhauses De Bijenkorf vier Spielplätze in Holland[4]. Diese Projekte werden von David Roditi geplant und umgesetzt. Die Gruppe beginnt sich zunehmend für eine *approche participative* zu interessieren: Das erste solche Projekt findet in Chalon-sur-Saône statt, wo sie auf Einladung des Maison de la Culture in der Innenstadt einen Bauspielplatz für die Jugendlichen aus den Vorstädten betreiben.

1972 verlässt David Roditi die Gruppe. Simon Koszel bleibt als „freies Element" dabei. Xavier de la Salle realisiert bis in die frühen 1990er Jahre Spielaktionen. Doch das soziale Klima in den französischen Grossiedlungen verschlechtert sich, Drogenkonsum und Jugendkriminalität nehmen zu. Ohne eine Gesamtstrategie können punktuelle Spielaktionen nichts mehr ausrichten, weshalb sich de la Salle zurückzieht. GB

Liste von Projekten (Auswahl):

(V VF=Village de Vacances Familles / Familienferiendorf)
(ZUP=Zone à urbaniser en priorité / Zone mit vorrangigem Entwicklungsbedarf)

• Sous-marin, Les Mathes / La Palmyre – Village de vacances des Pins de Cordouan, Royan, 1969
• Les logis du Clapet, Royan, 1969
• Quartier "La Grande Delle" (ZUP–ville nouvelle), Hérouville Saint-Clair, 1969
• Rue de Boucry, Paris, 1969
• Lozari V VF, Korsika, 1970
• Anglet V VF, 1970
• La Grande Motte V VF, 1969–1970
• Rembrandt Park, Amsterdam, im Auftrag von De Bijenkorf, 1970
• Park Blijdorp, Rotterdam, im Auftrag von De Bijenkorf, 1970
• Playground Eindhoven, im Auftrag von De Bijenkorf, 1970
• Zuiderpark, Den Haag, im Auftrag von De Bijenkorf, 1970

Old army material and waste products from industry, such as erstwhile molds for balloons, were inexpensive alternatives; this approach was first put into practice for the satellite town of Hérouville Saint-Clair outside of Caen,[2] where they built a kind of children's city with futuristic spheres that became the group's trademark. Such satellite towns were the first place where they had to deal with vandalism and the violent atmosphere of the French new towns; they went on to playgrounds in French vacation towns like La Grande Motte, Anglet, Biarritz, and Lotzari in Corsica.

In 1970, the Group Ludic was commissioned by the Centre de Création Industrielle (CCI) in Paris to design a play environment in Les Halles de Paris[3] before they were torn down. Many children, who all got in for free, attended the exhibition *jouer aux halles*, which was open daily for three months. As the event was advertised as an exhibition, the education authorities paid no attention to it and thus did not criticize it at all—but the media responded enthusiastically. The exhibition was a safe and welcome laboratory for new playground equipment, which the Group Ludic could then reuse in other contexts. In the same year, the Dutch department store De Bijenkorf commissioned four playgrounds by the group in Holland.[4] These projects were planned and built by David Roditi. The group then began to become more and more interested in a participatory approach: the first such project was in Chalon-sur-Saône, where the Maison de la Culture asked them to run a construction playground for teenagers form the suburbs.

In 1972, David Roditi left Group Ludic, leaving Simon Koszel who stayed on as a "free element." Xavier de la Salle continued organizing activities at playgrounds until the early 1990s. But the social climate in the large housing projects in the French suburbs kept deteriorating, with increasing drug consumption and juvenile crime. Without an overall strategy, occasional playground interventions no longer had any effect, so de la Salle stopped working on such projects. GB

Selected List of Projects:

(V VF=Village de Vacances Familles / Family Vacation Village)
(ZUP=Zone à urbaniser en priorité / Priority Urban Zone)

• Sous-marin, Les Mathes / La Palmyre – Village de vacances des Pins de Cordouan, Royan, 1969
• Les logis du Clapet, Royan, 1969
• Quarter "La Grande Delle" (ZUP–ville nouvelle), Hérouville Saint-Clair, 1969
• Rue de Boucry, Paris, 1969

- ZUP de Caucriauville, Le Havre (Normandie), 1970
- *jouer aux halles*, Les Halles, Paris, 1970
- Le Grand Large, Hôtel vacances Capricel, Biarritz, 1970
- Jardin d'acclimatation, Bois de Boulogne, Paris, 1971
- Abenteuerspielplatz, Chalon-sur-Saône (Burgund), 1972
- Biguglia VVF, Korsika, 1972
- Workshops, Foyer Rémois, Société Anonyme d'Habitations à Bon Marché (Gesellschaft für sozialen Wohnungsbau), Reims, 1973
- ZUP St-Jean des Vignes, Chalon-sur-Saône, 1973
- Internationales Jahr des Kindes, Jardin des Plantes, Paris, 1979

Anmerkungen:

1   Village de Vacances de la Caisse de retraite du Groupe Mornay, Les Pins de Cordouan, Royan
2   Quartier „La Grande Delle", Auftrag der Société d'Équipement de Basse Normandie (SEBN)
3   Pavillon 8 Halles de Baltard
4   Park Blijdorp, Rotterdam; Rembrandt Park, Amsterdam; Zuiderpark, Den Haag; Playground Eindhoven

- Lozari VVF, Corsica, 1970
- Anglet VVF, 1970
- La Grande Motte VVF, 1969–1970
- Rembrandt Park, Amsterdam, commission De Bijenkorf, 1970
- Park Blijdorp, Rotterdam, commission De Bijenkorf, 1970
- Playground Eindhoven, commission De Bijenkorf, 1970
- Zuiderpark, Den Haag, commission De Bijenkorf, 1970
- ZUP de Caucriauville, Le Havre (Normandy), 1970
- *jouer aux halles*, Les Halles, Paris, 1970
- Le Grand Large, Hôtel vacances Capricel, Biarritz, 1970
- Jardin d'acclimatation, Bois de Boulogne, Paris, 1971
- Adventure playground, Chalon-sur-Saône (Burgundy), 1972
- Biguglia VVF, Corsica, 1972
- Workshops, Foyer Rémois, Société Anonyme d'Habitations à Bon Marché (Corporation for social housing), Reims, 1973
- ZUP St-Jean des Vignes, Chalon-sur-Saône, 1973
- International Year of the Child, Jardin des Plantes, Paris, 1979

Notes:

1   Village de Vacances de la Caisse de retraite du Groupe Mornay, Les Pins de Cordouan, Royan.
2   Quartier de "La Grande Delle," commissioned by the Société d'Équipement de Basse Normandie (SEBN).
3   Pavillon 8 Halles de Baltard.
4   Park Blijdorp, Rotterdam; Rembrandt Park, Amsterdam; Zuiderpark, Den Haag; Playground Eindhoven

123

91-92   Group Ludic, Hérouville Saint-Clair (in der Nähe von / near
         Caën, Basse-Normandie), 1968

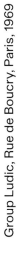

Group Ludic, ZUP de Caucriauville, Le Havre, 1970

101

129

Group Ludic, ZUP de Caucriauville, Le Havre, 1970

102

105   Group Ludic, Abenteuerspielplatz / Adventure playground
Chalon-sur-Saône, 1972

137

113 Egon Møller-Nielsen, *Tufsen*, Spielskulptur / Play sculpture,
Humlegården, Stockholm, 1949

Egon Møller≠Nielsen 1915–1959

Architekt und Bildhauer,
Stockholm

„Møller-Nielsen fing schon vor ein paar Jahren an, Spielskulpturen für seine dreijährige Tochter zu schaffen. Die Sehnsucht des kleinen Kindes, auf grossen Steinblöcken herumzuklettern, sich in einer Grotte zu verstecken oder einen Felsen herunterzurutschen – alle diese natürlichen kindlichen Instinkte sammelte ein glücklicher, spielerischer Vater in eine künstlerische Form und bald darauf stand auch die erste öffentliche Spielskulptur in einem Stockholmer Park.“[1] Diese Skulptur – genannt *Tufsen* – installiert die Stadtgärtnerei von Stockholm 1949 im Stadtpark. Es ist die erste abstrakte Spielskulptur im öffentlichen Raum und dies zu einer Zeit, in der Abstraktion überwiegend verhasst ist. Die Idee der Spielskulptur entsteht im Gespräch mit dem Stockholmer Stadtgärtner Holger Blom (1906–1996), unter dessen Leitung die Stadtparks eine neue Form und Funktion erhalten.[2] Für deren Gestaltung nimmt sich die Stadtgärtnerei die Natur zum Vorbild: statt Formalismus, Künstlichkeit und Inszenierung frei zugängliche Natur im Einklang mit der lokalen Topografie und Vegetation, statt repräsentativem Park ein grünes Wohn- und Spielzimmer. Die international viel beachtete Stockholm School of Park Design ist Teil eines politischen Programms, um die Lebensqualität in Stockholm zu verbessern. Schweden hatte sich nach dem Ersten Weltkrieg schnell von einem Agrarstaat zu einem industrialisierten Land gewandelt, mit verheerenden Auswirkungen auf die Wohnverhältnisse.

Tufsen[3] bleibt nicht die einzige Spielplastik von Møller-Nielsen. Er entwirft weitere Skulpturen, die in mehrfachen Abgüssen in schwedischen Städten aufgestellt werden. Seine Werke finden Eingang in einschlägige Publikationen, werden zum Modell der abstrakten Spielskulptur schlechthin und inspirieren Plastiker in ganz Europa und den USA. Für Künstler und Auftraggeber eröffnen sie zudem die Möglichkeit, die breite Öffentlichkeit mit abstrakter Kunst vertraut zu machen. „Trotzdem seine Spielplatzskulpturen sonderbar aussehen und nichts darstellen, haben sie nicht die Gegnerschaft der konservativen Kritik erweckt. Jetzt haben sich auch schon die Leute an diese nur-plastische und geheimnisvolle Form gewöhnt, die sie gleichwie zu einer teilnehmenden Attitüde lockt, den Kleinen zuwinkt herbeizukommen und bei dem lustigen Rutschen und Verstecken mit dabei zu sein. ‚Kleine Kinder haben nie verstehen können, warum sie nicht auf Skulpturen herumklettern dürfen' sagt Møller-Nielsen.“[4]

Der Erfolg von Møller-Nielsen geht unter andem auf den Architekturhistoriker, -kurator und -fotografen G. E. Kidder Smith zurück. In *Sweden Builds*[5], seiner einflussreichen Publikation, und der gleichnamigen Wanderausstellung im MoMA in New York macht Kidder Smith das Konzept des schwedischen Funktionalismus bekannt, die neuen Ideen für die Gestaltung des öffentlichen Raums sowie die Spielskulpturen von Møller-Nielsen. Die im Spieldesign tätige amerikanische

Architect and sculptor,
Stockholm

"Møller-Nielsen began making sculptures for play for his three-year-old daughter a few years ago. The little girl's desire to climb around on large stone blocks, to hide in a cave, or to slide down a rock—all these natural instincts of children were combined by a happy, playful father in an artistic way, and soon the first public play sculpture was installed in a park in Stockholm."[1] This sculpture, *Tufsen*, was installed in 1949 in the People's Park by Stockholm's Parks Department. At a time when abstraction was largely despised, it was the first abstract playground sculpture in a public space. The idea for a playground sculpture had come up in a conversation with Holger Blom (1906–1996), the head of the Parks Department, who was giving the city parks a new form and new functions.[2] The Parks Department took nature as a model for park design: instead of formalism, artifice, and fabrication, there would be easily accessible nature in harmony with the local topography and vegetation; instead of a representative park, there would be something like a green playroom and living room. The internationally renowned Stockholm School of Park Design was part of a political program to improve the quality of life in Stockholm, for Sweden's rapid transformation from an agrarian to an industrialized country after the First World War had had devastating effects on living conditions.

Tufsen[3] was not to be Møller-Nielsen's only such work; he went on to make further playground sculptures that were cast multiple times for use in Swedish cities. Once his works began to be mentioned in professional publications, they became the model of abstract playground sculpture as such and inspired sculptors all over Europe and in the United States. For artists and sponsors, they also helped make a broader public familiar with abstract art. "Although his playground sculptures look odd and do not represent anything, they have not made enemies of conservative critics. Now they have also gotten people used to forms that are nothing but shape and mystery. Such a sculpture draws people to participate, catching children's attention so that they rush over to be part of the joyful sliding and hiding. 'Small children have never understood why they are not allowed to climb around on sculptures,' says Møller-Nielsen."[4]

Part of Møller-Nielsen's success was thanks to the promotion of his work by the architectural historian, curator, and photographer G. E. Kidder Smith. In his influential book *Sweden Builds*[5] and the traveling exhibition of the same name at MoMA in New York, Kidder Smith drew attention to the concept of Swedish functionalism,

Firma Creative Playthings eröffnet Anfang der 1950er Jahre die neue Abteilung Play Sculpture für abstrakte Spielskulpturen. Deren Besitzer Frank Caplan reist unter anderem nach Schweden, wo er auch Møller-Nielsen trifft. Dieser wird unter Vertrag genommen und entwirft in der Folge die Skulptur *Spiral Slide*, die von Creative Playthings seriell hergestellt und vermarktet wird. GB

to new ideas for the design of public space, and to Møller-Nielsen's playground sculptures. Then, at the beginning of the 1950s, Creative Playthings, an American company active in playground design, opened a new department for abstract Play Sculpture. On his travels, the company's owner, Frank Caplan, visited Sweden and met and hired Møller-Nielsen, who then designed the *Spiral Slide* sculpture, which was mass-produced and marketed by Creative Playthings. GB

Anmerkungen:

1   E. Müller-Kraus, „Der Bildhauer, der spielen kann", in: *Abstrakte Kunst: Querschnitt 1953*, Sonderausgabe der Zeitschrift *Das Kunstwerk*, Woldemar Klein, Baden-Baden 1954, S. 83.
2   Biografie von Egon Møller-Nielsen auf http://sok.riksarkivet.se/sbl/Presentation.aspx?id=8679 (zuletzt aufgerufen am 1. Oktober 2015).
3   aus Kunststein in sechsfacher Ausführung hergestellt
4   Müller-Kraus, „Der Bildhauer" (s. Anm. 1), S. 83.
5   G. E. Kidder Smith, *Sweden Builds*, Reinhold Publishing Corporation, New York 1957, S. 230–231.

Notes:

1   E. Müller-Kraus, "Der Bildhauer, der spielen kann," in *Abstrakte Kunst: Querschnitt 1953*, special issue of *Das Kunstwerk*, Woldemar Klein, Baden-Baden 1954, p. 83.
2   Biography of Egon Møller-Nielsen on http://sok.riksarkivet.se/sb/Presentation.aspx?id=8679 (last accessed November, 2015).
3   Six copies were made in cast stone.
4   Müller-Kraus, "Der Bildhauer" (see note 1), p. 83.
5   G. E. Kidder Smith, *Sweden Builds*, Reinhold Publishing Corporation, New York 1957, p. 230–231.

 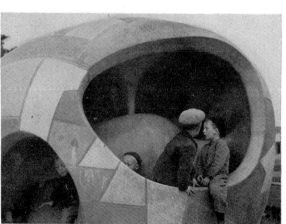

114   Seite aus / Page from G. E. Kidder Smith, *Sweden Builds*, Reinhold Publishing Corporation, New York 1957 (1950), p. 231.

115   Doppelseite aus / Spread from Paul Damaz, *Art in European Architecture. Synthèse des Arts*, Reinhold Publishing Corp., New York 1956, p. 208–209.

Play sculptures in Stockholm parks.

Sculptor/sculpteur: Egon Moller-Nielsen.

Sculptures-jardins dans les parcs de Stockholm.

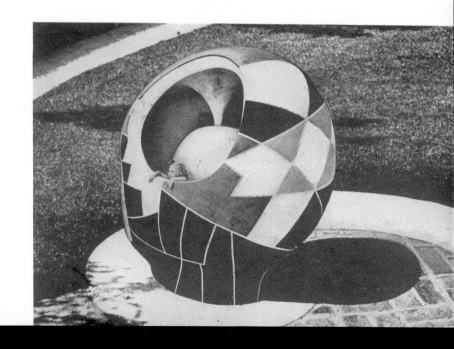

116   Egon Møller-Nielsen, *Tufsen*, Spielskulptur / Play sculpture,
Humlegården, Stockholm, 1949

145

117　Indoor-Spielplatz / Playground, *The Balloon*, Wohnsiedlung /
housing estate, Råby, Västerås, 1968–1969

Palle Nielsen
*1942

Künstler,
Kopenhagen

Artist,
Copenhagen

Bereits während seines Studiums an der Royal Danish Academy of Fine Arts berät Palle Nielsen den Stadtplaner einer Kopenhagener Vorortgemeinde in künstlerischen Belangen. Er nutzt seine Funktion, um Räume für Kinder zu entwerfen, die er *Spatial Formations* nennt. So eröffnet 1967 eine 5'000 m² grosse Spielumgebung, die zahlreiche Spielmöglichkeiten bietet, jedoch kaum die üblichen Geräte, und den Kindern stattdessen viel Raum für eigene Experimente und Begegnungen gewährt.

An einem Sonntagmorgen im Frühjahr 1968 verwandeln Nielsen und seine Gruppe von Aktivisten in einer spontanen Aktion den Hinterhof eines Arbeiterblocks in einen Abenteuerspielplatz. Auf Flugblättern fordern sie mehr Spielraum in Wohnquartieren. Zwei weitere illegale Plätze in Kopenhagen, die sie 1968 und 1969 „installieren", lösen ein grosses Echo in den Medien aus. Diese Guerilla-Spielplätze sind für die Gruppe um Nielsen ein Mittel, sich konstruktiv in die Stadtplanung einzumischen.[1]

Im Juni 1968 reist Nielsen nach Stockholm, um an der *Aktion Samtal* (Aktion Dialog) teilzunehmen. Die Aktion im öffentlichen Raum richtet sich gegen Kommerzialisierung, gegen gesichtslose Siedlungen und Plätze sowie gegen die Vorherrschaft des Autos in der Stadt. Bis Anfang der 1960er Jahre war Schweden mit seinem an den Bedürfnissen der Bewohner orientierten Funktionalismus international ein Vorbild für kommunalen Wohnungsbau, Wohnbaufinanzierung, Design und Grünraumgestaltung gewesen. In den 1960er und 1970er Jahren konzentriert sich die schwedische Wohnpolitik jedoch darauf, möglichst viele Wohnungen zu erstellen, wobei die urbane Qualität auf der Strecke bleibt und isolierte, trostlose Wohnghettos entstehen.[2]

Auch während der *Aktion Samtal* werden temporäre Spielplätze erstellt. Zusätzlich fordert Nielsen jedoch auch eine grössere Präsenz in den Medien, um die Anliegen der Aktion bekannt zu machen. Er schlägt vor, eine kulturelle Institution für ihre Zwecke einzuspannen, zum Beispiel das fortschrittliche Moderna Museet in Stockholm. Dies wird jedoch von *Aktion Samtal* als elitär kritisiert. Die Aktivisten wollen im Kollektiv agieren und nicht „egomane" Künstler sein. Trotzdem trifft sich Nielsen mit Carlo Derkert und Pontus Hultén, dem Kurator und dem Direktor des Moderna Museet. Sie willigen unter der Bedingung ein, dass die Gruppe ihr Projekt auf eigene Kosten und eigenes Risiko durchführt.[3]

Vom 30. September bis 23. Oktober 1968 findet die heute legendäre Ausstellung *Modellen – en modell för ett kvalitativt samhälle* (*Das Modell – ein Modell für eine qualitative Gesellschaft*) statt. Es ist eine raumfüllende, durch Holzstrukturen gegliederte Installation, ein Ort zum Theaterspielen, Musikhören, Bauen und Herumtoben. Nach dem Ende von *Modellen* gibt Nielsen in einem Zeitungsinterview bekannt, dass

Even while he was still a student at the Royal Danish Academy of Fine Arts, Palle Nielsen began working as a consultant on artistic issues with urban planners in a Copenhagen suburb. He used this position to design spaces for children that he called *Spatial Formations*. In 1967 he completed a 5,000m² playground that opened up countless ways to play, but had hardly any of the usual equipment, giving the children lots of space for their own experiments and encounters.

On a Sunday morning in the spring of 1968, Nielsen and his group of activists spontaneously turned the courtyard of a working-class apartment complex into an adventure playground and handed out flyers calling for more space for play in residential neighborhoods. When they "installed" two more illegal playgrounds in Copenhagen in 1968 and 1969, they got a great deal of publicity. For Nielsen and his group, these guerilla playgrounds were a way to get constructively involved in city planning.[1]

In June 1968, Nielsen traveled to Stockholm to take part in *Aktion Samtal* (Action Dialogue). This public happening opposed commercialization, faceless developments and squares, and the dominance of cars in the city. Until the beginning of the 1960s, Sweden's functionalism, which focused on the needs of residents, had been an international model for the design and financing of public housing, as well as for park design. However, in the 1960s and 1970s, Swedish housing policy began to concentrate on producing as many new apartments as possible, so the quality of city life was neglected, and isolated, grim residential ghettos were the result.[2]

Temporary playgrounds were set up during *Aktion Samtal*. But Nielsen also sought more media presence to publicize the purpose of the event. He suggested getting a cultural institution involved, such as the progressive Moderna Museet in Stockholm, but this was seen by *Aktion Samtal* as elitist. The activists wanted to act as a collective and not as "egotistical" artists. But Nielsen just went ahead and had a meeting with Carlo Derkert and Pontus Hultén, the curator and the director of the Moderna Museet. They agreed to help on condition that the group run the project at their own risk and expense.[3]

The now legendary exhibition *Modellen – en modell för ett kvalitativt samhälle* (*Model for a Qualitative Society*) took place from September 30 to October 23, 1968. The installation filled the room with wooden structures, creating a site for theater, music, building, and free play. After the exhibition was over, Nielsen announced in a newspaper interview that the playground

der Spielplatz zu kaufen sei, um ihn im Kontext einer Wohnsiedlung zu testen. Västerås, eine Gemeinde im Nordwesten von Stockholm, erwirbt *Modellen*.[4] Eine Immobilienfirma, die für den Erwerb und den Unterhalt aufkommt, will damit für ihre neu erstellte Siedlung Mieter anwerben. Jetzt *The Balloon* genannt, wird es im Frühjahr 1969 unter Protest der Anwohner geschlossen, nachdem die Immobilienfirma die Finanzierung einstellt.
GB

Anmerkungen:

1   Lars Bang Larsen (Hg.), *Palle Nielsen. The Model. A Model for a Qualitative Society* (1968), Museu d'art contemporani de Barcelona, 2009, S. 43–44.
2   Sveriges Arkitekturmuseum (Hg.), *Aufbruch und Krise des Funktionalismus. Bauen und Wohnen in Schweden 1930–80*, Stockholm 1976, S. 99–101.
3   Larsen, *Palle Nielsen* (s. Anm. 1), S. 45–49.
4   Ebd., S. 95–97.

was for sale so that it could be tested in the context of a housing development. *Modellen* was then acquired by Västerås, a city northwest of Stockholm.[4] In order to attract residents for its new development, a real-estate company agreed to pay for its purchase and upkeep. Now called *The Balloon*, it was closed in the spring of 1969 under protests from residents, after the company stopped financing it.
GB

Notes:

1   Lars Bang Larsen (ed.), *Palle Nielsen. The Model. A Model for a Qualitative Society* (1968), Museu d'art contemporani de Barcelona, 2009, p. 43–44.
2   Sveriges Arkitekturmuseum (ed.), *Aufbruch und Krise des Funktionalismus. Bauen und Wohnen in Schweden 1930–80*, Stockholm 1976, p. 99–101.
3   Larsen, *Palle Nielsen* (see note 1), p. 45–49.
4   Ibid., p. 95–97.

153

Isamu Noguchi, Kletterhügel und Planschbecken / Climbing mound and wading pool; Sachio Otani, Pavillons und Bodenbelag / Shelters and pavement, National Children's Land, Yokohama, c. 1965 / 1967

Isamu Noguchi
1904–1988

Bildhauer und Designer,
New York

Isamu Noguchi wächst als Sohn einer amerikanischen Mutter und eines japanischen Vaters auf. Von 1906 bis 1918 lebt er mit seiner Mutter und der jüngeren Halbschwester in Japan. Dann schickt ihn die Mutter auf ein Internat nach Indiana, USA. Mit sechzehn beschliesst er, Künstler zu werden, und benutzt von nun an den Familiennamen seines Vaters, Noguchi. Die legendäre Ausstellung von Constantin Brancusi im MoMA in New York 1926 leitet einen Wendepunkt in seinem künstlerischen Werdegang ein. Dank eines Guggenheim-Fellowship-Stipendiums wird er Assistent im Pariser Atelier von Brancusi, wo er die Sprache der Abstraktion und der Avantgarde kennenlernt. 1933 kehrt er von einem längeren Aufenthalt in China und Japan nach New York zurück. Er beginnt sich für Gärten, Landschaften und Parks zu interessieren, besonders für indianische und prähistorische Geländegestaltungen. Fasziniert von der Welt der Kinder entwirft er noch im gleichen Jahr den Spielplatz *Play Mountain*, der nur aus Erdmodellierungen besteht. Diese einfache Ausformung bietet unerschöpfliche Spielmöglichkeiten und wird für den Künstler zum Schlüsselwerk: „*Play Mountain* war der Kern, aus dem alle meine Ideen, die Skulptur mit der Erde zu verbinden, entsprangen. Er ist auch Vorläufer für den Spielplatz als skulpturale Landschaft."[1] Noguchi stellt seine revolutionäre Idee des Spielplatzes ohne Spielgeräte dem New Yorker Parkdirektor Robert Moses vor. Dieser steht am Anfang seiner Karriere und räumt der Planung von Spielplätzen oberste Priorität ein. Moses lehnt jedoch Noguchis Projekt ab und überzieht die Stadt stattdessen mit 400 standardisierten Spielghettos. 1940 erhält Noguchi von Lester McCoy, Parkdirektor von Honolulu, Hawaii, den Auftrag, ein Set von Spielgeräten zu entwerfen. Der vorzeitige Tod von McCoy verhindert jedoch den Abschluss des Projekts. Noguchi versucht die Geräte dem New Yorker Park Department zu verkaufen, erhält aber von Moses erneut eine Absage. 1941 entwirft Noguchi den *Contoured Playground*, eine abwechslungsreiche Spiellandschaft aus Mulden, Pyramiden und Hügeln. Mit dem Kriegseintritt der USA werden jedoch die öffentlichen Bauprojekte sistiert. 1946 ist *Contoured Playground* Teil der Ausstellung *Fourteen Americans* im MoMA.[2] Noguchis wachsender Erfolg als Künstler weckt nun zunehmend Aufmerksamkeit für seine Spielplatzprojekte. Als die Philanthropin Audrey Hess vom geplanten Spielplatz beim Hauptsitz der Vereinten Nationen in New York erfährt, versucht sie, Noguchi als Designer zu vermitteln. 1951 entwirft er für die Vereinten Nationen eine Spiellandschaft, die anstelle von Erdmodellierungen mit skulpturalen Objekten arbeitet. Moses gelingt es jedoch, „sein" Projekt durchzusetzen.[3] Sechs Monate später stellt das MoMA Noguchis abgelehntes Modell aus und die Zeitschrift *Architectural Record* beschreibt im Oktober 1952 den Entwurf als „den kreativsten und phantasievollsten Spielplatz, der je erfunden wurde"[4]. Es gibt mehr und mehr Stimmen, die New Yorks ideenlosen Umgang mit Spielplatzdesign kritisieren.

Sculptor and designer,
New York

Isamu Noguchi was the son of an American mother and a Japanese father. From 1906 to 1918 he lived with his mother and his younger half-sister in Japan; then his mother sent him to a boarding school in Indiana. At 16 he decided to become an artist and began to use his father's last name, Noguchi. The legendary Constantin Brancusi exhibition in 1926 at MoMA in New York was a turning point in his artistic development: he received a Guggenheim Fellowship to work as Brancusi's assistant in Paris, where he learned the language of abstraction and the avant-garde. In 1933, after a long stay in China and Japan, he returned to New York and began to be interested in gardens, landscapes, and parks, and especially in Indian and prehistoric landscaping. Fascinated by the world of children, he designed the playground *Play Mountain* that same year, which was made up of nothing but landscaping. This simple shaping offered inexhaustible possibilities for play and was a key moment in Noguchi's development: "*Play Mountain* was the kernel out of which have grown all my ideas relating sculpture to earth. It is also the progenitor of playgrounds as sculptural landscapes."[1] Noguchi then presented his revolutionary idea of a playground without equipment to New York's Parks Commissioner, Robert Moses, who, at the beginning of his career, was making playground planning a top priority. But Moses rejected Noguchi's project and overran the city with 400 standardized play ghettos instead. In 1940, Noguchi was asked by Lester McCoy, the Parks Director in Honolulu, Hawaii, to design a set of playground equipment. Unfortunately McCoy's premature death prevented the project from being completed, and when Noguchi tried to sell the equipment to the Parks Department in New York, he was again turned down by Moses. In 1941 he designed the *Contoured Playground*, a varied landscape for play made of hollows, pyramids, and hills. But with the American entrance into the war, public building projects were cancelled. Still, in 1946, the *Contoured Playground* was part of a MoMA exhibition, *Fourteen Americans*,[2] and Noguchi's increasing success as an artist drew attention to his playground projects. When the philanthropist Audrey Hess learned about the playground planned for the headquarters of the United Nations in New York, she tried to get Noguchi the commission for the design. In 1951, he presented a design to the UN for a playground landscape that worked with sculptural objects instead of landscaping. But Moses managed to push "his" project through instead.[3] Six months later, when MoMA exhibited Noguchi's rejected model, the *Architectural Record* described it in

Inzwischen wächst Noguchis Reputation weiter, und Hess setzt alles dran, ein Projekt von ihm umzusetzen. Eine neue Gelegenheit zeichnet sich 1960 ab: Zusammen mit dem Architekten Louis I. Kahn erarbeitet Noguchi mehrere Vorschläge für den Adele Levy Memorial Playground in New York (1961–1965). Auch mehrfache Anpassungen bringen die Einwände aus dem Parks Department, von dessen Spitze Moses 1961 zurückgetreten war, und von Seiten des Quartiers nicht zum Verstummen. Schliesslich bringt eine Klage das Projekt 1966 zu Fall. Zur gleichen Zeit kann Noguchi in Yokohama in Zusammenarbeit mit dem Architekten Sachio Otani für das National Children's Land eine erste Spiellandschaft realisieren. Wenig später entwirft er 1968 *Octetra*, ein Spielmodul aus rotem Beton, das im italienischen Spoleto im Rahmen des *Festival dei Due Mondi* erstmals installiert und bis heute produziert wird.

1976 realisiert Noguchi seinen ersten Spielplatz in den USA. Playscape in Atlanta wird vom High Museum of Art in Auftrag gegeben und 2009 restauriert. Hier arbeitet er nicht mit Geländeformen, sondern komponiert mit seinen skulpturalen Spielgeräten eine auf den Ort abgestimmte Spielwelt.

Noguchi hat als Grenzgänger zwischen westlicher und östlicher Kultur, zwischen Skulptur und Landschaftsarchitektur, zwischen Kunst und Gebrauchsobjekt grenzüberschreitend Freiräume erschlossen und bis heute gültige künstlerische Massstäbe gesetzt. Er war der Pionier des Spielplatzes als Landschaft, und seine Projekte für Spielplätze ohne Geräte waren der Zeit voraus. Vergleichbar mit den progressiven Ideen von Sørensen im Dänemark der 1930er Jahre, haben seine Entwürfe Architekten wie Richard Dattner und Landschaftsarchitekten wie M. Paul Friedberg inspiriert und ermutigt, für Spielplatzgestaltungen neue Wege zu gehen. GB

Entwürfe für Spielplätze und -geräte:

• *Play Mountain*, Spielplatz für New York, 1933; nicht realisiert
• Set von Spielgeräten für Ala Moana Park, Honolulu, Hawaii, 1940; nicht realisiert
• *Contoured Playground*, 1941; nicht realisiert
• Playground for United Nations Headquarter, New York, 1952; nicht realisiert
• Riverside Drive Playground, New York, zusammen mit Louis I. Kahn (Adele Levy Memorial Playground), 5 Vorschläge, 1961–1966; nicht realisiert
• National Children's Land, Yokohama, 1965–1967; temporäre Installation
• Abstract Moonscape, US Pavilion für *Expo '70*, Osaka, 1968; nicht realisiert
• *Octetra*, Spielmodul, 1968 in Japan mehrfach eingesetzt
• Playscape, Piedmont Park, Atlanta, 1976 (2009 restauriert)

Anmerkungen:

1	Isamu Noguchi, *A Sculptor's World*, zitiert in: Michael Gotkin, „The Politics of Play. The Adventure Playground in Central Park", in: Charles A. Birnbaum (Hg.), *Preserving Modern Landscape Architecture. Papers from the Wave Hill National*

its October 1952 issue as "the most creative and imaginative play area yet devised."[4] Meanwhile, there were more and more critiques of New York's unimaginative approach to playground design.

Noguchi's reputation continued to grow, and Hess did everything she could to realize one of his projects. A new opportunity came up in 1960: collaborating with the architect Louis I. Kahn, Noguchi made a series of designs for the Adele Levy Memorial Playground in New York (1961–1965). By 1961 Moses had retired as Parks Commissioner, but Noguchi's repeated modifications of the plans still did not overcome the objections from the Parks Department or those of local residents, and a lawsuit ended the project in 1966. At the same time, Noguchi was able to collaborate with the architect Sachio Otani to build his first playground landscape for the National Children's Land in Yokohama. Soon after that, in 1968, he designed *Octetra*, a playground module made of red concrete, which was first installed in Spoleto in Italy as part of the *Festival dei Due Mondi* and is still being produced today.

In 1976 Noguchi was finally able to build his first playground in the United States. Playscape in Atlanta was commissioned by the High Museum of Art and was restored in 2009. Here he did not work with landscape forms, but used his sculptural playground equipment to compose a world to play in and coordinated it with the site.

From his position between Western and Eastern culture, between sculpture and landscape architecture, and between art and everyday objects, Noguchi opened up free spaces that crossed borders, while also establishing artistic standards that are still valid today. He was the pioneer of the playground as a landscape, and his projects for playgrounds without equipment were ahead of their time. Like the progressive ideas of Sørensen in Denmark in the 1930s, his work inspired architects such as Richard Dattner and landscape architects such as M. Paul Friedberg, and encouraged them to explore new approaches to playground design. GB

Designs for Playgrounds and Playground Equipment:

• *Play Mountain*, playground for New York, 1933; unbuilt
• Set of playground equipment for Ala Moana Park, Honolulu, Hawaii, 1940; unbuilt
• *Contoured Playground*, 1941; unbuilt
• Playground for United Nations Headquarters, New York, 1952; unbuilt
• Riverside Drive Playground, New York, with Louis I. Kahn (Adele Levy Memorial Playground), 5 designs, 1961–1966; unbuilt

Park Service Conference, Spacemaker Press, Cambridge, Massachusetts 1999, S. 22.

2   Shaina D. Larrivee, „Playscapes. Isamu Noguchi's Designs for Play", in: *Public Art Dialogue,* Jg. 1, Nr. 1, 2011, S. 54–64.

3   Susan G. Solomon, *American Playgrounds. Revitalizing Community Space*, University Press of New England, Hanover 2005, S. 10–11 und 24–25.

4   Zitiert in: Hilary Ballon und Kenneth T. Jackson, *Robert Moses and the Modern City. The Transformation of New York*, W.W. Norton and Company Inc., New York 2007, S. 313.

•   National Children's Land, Yokohama, 1965–1967; temporary installation
•   Abstract Moonscape, US Pavilion for *Expo '70,* Osaka, 1968; unbuilt
•   *Octetra*, playground module, 1968, used in multiple places in Japan
•   Playscape, Piedmont Park, Atlanta, 1976 (restored in 2009)

Notes:

1   Isamu Noguchi, *A Sculptor's World*, cited in Michael Gotkin, "The Politics of Play. The Adventure Playground in Central Park," in Charles A. Birnbaum (ed.), *Preserving Modern Landscape Architecture. Papers from the Wave Hill National Park Service Conference*, Spacemaker Press, Cambridge, Massachusetts 1999, p. 22.

2   Shaina D. Larrivee, "Playscapes. Isamu Noguchi's Designs for Play," in *Public Art Dialogue*, vol. 1, no. 1, 2011, p. 54–64.

3   Susan G. Solomon, *American Playgrounds. Revitalizing Community Space*, University Press of New England, Hanover 2005, p. 10–11 and 24–25.

4   Cited in Hilary Ballon and Kenneth T. Jackson, *Robert Moses and the Modern City. The Transformation of New York*, W.W. Norton and Company Inc., New York 2007, p. 313.

125–126 Isamu Noguchi, Kletterhügel und Planschbecken / Climbing mound and wading pool; Sachio Otani, Pavillons und Bodenbelag / Shelters and pavement, National Children's Land, Yokohama, c. 1965/1967

127　Isamu Noguchi, Kletterhügel und Planschbecken / Climbing
mound and wading pool; Sachio Otani, Pavillons und Bodenbelag /
Shelters and pavement, National Children's Land, Yokohama, c. 1965 / 1967

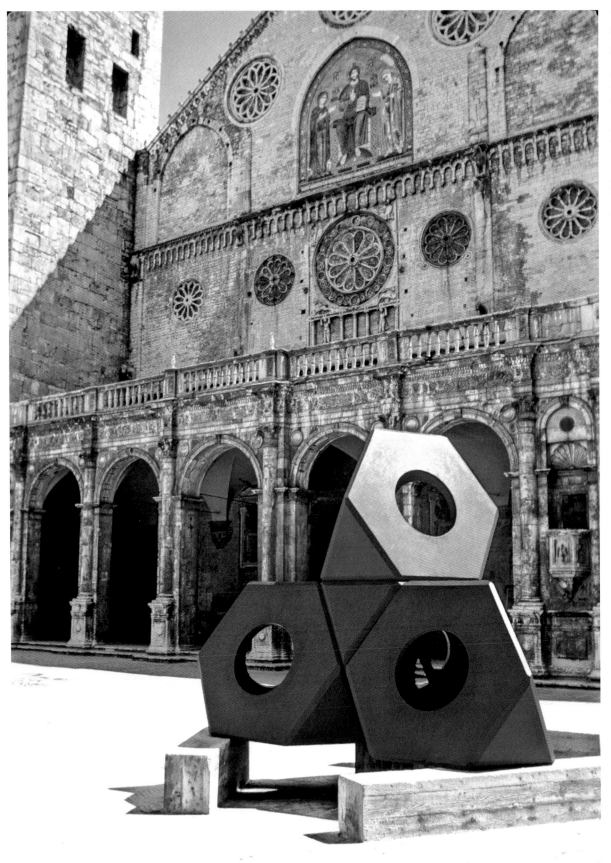

128   Isamu Noguchi, Spielskulptur / Play sculpture Octetra, Festival
dei Due Mondi, Spoleto, 1968

Auftrag: Stadtgartenamt Wien

SPIELPLASTIK 8
1958
Kunstmarmor – Glasmosaik 120x190x65cm
1030 Wien Arenbergpark

Josef Schagerl
*1923

Plastiker,
Wien

Nach der Tischlerlehre von 1938 bis 1941 arbeitet Josef Schagerl zunächst im Atelier seines Vaters, des Künstlers Josef Johannes Schagerl. Bald wird er jedoch zum Kriegsdienst eingezogen und kehrt erst 1946 aus der Gefangenschaft zurück. Danach studiert er bis 1952 an der Akademie der bildenden Künste Wien, wo er mit dem Diplom als Bildhauer abschliesst.

Nach dem Zweiten Weltkrieg muss die Stadt Wien die kriegszerstörten öffentlichen Gartenanlagen erst wieder instand setzen. Im Zuge von Neubepflanzungen und Umgestaltungen entstehen hier auch Kinderspielplätze.[1] 1949 gibt der Wiener Bürgermeister Theodor Körner unter dem Titel „Spielplatznot" eine Untersuchung zur Spielplatzplanung in Auftrag. Seine Forderung lautet: „Kein Wiener Kind darf weiter von einem Kinderspielplatz wohnen als 5 Minuten."[2] Daraufhin entstehen in den 1950er Jahren über das ganze Stadtgebiet verteilt Kinder- und Ballspielplätze mit gängigen Spieleinrichtungen.[3] Gleichzeitig etabliert die Stadt ein umfangreiches Programm für Kunst am Bau und Kunst im öffentlichen Raum. Zahlreiche Wiener Künstler erhalten Aufträge, um Spielskulpturen und -geräte für öffentliche Parks und Wohnanlagen zu entwickeln. In keiner anderen Stadt engagieren sich so viele Künstler auf diesem Gebiet, wobei Schagerl und Josef Seebacher (1918–1981) zu den aktivsten unter ihnen gehören.[4] Schagerl teilt das Atelier mit Seebacher, der in Dänemark die Spielskulpturen von Egon Møller-Nielsen kennengelernt hatte. Schagerl entwirft, nachdem er 1949 den endgültigen Schritt in die Abstraktion vollzogen hat, 1953 die erste abstrakte Spielskulptur, angeregt von Seebacher. Die *Doppelrutsche* wird jedoch von der Stadt abgelehnt. 1956 kommt schliesslich die *Elefantenrutsche* aus Stahlrohr, gegossenem Kunststein und Glasmosaiken auf dem Wiener Rabenhof zu stehen. Diese aufwendig produzierte, abstrakte „Gebrauchskunst" ist eine Möglichkeit, die Bevölkerung mit abstrakter Kunst vertraut zu machen und deren Akzeptanz zu fördern. In diesen Objekten gelingt es Schagerl, die auf Autonomie bedachte Sprache der modernen Plastik mit dem Wunsch nach Spiel und Funktion zu verbinden.

Schagerl hat zunehmend Mühe, neben dem politisch gut vernetzten Seebacher Aufträge von der Stadt zu erhalten. Angeblich entsprechen seine Plastiken nicht den Sicherheitsnormen. 1965 realisiert Schagerl im Hof eines Wohnblocks[5] im Auftrag des Vereins der Freunde des Wohneigentums die letzte Spielplastik. Danach widmet er sich ganz der Plastik aus Stahl. Im Verlauf der Jahre verschwinden sämtliche Spielskulpturen Schagerls sowie der anderen Künstler aus dem öffentlichen Raum. Eine Ausnahme bildet *Salamander* (in einer Wohnanlage an der Grinzingerstrasse 54, Wien 19), die nun jedoch ein Kunstobjekt ist und ihre ursprüngliche Funktion nicht mehr erfüllt.

Im Jahr 1973 erwirbt Schagerl die verfallene gotische Johanniskapelle in Rafing bei Pulkau, Niederösterreich,

Sculptor,
Vienna

After training as a carpenter from 1938 to 1941, Josef Schagerl first worked in the studio of his father, the artist Josef Johannes Schagerl. But he was soon drafted to serve in the war and only returned from a prisoner of war camp in 1946. From then until 1952, he completed a degree in sculpture at the Academy of Fine Arts in Vienna.

After the Second World War, the city of Vienna began to restore the public parks and gardens that had been destroyed during the war. Along with the replanting and redesigning of the parks, playgrounds were built.[1] In 1949, Vienna's Mayor Theodor Körner commissioned a study of playground planning called "Playground Emergency": "No child in Vienna should live further than five minutes from a playground."[2] So in the 1950s, playgrounds and ball fields were constructed all over Vienna with the usual equipment.[3] At the same time, the city established an extensive program for the "percent for art" [Kunst am Bau] and art in public spaces. Numerous Viennese artists were commissioned to design playground sculptures and equipment for public parks and housing projects. In no other city were so many artists active in this field, with Schagerl and Josef Seebacher (1918–1981) among the most active of them.[4] Schagerl shared a studio with Seebacher, who had seen playground sculptures by Egon Møller-Nielsen in Denmark. After making the definitive step into abstraction in 1949, Schagerl was encouraged by Seebacher to make the first abstract playground sculpture in 1953, but the *Double Slide* was turned down by the city. Finally, in 1956, the *Elephant Slide* of steel pipes, cast stone, and glass mosaics was set up at the Rabenhof in Vienna. This laboriously produced, abstract "applied art" was one way to make the public familiar with abstract art and encourage its acceptance. In these objects, Schagerl managed to combine the autonomy-based language of modern sculpture with the goals of play and functionality.

Compared to Seebacher, who had excellent political connections, Schagerl had increasing difficulty getting commissions from the city; his sculptures supposedly did not meet security standards. His last playground sculpture was commissioned in 1965 by the Association of Friends of Residential Property for the courtyard of an apartment complex.[5] From then on, he focused only on steel sculptures. Over the years, almost all of his playground sculptures, as well as those of other artists, have disappeared from public places. One exception is *Salamander* (at Grinzingerstrasse 54, Vienna 19), but it is now seen as an artwork and no longer serves its original purpose as a playground sculpture.

die er renoviert und zu einem Gesamtkunstwerk und Kulturort ausbaut. GB

Anmerkungen:

1   Alfred Auer, „Das öffentliche Grün", in: Stadt-
bauamt Wien (Hg.), *Der Aufbau. Fachschrift für Planen, Bauen,
Wohnen und Umweltschutz der Stadtbaudirektion Wien &
Fachschrift der Stadtbaudirektion Wien*, Wien, Nr. 9, 1954,
S. 212.
2   Cordula Loidl-Reisch, „Im Freien. Von Spielorten,
Spielplätzen und der bespielbaren Stadt", in: Ernst Strouhal,
Manfred Zollinger und Brigitte Felderer (Hg.), *Spiele der Stadt.
Glück, Gewinn und Zeitvertreib*, Springer, Wien 2012, S. 208.
3   J. Thaler, „Kinderspielplätze in den öffentlichen
Gartenanlagen der Stadt Wien", in: Stadtbauamt Wien (Hg.),
Der Aufbau (s. Anm. 1), S. 210–211.
4   Irene Nierhaus, *Kunst-am-Bau im Wiener kommu-
nalen Wohnbau der fünfziger Jahre*, Böhlau Verlag, Wien 1993,
S. 35.
5   An der Braunhirschengasse 26, 15. Bezirk, Wien.

In 1973 Schagerl bought a rundown Gothic chapel, the Johanniskapelle, in Rafing bei Pulkau in Lower Austria, which he renovated and turned into a *Gesamtkunstwerk* and a venue for cultural events. GB

Notes:

1   Alfred Auer, "Das öffentliche Grün," in Stadtbauamt Wien (ed.), *Der Aufbau. Fach-schrift für Planen, Bauen, Wohnen und Umwelt-schutz der Stadtbaudirektion Wien & Fachschrift der Stadtbaudirektion Wien*, Vienna, no. 9, 1954, p. 212.
2   Cordula Loidl-Reisch, "Im Freien. Von Spielorten, Spielplätzen und der bespielbaren Stadt," in Ernst Strouhal, Manfred Zollinger, and Brigitte Felderer (eds.), *Spiele der Stadt. Glück, Gewinn und Zeitvertreib*, Springer, Vienna 2012, p. 208.
3   J. Thaler, "Kinderspielplätze in den öffentlichen Gartenanlagen der Stadt Wien," in Stadtbauamt Wien (ed.), *Der Aufbau* (see note 1), p. 210–211.
4   Irene Nierhaus, *Kunst-am-Bau im Wiener kommunalen Wohnbau der fünfziger Jahre*, Böhlau Verlag, Vienna 1993, p. 35.
5   Braunhirschengasse 26 in Vienna's 15th District.

131–132   Josef Schagerl, *Elefant*, Rutsche / Slide, Rabenhof, Wien /
Vienna, 1954 / 1956

Foto LUK.

Foto SCHAG

134–135   Josef Schagerl, *Zwieselrutsche*, Hütteldorferstrasse 266,
Wien / Vienna, 1957

136   Josef Schagerl, Rutsche / Slide, Arenbergplatz, Wien /
Vienna, 1958

170

171

139   Josef Schagerl, Spielplastik / Play sculpture, Baumgartner-
Casino-Park, Wien / Vienna, 1956 / 1957

140   Mitsuru Senda, *Giant Path Play Structure*, Mukoyama
Children's Park Sendai, Miyagi Prefecture, 1969

Mitsuru (Man) Senda
*1941

Architekt,
Tokyo

Es gibt kaum einen anderen Architekten, der sich so lange und intensiv mit den Bedürfnissen von Kindern auseinandergesetzt und so zahlreiche Spielplätze und Einrichtungen für sie entworfen hat wie Mitsuru Senda.

1964, nach Abschluss des Architekturstudiums in Tokyo, arbeitet Senda vier Jahre für den renommierten Architekten Kiyonori Kikutake (1928–2011), einen Mitinitianten der Metabolistenbewegung, der japanischen Architektur-Avantgarde.[1] Im Auftrag von Kikutake arbeitet er für das National Children's Land, einen Kinderpark in Yokohama, der nach dem Masterplan von Takashi Asada, einem weiteren Metabolisten, realisiert wird. Dort trifft Senda auch auf den amerikanisch-japanischen Künstler Isamu Noguchi, der für diesen 1965 eröffneten Kinderpark eine Spiellandschaft baut. Kikutakes visionäre Architektur und Noguchis sorgfältiges Gestalten beeindrucken den jungen Architekten tief. Senda selbst entwirft ein Planschbecken und drei Bauten für den Park, weitere kommen in den 1980er Jahren hinzu. Das National Children's Land besteht bis heute.[2]

1968 eröffnet Senda in Tokyo sein eigenes Büro, das Environment Design Institute. Der erste Auftrag ist ein Spielplatz für die Central Children's Hall in Sendai. Senda beobachtet mit Sorge, wie seit dem Krieg die natürlichen Spielräume für Kinder nach und nach verschwinden: „Diese aufregenden Erfahrungen in natürlicher Umgebung; das Vergnügen in den Feldern herumzurennen, die Vertrautheit der Strassen, die Freiheit des Schrottplatzes und das Vergnügen des Versteckens."[3]

Er fasst den Entschluss, den Entwurf von Spielumgebungen zu seiner Hauptbeschäftigung zu machen. Anfangs entwirft er, was ihm Spass macht. Als Senda aber während eines Vortrages gefragt wird, ob Kinder nicht von sich aus Plätze zum Spielen entdecken, beginnt er sich ernsthaft mit dieser Frage auseinanderzusetzen. Wegweisend für sein umfassendes Verständnis von Architektur als Spielstruktur ist dabei der Aufbau des traditionellen japanischen Hauses, das mit seinen Korridoren, Veranden und Durchgängen auch eine offene und poröse (Spiel-)Struktur ist. Diesen Ansatz verfolgt Senda konsequent für den Entwurf von Kindergärten, Schulen, Kindermuseen und Spielumgebungen. 1974 erhält er ein Stipendium der Toyota Foundation. Die Resultate seiner Forschungen veröffentlicht er 1977 in der japanischen Zeitschrift *Architektur und Kultur*. Als 1976 in der Publikation *Spielraum für Kinder* erstmals seine Spielumgebungen vorgestellt werden, wird auch der Westen auf Sendas Werk aufmerksam.

Anfang der 1980er Jahre schreibt Senda eine Dissertation, die er unter dem Titel *Children's Play Environments* veröffentlicht. Er lehrt an verschiedenen Universitäten und erhält erneut Stipendien, um auf dem Gebiet weiter zu forschen. Senda definiert die wichtigsten Komponenten einer guten Spielstruktur folgendermassen: Das Spiel soll sich kreisförmig

Architect,
Tokyo

There has hardly ever been another architect who has designed as many playgrounds and facilities and thought so much and so intensively about the needs of children as Mitsuru Senda.

After finishing his degree in architecture in Tokyo in 1964, Senda spent four years working for the renowned architect Kiyonori Kikutake (1928–2011), one of the founders of the Metabolist movement, the architectural avantgarde in Japan.[1] Kikutake assigned him projects for the National Children's Land, a children's park in Yokohama that was built according to the designs of Takashi Asada, another Metabolist. In Yokohama, Senda met the Japanese-American artist Isamu Noguchi, who was building a playground for the park's opening in 1965. Kikutake's visionary architecture and Noguchi's careful design deeply impressed Senda. The young architect designed the wading pool and three buildings for the park, as well as further projects there in the 1980s. The National Children's Land is still in use today.[2]

In 1968, Senda founded the Environment Design Institute in Tokyo. His first commission was for a playground for the Central Children's Hall in Sendai. Senda was concerned about how natural space for children to play had been gradually disappearing since the war: "Those thrilling experiences in the natural environment; the enjoyment of running around the fields, the intimacy of the streets, the freedom of the scrap yard and the pleasure of the hide out."[3]

He decided to make the design of spaces for play his primary focus. At first, he designed whatever he thought was fun. But when Senda was asked during a lecture whether children find their own places to play, he began to take the question seriously. The organization of the traditional Japanese house, with its halls, verandas, and passages that make it an open and porous place to live (and to play) in, became fundamental to his sweeping sense of architecture in general as a set of constructions for play. Senda rigorously pursued this approach in his designs for kindergartens, schools, children's museums, and playgrounds. In 1974, he received a fellowship from the Toyota Foundation; he published the results of his research in 1977 in the Japanese journal *Architecture and Culture*. The 1976 book *Children's Play Spaces* first introduced the West to his playgrounds.

At the beginning of the 1980s, Senda wrote a dissertation that he published as *Children's Play Environments*. He taught at a number of universities and received further fellowships to continue his research in the field. Senda defines the most important components of a good

entwickeln können, es muss Momente des „Nervenkitzels" geben sowie Möglichkeiten zum Verstecken und Abkürzen. Das Gefühl des Schwindels – *Vertigo* –, wie es der französische Philosoph Robert Caillois in seinem einflussreichen Buch *Les jeux et les hommes* 1958 beschreibt, ist dabei zentral: „*Ilinx.* – Eine letzte Kategorie fasst jene Spiele zusammen, die auf dem Begehren nach Rausch beruhen und deren Reiz darin besteht, für einen Augenblick die Stabilität der Wahrnehmung zu stören und dem klaren Bewusstsein eine Art wollüstiger Panik einzuflössen."[4] Sendas Überlegungen finden kontinuierlich Eingang in seine architektonische Praxis, und das bis heute. Er begründet ein architektonisches Denken, das die Trennung zwischen Architektur und Spielplatz aufhebt. Dieser Ansatz wird unter anderem von den Architekten Takaharu und Yui Tezuka aufgenommen und für den viel beachteten Fuji-Kindergarten (2007) in Tokyo weiterentwickelt. GB

structure for play as follows: play should be able to develop in a circle; it has to have "thrilling" moments as well as hiding places and short cuts. The feeling of vertigo described by the French philosopher Roger Caillois in his influential 1958 book *Les jeux et les hommes* is central to Senda: "*Ilinx.*— The last kind of game includes those which are based on the pursuit of vertigo and which consist of an attempt to momentarily destroy the stability of perception and inflict a kind of voluptuous panic upon an otherwise lucid mind."[4] Senda's ideas continually flow into his architectural practice, even today. He has founded an architectural mode of thinking that eliminates the separation between architecture and playground. This approach has been taken up by the architects Takaharu and Yui Tezuka, among others, and developed further in the well-received Fuji kindergarten in Tokyo (2007). GB

1	Mitsuru Senda, *Design of Children's Play Environments*, McGraw-Hill, New York 1992, S. viii.
2	http://www.kodomonokuni.org / english / (zuletzt aufgerufen am 1. Oktober 2015).
3	Mitsuru Senda, „Playground Types in Japan", in: *Process: Architecture. Playgrounds and Play Apparatus*, Tokyo, Nr. 30, 1982, S. 19–20.
4	Roger Caillois, *Die Spiele und die Menschen. Maske und Rausch*, Ullstein, Berlin 1982 (1958), S. 32.

Notes:

1	Mitsuru Senda, *Design of Children's Play Environments*, McGraw-Hill, New York 1992, p. viii.
2	http://www.kodomonokuni.org / english / (last accessed December, 2015).
3	Mitsuru Senda, "Playground Types in Japan," in *Process: Architecture. Playgrounds and Play Apparatus*, Tokyo, no. 30, 1982, p. 19–20.
4	Roger Caillois, *Men, Play, and Games*, University of Illinois Press, Champaign 1961 (1958), p. 23.

141   Mitsuru Senda, *Giant Path Play Structure*, Mukoyama
Children's Park Sendai, Miyagi Prefecture, 1969

142   Mitsuru Senda, *Escargot*, 1977

Mitsuru Senda, *Giant Path Play Structure*, Mukoyama Children's Park Sendai, Miyagi Prefecture, 1969

Mitsuru Senda, *Panel Tunnel*, 1976

Mitsuru Senda, *Cosmos*, 1975

145

Parc de jeux à Miyagi, Japon

Conception: Mitsuru Senda, Mikio Shiga,
et Atelier Man & Space
Mise en service: 1969

L'aménagement stylisé de la grande plaine de
jeux n'est absolument pas en contradiction
avec la proximité de la forêt de pins. Dans
la plupart des pays, un tel projet serait
irréalisable, car c'est encore le monde du
"policé". Mitsuru Senda dit: "Le danger fait
partie de la vie, il peut être maîtrisé par
le jeu". (Affirmation difficilement acceptée
par beaucoup de constructeurs.) Tous les pro-
jets de Senda baignent dans une vallée, une
colline, une forêt, et jamais dans une nature
reprise ou stylisée. L'intervention est hors
d'échelle traditionnelle, spacieuse et ne peut
que conquérir favorablement les enfants. Pour
eux, c'est la fantaisie débridée, la libéra-
tion de leurs énergies, le test de l'agilité.
Ici un serpent volant parcourt 150 m (4) entre
une pyramide en béton lisse, et un toit en
résille métallique (2), qui donne accès à
un entonnoir ("fourmi-lion") par des tobog-
gans-fusées (1).

1 passerelle annulaire
2 pyramide
3 "désert"
4 "oasis"
5 "fourmi-lion"
6 résille métallique
7 "place de violon"
8 auge "guru-guru"

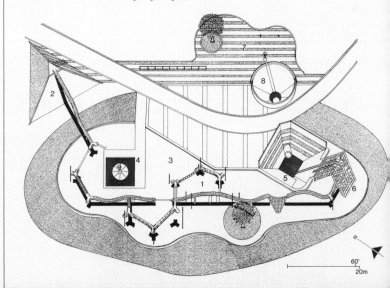

60'
20m

1	2		
3		4	

5	6	(6)	(5)

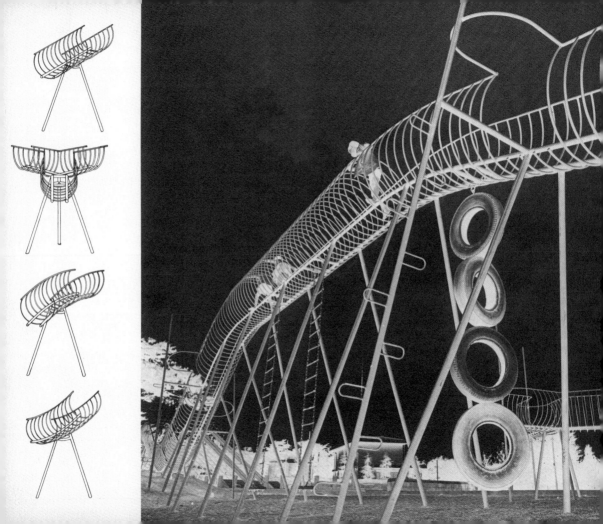

148   Skrammellegeplads (Gerümpelspielplatz / junk playground),
Emdrup, Kopenhagen / Copenhagen, 1943

Carl The**odo**r Sørensen 1893–1979

Landschaftsarchitekt,
Kopenhagen

Landscape architect,
Copenhagen

Carl Theodor Sørensen arbeitet ab den 1920er Jahren als frei-beruflicher Landschaftsarchitekt in Kopenhagen. Er entwirft eine Vielzahl von Gärten und Parks für private und öffentliche Auftraggeber. Sørensen und der Pädagoge Hans Dragehjelm (1875–1948), der sich bereits 1909 mit der Publikation *Das Spielen der Kinder im Sande*[1] profiliert hat, sind Vorkämpfer für das „natürliche" Kinderspiel. Sie wollen dem Stadtkind ohne mora-lischen Hintergedanken ein Stück Natur zurückgeben, mit dem Wunsch, die kindliche Kreativität zu beflügeln. Ihre Forderungen fallen auf fruchtbaren Boden, weil sich die nordischen Staaten zu dieser Zeit anstrengen, die Wohn- und Lebensqualität in ihren Städten mit modernen Bauten und familienfreundlichen Aussenräumen mit Kinderspielplätzen zu verbessern. Die im 20. Jahrhundert aufkommende Kinderpsychologie liefert zudem den wissenschaftlichen Beweis, dass das Spiel von grosser Wichtigkeit für die kindliche Entwicklung ist. Die Erkenntnisse werden in Dänemark durch populär-wissenschaftliche Bücher und Zeitschriften verbreitet.

Ab 1925 gestaltet Sørensen die Aussenräume von mehreren dänischen Baugenossenschaften. Dabei konzipiert er den städtischen Spielplatz als natürlichen, ländlichen Ort. Im Zentrum steht die radikale Aufforderung an die Kinder, ihre Umgebung selbst zu gestalten. Ein grosser Sandkasten steht für den Strand, ein Planschbecken für das Meer und weite Grasflächen mit Büschen und Pfaden stehen für Wiese und Wälder. Idealerweise können die Kinder auch Haustiere halten.[2] Als Spielgeräte sind nach Sørensens Auffassung höchstens Schwingen oder Schaukeln notwendig, wie etwa ein Kletter-baum oder hängende Autoreifen. Nicht alle Genossenschafter sind jedoch von Sørensens Ideen begeistert, sie wollen nicht, dass ihre Kinder im Sand und Wasser schmutzig werden. Die meisten Planschbecken werden bereits nach kurzer Zeit zu Blumenbeeten umgewandelt. Trotzdem lässt Sørensen nicht von seinen progressiven Ideen ab. Er veröffentlicht zahlreiche Bücher, darunter 1931 das einflussreiche *Parkpolitik i Sogn og Købstad* (*Park-Politik in Pfarrei und Gemeinde*). Es ist ein Bekenntnis zum öffentlichen Grünraum und seiner sozialen Funktion nach dem Vorbild des amerikanischen oder deutschen Volksparks. Sørensen zieht umfangreiches Bildmaterial herbei, um zu zeigen, wie vielfältig Parks als Orte der Freizeit genutzt werden können.[3] Erstmals taucht darin die Idee auf, Kindern einen freien Platz mit Baumaterial und Werkzeugen zur Ver-fügung zu stellen, von ihm „Skrammellegeplads" (Gerümpel-spielplatz) genannt. In einem weiteren Artikel schreibt er 1935: „Schliesslich sollten wir wohl irgendwann damit experimen-tieren, was man einen Gerümpelspielplatz nennen könnte. Ich denke dabei an einen Bereich, nicht zu klein, mit dichtem Grün

In the 1920s, Carl Theodor Sørensen began working as a freelance landscape architect in Copenhagen and was given many private and public commissions for gardens and parks. Sørensen and the teacher Hans Dragehjelm (1875–1948), author of the 1909 book *Das Spielen der Kinder im Sande* (*Children Playing in Sand*),[1] were pioneers of "natural" children's play. Without any hidden moral agenda, they wanted to give a bit of nature back to children in the city, so as to inspire their creativity. Such ideas were very well received at the time because the Nordic countries were busy striving to improve the quality of housing and of urban life in general, with modern buildings and family-friendly outside areas, including playgrounds. Child psychology was in its early years at the beginning of the 20th century, and it offered scientific evidence that play was very important for childhood develop-ment—ideas that were popularized in books and magazines in Denmark.

Starting in 1925, Sørensen began to work on designing the outdoor parts of a number of Danish housing complexes, and developed the idea of the urban playground as a natural, rural environment. At the heart of his concepts was a radical challenge to children to shape their own environments. A large sandbox stood for the beach, a wading pool for the sea, and wide grassy areas with bushes and paths for fields and woods. Ideally, the children would be able to keep pets, too.[2] As for playground equipment, Sørensen thought that nothing more than swings and climbing opportunities should be necessary, such as hanging tires or a climbing tree. But not all of the residents liked Sørensen's ideas; they did not want their children to get dirty in sand and water. Most of the wading pools were soon turned into flowerbeds. Nevertheless, Sørensen contin-ued to pursue his progressive ideas and published a number of books, the most influential of which was the 1931 *Parkpolitik i Sogn og Købstad* (*Park Policy in Parish and Town*), a testimonial to public parks and their social function, with American and German parks as models. Sørensen used nu-merous illustrations to show the many ways that parks could be used for recreation.[3] This was the first appearance of the idea that children could be given a "Skrammellegeplads" (junk playground) with building materials and tools. He wrote about them further in a 1935 article: "Finally we should probably at some point experiment with what one could call a junk playground. I am thinking in terms of an area, not too small in size, well closed off from its surroundings by thick greenery, where we should gather, for the amusement of older children,

185

gut von seiner Umgebung abgetrennt, wo wir für das Vergnügen grösserer Kinder alle Art von altem Abfall sammeln sollten, mit dem die Kinder der Wohnblocks spielen dürfen, wie es die Kinder auf dem Land und in den Vorstädten bereits tun. Es könnte da Äste und Abfall vom Baum- und Gebüschbeschnitt haben, alte Kartonboxen, Bretter und Platten, ‚tote' Autos, alte Reifen und viele andere Sachen. Gesunde Knaben würden damit mit Freude etwas anstellen. Natürlich würde es schrecklich aussehen…" 4

Noch während der deutschen Besetzung Dänemarks wird 1943 ein solcher Skrammellegeplads in Emdrup bei Kopenhagen inmitten einer Siedlung mit über 700 grossen Familienwohnungen realisiert. Während Sørensens progressive Schriften ausserhalb Dänemarks kaum Verbreitung finden, wird dieser Skrammellegeplads international zum Symbol des Aufbruchs und zum Aufruf, der kindlichen Kreativität Freiraum zu geben. GB

Anmerkungen:

1   Hans Dragehjelm, *Das Spielen der Kinder im Sande. Praktische Ratschläge und Winke zur Förderung des Sandspielens für Haus, Schule, Spielplatz und Behörde, zusammengestellt auf Grundlage amtlicher und anderer Berichte aus den verschiedenen Ländern*, autorisierte Übers. aus dem Dänischen von Alf. Dietrich, Tillge, Kopenhagen 1909.
2   Ning de Coninck-Smith, *Natural Play in Natural Surroundings. Urban Childhood and Playground Planning in Denmark*, c. 1930–1950, Working Paper 6, Department of Contemporary Cultural Studies, The University of Southern Denmark, Odense 1999, S. 13.
3   Ken Worpole, *Here Comes the Sun. Architecture and Public Space in Twentieth-Century European Culture*, Reaktion Books, London 2000, S. 89.
4   Carl Theodor Sørensen, „Etagehusets Have", in: *Arkitektens Månedshæfte*, 1935, S. 61, zitiert in: de Coninck-Smith, *Natural Play* (s. Anm. 2), S. 13.

all sorts of old scrap that the children from the apartment blocks could be allowed to work with, as the children in the countryside and in the suburbs already have. There could be branches and waste from tree polling and bushes, old cardboard boxes, planks and boards, scrapped cars, old tires, and more. Which would be a joy for healthy boys to use for something. Of course it would look terrible … " 4

During the German occupation of Denmark, the first Skrammellegeplads was established in a development with over 700 large apartments for families in Emdrup, a suburb of Copenhagen. Although Sørensen's progressive writings were hardly read outside of Denmark, the Skrammellegeplads became an international symbol of change, as well as a call to provide more space for children's creativity. GB

Notes:

1   Hans Dragehjelm, *Das Spielen der Kinder im Sande. Praktische Ratschläge und Winke zur Förderung des Sandspielens für Haus, Schule, Spielplatz und Behörde, zusammengestellt auf Grundlage amtlicher und anderer Berichte aus den verschiedenen Ländern*, authorized German translation from the Danish by Alf. Dietrich, Tillge, Copenhagen 1909.
2   Ning de Coninck-Smith, *Natural Play in Natural Surroundings. Urban Childhood and Playground Planning in Denmark, c. 1930–1950*, Working Paper 6, Department of Contemporary Cultural Studies, The University of Southern Denmark, Odense 1999, p. 13.
3   Ken Worpole, *Here Comes the Sun. Architecture and Public Space in Twentieth-Century European Culture*, Reaktion Books, London 2000, p. 89.
4   Carl Theodor Sørensen, "Etagehusets Have," in *Arkitektens Månedshæfte*, 1935, p. 61, cited in de Coninck-Smith, *Natural Play* (see note 2), p. 13.

149 Skrammellegeplads (Gerümpelspielplatz / junk playground),
Emdrup, Kopenhagen / Copenhagen, 1943

187

150–151   Skrammellegeplads (Gerümpelspielplatz / junk playground),
Emdrup, Kopenhagen / Copenhagen, 1943

Early experience from Emdrup

by John Bertelsen

Dedicated to LADY ALLEN OF HURTWOOD

The children who flocked to the adventure playground in Emdrup when it opened on 15 August 1943, in the middle of war and occupation, were from a broad cross-section of the population, from the relatively well-off to the far less fortunate. A dividing line of sorts could perhaps be drawn between children from families where the borough paid a rent contribution, and children from families who could manage without such help. The most fortunate children were those who, regardless of social status, had enjoyed love and acceptance all their lives, but this is sometimes hard for parents to provide when living in difficult circumstances, or when one has accepted mediocrity and average social standards as the yardstick.

Children's play development is closely related to their environment—the physical and the psychical—to adults' and society's attitudes towards play. The children's behaviour and play at the adventure playground demonstrated this, and the influence of various conditions was clearly reflected. It is not sufficient for adults and society merely to provide facilities for play—they must offer a positive, individual attitude towards it, so that the psychical climate for the child's growth, through play, is created. Today, we create a somewhat better physical environment for children's wellbeing and development through play, but we nevertheless have difficulty in accepting that a *pro-child* physical environment also needs a *pro-play* psychical background if the children are to use the possibilities afforded in a positive and appropriate way.

We tend to let new forms enshrine outmoded concepts; something acceptable for adults as well as for society in general; something respectable, because our inner sense cannot always keep abreast of the latest ideas—although we, of course, pretend that we are very 'with it'. In principle, we are like the Chinese visitor who, having flown from Peking to London, was asked what it was like to travel such a distance in so short a time. He answered, sensibly and honestly, 'It was a lovely experience but my soul has not yet caught up'. If only more of us possessed the same awareness, it would help greatly in many ways.

It is vital for the child that there should be a link between the physical environment and the psychical: that the facilities for play be accompanied by an appropriate psychological environment and a positive attitude towards the whole concept of play. Children are gluttons for life and have a need for all the various experiences which play can offer.

No one can claim that adults, and society, have any monopoly of truth. It is only convention which makes our physical and psychical arteriosclerosis acceptable.

Play has something to do with attacking life in an unconventional manner. The experiment in Emdrup, which I directed in 1943–47, was very gratifying. There, all activities were accepted as normal and matter-of-course. The outside world made a sensation of the experiment, and this attitude has scarcely changed today. We are still far from an acceptance of what, rightly, should be considered normal, and our present attitudes often label the 'normal' as sensational when it is put into practice.

The pages which follow give extracts from a diary of the first year of the Emdrup adventure playground where I joined the children and young people in 'Let's do it—play'. I think that the underlying message is still valid today, 27 years after the diary was written. Judge for yourself!

1943

At 10.45 am today the playground opened. The weather was cool and the sky overcast. In spite of this, by 9.30 the children were already pushing at the door to the promised land. Due to a slight misunderstanding I didn't have the key until 10.15 and was unable to open up until fifteen minutes later than planned.

By this time some fifty to seventy-five children, together with a few mothers and grandmothers, had gathered. Grumbling dissatisfaction at the still-locked door increased each minute, as did the number of children, and the situation was beginning to look almost threatening.

Then at last the company's carpenter arrived with the key, the door was opened and the children burst through, completely taking over the playground, appropriating wheelbarrows and everything.

We began by moving all the building material in the open shed. Bricks, boards, fir-posts and cement pillars were moved to the left alongside the entrance, where building and digging started right away. The work was done by children aged 4 to 17. It went on at full speed and all the workers were in high spirits; dust, sweat, warning shouts and a few scratches all created just the right atmosphere. The children's play- and work-ground had opened, and they knew how to take full advantage of it.

When I eventually closed the door at 6.15 pm, approximately 900 children had visited the playground.

Today was flagpole day. At noon, to the accompaniment of a siren and cheers from the crowd, the 'skull and cross-bones' was raised on a fir-post outside hut 3, block 1. There was an awesome moment as the flag was unfurled and the empty eye-sockets were revealed, glaring out over the playground, but the tense feeling soon passed, as it quickly became evident that this was just a routine 'topping out' ceremony, with which the usual cakes and lemonade were enjoyed.

During the day no less than five 'flagpoles' made their appearance, but their owners took a more conventional view, preferring to hoist the honourable banner of their forbears. Either this, or they lacked the imagination for anything else. Whatever the reason, they all raised the Danish flag.

As most of the building material had been used in putting up small huts the previous day, the 'homeless' children set to work and built a large wigwam of fir-posts. This wigwam was intended as a sort of communal hut for all those who, for the time being, had no house to call their own. During the afternoon there was a bustle of activity—putting the final touches to the houses and fixtures, such as chairs and tables, and some even arranged flowers in an empty beer bottle to place on the table. The only discouraging thing is that we are sadly in need of materials, which means that the children are not able to realise their ambitions in creating the adventure playground.

The work today has been based on the slogan: 'Back to the land'. The plot, from which the turf had been lifted, is now filled with earth caves. An especially large cave houses the ground's police. No sooner was it finished than a flag marked 'Police' was hoisted

Group Ludic

Xavier de la Salle

159–160 Group Ludic, Im U-Boot / In the submarine, Les Mathes /
La Palmyre – Les Pins de Cordouan, Royan (Poitou-Charentes), 1969

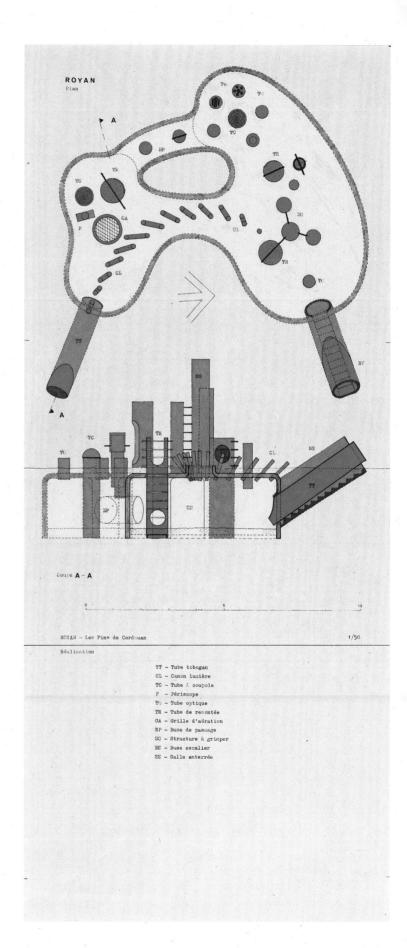

ROYAN
Plan

Coupe **A – A**

| 0 | | | | | 5 | | | | | 10 |

ROYAN – Les Pins de Cordouan   1/50

Réalisation

TT – Tube tobogan
CL – Canon lumière
TC – Tube à coupole
P – Périscope
TO – Tube optique
TR – Tube de remontée
GA – Grille d'aération
BP – Buse de passage
SG – Structure à grimper
BE – Buse escalier
SE – Salle enterrée

Es fühlt sich an, als sei es erst gestern gewesen. So kann es - fast ein halbes Jahrhundert nach der Gründung von Group Ludic - verschiedene Gründe geben, noch einmal darüber zu sprechen. Der eine, scherzhafte, wäre der Versuch nachzuweisen, dass das Gestalten und Realisieren von Spielplätzen ein bewährtes Mittel ist, um das vorzeitige Altern ihrer Gestalter zu vermeiden. Der andere, ernsthaftere, wäre die Beteuerung, dass das Thema, ungeachtet der Anstrengungen unseres Teams und vieler anderer jener Zeit, von unverminderter Aktualität ist, denn es ist nach wie vor notwendig, dass sich junge Gestalter dieser Aufgabe widmen und auf diesem Weg weitergehen.

Um den Werdegang unseres aus David Roditi, Simon Koszel und mir bestehenden Teams zu veranschaulichen, werde ich in diesem Artikel die entscheidenden Faktoren benennen, die unser Vorhaben in Gang gebracht und die Verwirklichung neuer Methoden in jener Zeit ermöglicht haben. Aus mehr als hundert realisierten Projekten und bedeutenden Ereignissen entstanden neue Konzepte.

Eine Zeit der Öffnung und Kreativität

Zunächst jedoch spielte sich in Frankreich das ab, was man „die Ereignisse von 1968" nannte. Einige Monate davor hatten sich die drei Gründungsmitglieder von Group Ludic kennengelernt, und ohne dass es dafür eine rationale Erklärung gibt oder der Zufall allein es erklären kann, war uns dreien ein ungewöhnliches Profil gemein: Wir waren junge Künstler um die Dreissig, stammten aus verschiedenen Ländern und Kulturen (Grossbritannien, Polen, Frankreich), mit jeweils sehr unterschiedlichen beruflichen Erfahrungen in ziemlich spezialisierten Kreativbereichen (Mode, Grafikdesign, Film, Architektur, Kommunikation, Malerei, Skulptur usw.). Jeder von uns hatte, aktuell oder in der Vergangenheit, im Ausland und in Frankreich berufliche Verantwortung übernommen, wusste die Erfahrungen in die Praxis umzusetzen und war fähig, eine Fülle von Informationen oder multiplen Bezügen zu verarbeiten und zu integrieren. Dies war die Zeit, in der „Kreativität" eine allgegenwärtige Grundhaltung war, die sämtliche Aspekte des Alltags durchzog.

Um sich ein Bild von der Welt zu machen, in der dieses Trio verkehrte und die es sich aneignete, muss man sich zunächst einen Raum vorstellen, der in einer Superstruktur von Buckminster Fuller entstand, im Schutze eines Seilnetzdachs Frei Ottos, das ein Projekt von Yona Friedman beherbergte, in dem Buster Keaton Jean Piagets Gedichte nach einer Adaption von Fernand Deligny inszenierte, wo Françoise Dolto Ideen vortrug, kommentiert und analysiert von Gaston Bachelard, arrangiert und umgesetzt von Félix Guattari. Die Klangstrukturen der Brüder Baschet und zwischendurch auch Frank Zappa produzierten den Sound.

Die ersten Schritte

Nachdem wir beschlossen hatten, gemeinsam für die Welt des Kindes zu arbeiten - Kinder und ihre Spiele, Räume für Kinder, Kinderwelten - trafen wir uns zunächst in der Nähe von David, der damals auf einem im Zentrum von Paris liegenden Hausboot lebte. Wir benutzten das Ufer der Seine und die nähere Umgebung als Treffpunkt und Produktionsstätte - Diskussionen, Projekte, Skizzen für räumliche Arrangements, Architek-

It feels like it was just yesterday, so agreeing to talk about it again—nearly half a century after the partnership known as Group Ludic was formed—may reflect various motives. One, on a flippant level, would be the inclination to demonstrate that the design and construction of playgrounds for children is a tried-and-true way for the designers involved to avoid growing prematurely old; the other, more serious, motive would concern the assertion that, despite the efforts of our own team and many other designers of the day, the subject is more relevant than ever. There still remains a pressing need for newcomers to choose this path and pursue it.

In an attempt to elucidate our career—a team composed of David Roditi, Simon Koszel, and myself—this article will highlight the key factors that inspired our approach and forged the new methods used at the time, giving rise to new concepts developed from over one hundred actual projects and major events.

An Era of Open-Mindedness and Creativity

First, France was at the center of what is know as "the events of 1968." The three founding partners of Group Ludic met a few months prior to that date. Although there is no evidence for a rational explanation of that encounter, and although chance alone cannot explain every motivation, the three of us nevertheless all shared an unusual profile: we were young artists, each about 30 years old, from different countries and cultures (Great Britain, Poland, France), with widely varying professional experience in fairly specialized artistic fields (fashion, graphic design, movies, architecture, public relations, painting, sculpture, etc.). Each had well-proven responsibilities in France or abroad, demonstrating not just a transversal application of skills, but also an ability to manage and incorporate wide-ranging input and references from diverse geographical origins. It should also be noted that this was a period when "creativity" was considered a vital quality of behavior that should imbue all aspects of daily life.

In order to provide a picture of the world frequented and adopted by the trio, we must first imagine a sphere that emerged and grew within a superstructure devised by Richard Buckminster Fuller, was shielded by Frei Otto's tensile structures, and was open to the implementation of a project by Yona Friedman; it was a site of vitality and development, where Buster Keaton would stage Jean Piaget's poems as adapted by Fernand Deligny, where Françoise Dolto would come to distill ideas, which were discussed and analyzed by Gaston Bachelard, and then rearranged by Félix Guattari, who would propose

turmodelle usw. David realisierte damals die ersten Prototypen einer riesigen Spielstruktur, die auf verschiedenen Modulen basierte und die er dann auf dem Quai mit seinen Kindern oder den Kindern von Passanten ausprobierte.

Zugleich näherten wir uns der Welt des Kindes über theoretisches Wissen, das wir aus den USA, Grossbritannien und verschiedenen skandinavischen Ländern mitgebracht hatten, da diese uns auf dem Gebiet öffentlicher Parks, städtischer Naherholungsgebiete und Landschaftsanlagen voraus waren. Nicht zu vergessen sind Verweise auf theoretische und praktische, damals vielgelesene Texte (von der „freien" Schule in Summerhill über die methodologischen Einsichten Maria Montessoris und Célestin Freinets bis hin zu den Recherchen Jean Piagets). Ebenso lasen wir die Arbeiten über die institutionelle Analyse (Psychothérapie institutionnelle) von Fernand Deligny und seinen Schülern, die Simon sehr gut kannte.

Es ging uns darum, in den Raum einzugreifen, um die Art, wie man ihn konstruiert, besetzt und für Kinder zugänglich macht. Dabei wurde das „Warum" zu einer der entscheidenden Komponenten, egal ob es um Bildung, Entwicklung, Erziehung, Wohlbefinden, Komfort, Entdecken oder etwas anderes ging.

Unsere ersten Vorschläge, die wir später immer wieder aufgriffen und die als Grundlage all unserer Projekte dienten, beruhten auf einer Konkretisierung des Raums, der aus Grund- und Elementarformen zusammengesetzt war (Kuben, Zylinder, Kugeln, Pyramiden). Diese wiederum schufen komplexe Raumorganisationen (etwa eine Assemblage kleiner Volumina, Durchgänge, grosse Volumina, Verbindungsstege, offene Räume, geschlossene Räume usw.). Die sich daraus ergebenden räumlichen Kontinuitäten oder Brüche waren auf unterschiedliche Weise (Rutschen, Leitern) und von verschiedenen Standpunkten (Beobachten, Sich-Verbergen) zugänglich, boten physische Herausforderung (Klettern, Schaukeln, Hängen, Rutschen) und andere spontane, mit dem jeweiligen Ort zusammenhängende Beschäftigungen (Plaudern, Einschlafen, Beobachten, Lesen, Erfinden gemeinsamer Spiele, aber auch das Tauschen von Spielzeug oder anderem Spielmaterial).

Wir bezweckten durch die Präsenz einfacher Formen und Volumina komplexe Raumanordnungen und einladende, inspirierende Strukturen zu schaffen, die sich ganz nach Bedürfnis und Belieben in eine Höhle, eine Raumkapsel, eine einsame Insel, einen Piratenschlupfwinkel, ein Restaurant, einen Zuckerwattestand oder was auch immer verwandeln liessen.

Diese Volumina sollten keine Abfolge von Raumkörpern mit festgelegten Funktionen sein, sondern eigenständige Räume mit einer eigenen plastischen und ästhetischen Wirkung. Die Wirkung entstand durch die Art der Materialien, Oberflächenbeschaffenheit, Farbe, Beleuchtung, die volumetrischen und räumlichen Organisationen und Beziehungen. Da ihnen keine Gebrauchsanweisung beigefügt war, konnten die Kinder sie nutzen wie sie wollten, entweder um sich zu bewegen (Rutschen, Klettern, Kriechen, Schaukeln) oder unter dem Gesichtspunkt von Imagination oder Projektion („Das ist unsere Höhle..." / „Das ist unser Bootsdeck..." / „Das wäre..."). Der von uns damals verwendete Begriff „Struktur des Spiels" (structure du jeu) sollte nicht „chic" sein, sondern den Erwachsenen klarmachen, dass man hier eine andere Welt betrat.

applications; the accompanying music would be provided by the Baschet Brothers' sound installations, which sometimes included the presence of Frank Zappa.

First Steps

Having decided to work together within the world of children—children and their games, children's spaces, a child's world—we initially met not far from David's home—he was living at the time on a barge moored in central Paris. We used the riverside and surrounding spaces as our rallying point and production zone. Discussions, plans, sketches of spatial arrangements, models: David would make the early prototypes of the giant play structures based on modular elements tested on the quay with his own children or those of passersby.

At the same time, our theoretical approach to the world of children was stimulated by ideas we brought back from the United States, Great Britain, and northern European countries, given their advance in the realm of public parks, urban recreation zones, and landscape gardens, not forgetting references to theoretical and practical texts widely read at the time (from the "free" school at Summerhill to Jean Piaget's research, via methodological input from Maria Montessori and Célestin Freinet). We also consulted the work on therapeutic communities developed by Fernand Deligny and his followers, about which Simon knew a great deal.

It was a question of acting upon a space, upon the way space was constructed, paying attention to how it was made available to children. The "why" became a key element in the equation: whether for learning, development, upbringing, wellbeing, convenience, discovery, and so on.

Our first proposals—which subsequently served as the foundations of all our projects—were based on a concretization of space composed of basic, elementary shapes (cubes, cylinders, spheres, pyramids) that created complex spatial arrangements (for example, an assembly of small volumes, passageways, large volumes, connecting bridges, open spaces, closed spaces ...). The resulting spatial continuities or disruptions could be accessed in various ways (ladders, slides), from different viewpoints (watching, hiding), offering physical challenges (climbing, swinging, hanging, sliding), and included other spontaneous activities associated with such places (chatting, falling asleep, watching, reading, not forgetting the invention of joint games and the swapping of toys or game material).

In fact, it involved an assembly of simple shapes and volumes to create complex spatial arrangements that were easy to approach,

Auch wurde die Umgebung der Spielstrukturen – öffentliche Garten- oder Parkanlagen, Wohnsiedlungen – als Landschaft gestaltet, bepflanzt, die Böden an die Bedürfnisse des Spielens angepasst, um die Aneignung dieses neuen Ortes zu erleichtern. Der öffentliche Raum wurde ein Ort, wo Kinder einem „Ereignis" begegnen konnten. Hier wurde ihnen die Möglichkeit geboten, eine ganz spezielle und unerwartete Erfahrung zu machen, auf unbekannten Raumkörpern herumzurutschen, hindurchzukriechen, um sie herumzurennen, sich zu verstecken, hinaufzuklettern, Fangen zu spielen – sprich die Summe der Möglichkeiten, die sich aus dem Zusammensein ergeben.

Zahlreiche Niederlagen, erste Erfolge

Als Gestalter von Räumen für Kinder hatten wir die ebenso grosszügige wie naive Vorstellung, Menschen aus der Bildung, der Immobilienentwicklung, dem sozialen Wohnungsbau oder der Gestaltung von kreativem Design und öffentlichen Räumen überzeugen zu müssen. Diese waren jedoch zum damaligen Zeitpunkt die falschen Zielgruppen. Man liess uns abblitzen, konfrontierte uns mit einer Fülle negativer Meinungen, weigerte sich, uns zu treffen, ignorierte unsere Vorschläge oder vertrat ablehnende, engstirnige Positionen – eine Entmutigung selbst für den stärksten Samurai. Dann, eines Tages, kontaktierte uns der Architekt Alain Villeminot, angetan von „den Vorzügen des freien Spiels als Lernerfahrung für das Leben". Er lud uns ein, einen Vorschlag für einen Kinderspielplatz als Zentrum des geplanten Feriendorfes in Royan direkt an der französischen Atlantikküste zu erarbeiten (Abb. 158–164).

Da erwachte unser Team zum Leben: Pläne, Modelle, dann der Auftrag, sechs Monate unentwegter Arbeit, Tag und Nacht, eine intensive Auseinandersetzung mit allen Fragen, die es zu lösen galt. Wir mussten bei diesem Projekt grundlegende, sehr präzise technische Vorgaben erfüllen und zugleich eine Fülle von Fakten über die Welt des Kindes erheben und auswerten, was wenig mit dem Bild von verträumten Künstlern zu tun hatte, mit dem man uns damals häufig in Verbindung brachte.

Dieses Projekt in Royan war ein voller Erfolg, sowohl bei den Kindern als auch bei den Erwachsenen (die zu anderen Stunden in das „U-Boot" hinabstiegen). Dieser Erfolg brachte uns Beachtung und lobende Worte der Medien, doch vor allem zog er eine Reihe von Aufträgen für Projekte eines anderen Touristikunternehmens, des Touring Clubs, nach sich, dann Aufträge von Village de Vacances Famille (VVF) und Village de Vacances Tourisme, für die wir innerhalb von drei Jahren etwa zehn grosse Spielplätze oder Freizeitanlagen realisierten. Um den ernsthaften Charakter unserer „Disziplin" zu untermauern, beobachteten wir jedes Projekt ausführlich nach dessen Fertigstellung. Das Ziel dieser „Manöverkritik" war es, bestimmte negative Aspekte zu beheben (Änderung bestimmter Raumvolumina, um die Höhe oder den Eingangsbereich eines Raumes anzupassen, Verbesserung des natürlichen Lichteinfalls usw.). Vor allem aber gelangten wir durch die täglichen Beobachtungen nach und nach zu einem besseren Verständnis gewisser Fakten, die von grundlegender Bedeutung waren: Hierzu zählten etwa die Risikobereitschaft von Kindern unterschiedlichen Alters und in verschiedenen Situationen, die Nutzung des Raums in der Funktion der Volumina oder der

allowing for all kinds of appropriations and fantasies of multiple universes, capable of being transformed by need or desire into a cave, a space capsule, a deserted island, a pirates' lair, a restaurant, a cotton-candy stall, and so on.

It was important that these spaces or volumes did not constitute a series of predefined volumes, but rather autonomous spaces with their own visual and aesthetic impact, emanating from the very nature of the materials of which they were made, from their spatial and volumetric arrangement, from their texture, color, and lighting, and from the volumetric relationships established between them. Since they came with no user's manual, children could appropriate them as they wished, either in basic terms (sliding, climbing, crawling, swinging) or in terms of imagination or projection ("This is our cave ... " / "This is the deck of our ship ... " / "Let's say this is ... "). The term we used at the time, "play structure" (structure de jeu), was not designed to be "fashionable," but rather to make adults understand that here you entered another world.

Furthermore, we also addressed the environment in which these structures were installed—public parks, gardens, housing projects—that is to say, the surrounding space was also landscaped, planted, given suitable playground surfaces, designed, and organized to favor an appropriation of this new vital space. The public sphere became a place where children could encounter an "event" that allowed them to have a very special, unexpected experience, sliding along unfamiliar shapes, ducking beneath them, running around them, hiding in them, climbing over them, chasing others through them—in short, all the inventiveness that arises just by being and playing together.

Numerous Failures, Initial Successes

In our view—as naive as it was generous—our approach to the field of the design of children's areas should have won over people in the worlds of education, real-estate development, low-cost housing, architecture for creative design and public spaces, and such-like: but we were targeting the wrong people at the time. We were shown the door, and received a series of negative opinions, refusals to meet, lack of responses to our proposals, and negative, narrow-minded stances that would have discouraged the most hardened veterans. Then one day an architect, Alain Villeminot, attracted by "the virtues of free play as a learning experience," wanted the children's recreation zone to become a major focus of a seaside vacation village he was planning at Royan, on France's Atlantic coast, and asked us to come up with a plan (ill. 158–164).

Gruppen, das Verhalten eines Kindes in einem bestimmten Raum, allein oder in Begleitung, usw.

Wir hatten keinen Anspruch, wissenschaftliche Studien durchzuführen, unsere Beobachtungen in Theorie übersetzten zu müssen oder zu wollen oder gar „auf die Gestaltung des öffentlichen Raums spezialisierte Künstler" zu werden. Andererseits versuchten wir, gute Gestalter und Erbauer von Spiel- und Lebensräumen für Kinder zu sein. Wir wollten verantwortungsvolle Schöpfer von „Alltagsobjekten" im Einklang mit ihrer Umwelt sein und die an uns gestellten Erwartungen auf technische und möglicherweise auch poetische Art erfüllen.

Von der Forschung und Experimenten in die harte Wirklichkeit

Das „echte Terrain" bestand für uns aus schwierigen Quartieren und „Schlafstädten", d.h. Städten, wo das lebendige Strassentreiben dem Monofunktionalismus geopfert worden war, den viele Planer im Namen der „Charta von Athen" stumpfsinnig umgesetzt hatten. Wir bezeichneten solche Gegenden einfach nur als „Städte ohne Stadt".Der Architekturstudent Jean-Jacques Johannet, der Praktikant in einem Architekturbüro war, das gerade ein neues Stadtviertel auf einem ehemaligen Zuckerrübenfeld mitten im Nichts plante, überzeugte seinen Chef, uns für die Planung eines Spielplatzes einzuladen. Der Spielplatz wurde nach zahlreichen Besuchen vor Ort auf der Baustelle entworfen und schlussendlich vom Team umgesetzt, als die Bauarbeiten noch im Gang waren und die Bewohner der ersten fertiggestellten Wohneinheiten bereits einzogen. Das Projekt veranschaulichte so den Reichtum einer engen Zusammenarbeit zwischen Gestaltern und Bewohnern, sei es, indem wir Rückschlüsse aus den Kommentaren der Benutzer zogen oder sei es durch die Aneignung von dem, was nun zu ihrem öffentlichen Raum wurde.

Daraus entwickelte sich der partizipatorische Ansatz, den unser Team fortan anwendete und anhand dessen die Beziehungen zwischen Gestaltern und Bewohnern bei Verhandlungen reflektiert und einfache und effiziente Regeln definiert wurden.

Eine bemerkenswerte Begegnung

Dies ist die treffendste Beschreibung unserer Begegnung mit François Mathey, Direktor des Centre de Création Industrielle (CCI) am Musée des Arts Décoratifs in Paris, als er zusammen mit François Barré, dem jungen und brillanten Initianten im Designbereich, die Eröffnung des zukünftigen CCI plante. Gemeinsam erteilten sie uns den Auftrag, in einem der abrissgeweihten Pavillons von Les Halles de Baltard (die zentralen Markthallen von Victor Baltard), eine Vor-Ausstellung zu planen, zu organisieren und zu betreiben, während eigentlich alle Augen auf die Errichtung des heutigen Centre Beaubourg gerichtet waren. Mathey und Barré hatten sich nicht nur von der Gestaltung unserer Projekte beeindrucken lassen, sondern auch von den sozialen Fragen, auf die wir mit der Installation im öffentlichen Raum abzielten.

Sie liessen uns völlig freie Hand, dieses legendäre, mehrere Tausend Quadratmeter grosse Grundstück in

The team sprang to life: plans, models, then the commission, six months of sleepless nights running through all the questions that needed to be resolved. We had to build to crucial, highly specific technical requirements, and also explore data on the world of children; in short, we had to assimilate a mass of data that went far beyond the image of dreamy artists often ascribed to us at the time.

This project in Royan proved highly popular among both children and adults (who used the "submarine" at times when children did not). This success earned us media attention and praise, and above all a series of commissions for new sites by another holiday firm, the Touring Club, followed by Village de Vacances Familles (VVF), and Village de Vacances Tourisme, for whom we produced roughly ten major playgrounds or sites over a three-year period. In order to reinforce the seriousness of our "field," every project was subsequently followed by observations over a relatively long period. The interest of these observations lay in the possibility of altering certain negative features—changing certain volumes to modify the height or access to a space, improving the natural lighting, etc.—but above all the daily observations progressively yielded deeper insight into certain data that were more crucially important to us, such as children's risk-taking at various ages and in various situations, the occupation of the space as a function of the nature of volumes or groups, the behavior of a child in a given space when alone or when accompanied, and so on.

We had no pretensions of carrying out scientific investigations, or of being obliged or able to write up theoretical articles on our observations, or even of becoming "artists specialized in the designing public spaces." On the other hand, we were trying to be good designers and makers of playground zones and living spaces for children; we wanted to be responsible creators of "lifestyle objects" adapted to their environment, making a positive contribution to expectations that were explicit, technical, and perhaps also poetic.

Moving from Research and Experimentation to "Real Terrain"

For us, the "real terrain" was composed of tough urban neighborhoods and housing projects in cities where varied local life was dying out in the name of mono-functionalism, stupidly applied by designers who waved the Athens Charter. We called such places simply "towns without a town." Jean-Jacques Johannet, an architecture student working as an intern for an architectural firm designing a new urban zone on a former sugar-beet

165   Group Ludic, Hängebrücke über Kanal / Suspension bridge over the canal, Blijdorp Park, Rotterdam, Auftrag des Warenhauses / commission by the department store De Bijenkorf, 1970

166   Group Ludic, Rembrandt Park, Amsterdam, Auftrag des Warenhauses / commission by the department store De Bijenkorf, 1970

Beschlag zu nehmen. Sie sorgten aber für die Berichterstattung in den Medien und eine offizielle Anerkennung unseres Vorgehens, indem sie ein Projekt in Originalgrösse ermöglichten, das nicht nur den Umgang mit öffentlichen Räumen für Kinder thematisierte, sondern es Zehntausenden von diesen auch tatsächlich ermöglichte, zum „Spielen in Les Halles" zu gehen. Die Kinder kamen allein oder mit ihren Eltern, die anwesend und sichtbar blieben, aber ausserhalb des Spielbereichs, um ihnen die völlige Freiheit zu gewähren. Mit unterschiedlichen Installationen wollten wir auf die Absurdität bestimmter Tabus oder Verbote hinweisen, wie Risiko, Gefahr, Angst vor dem Unbekannten oder der Durchmischung verschiedener Altersgruppen.

Vom kreativen Standpunkt betrachtet war Les Halles auch das Projekt, bei dem wir auf Drängen Simons sehr ausführlich mit der Aneignung von Industrieobjekten experimentierten. Das heisst, dass wir bestimmte Industrieobjekte für einen anderen als den eigentlich vorgesehenen Zweck benutzten. So verwendeten wir beispielsweise ein extrem grosses aufblasbares Kissen, mit dem normalerweise Flugzeuge aus dem Schlamm gezogen werden (das musste man erstmal finden!) als riesige Sprungmatte, ein Vorläufer der heutigen Hüpfburgen (Abb. 171–172).

In dieser Zeit war David für vier Projekte in Holland zuständig, in Amsterdam, Rotterdam, Eindhoven und Den Haag. Das Kaufhaus De Bijenkorf schenkte diesen Städten anlässlich des Gründungsjubiläums des Unternehmens je einen riesigen Spielplatz, mit bis dahin unbekannten Attraktionen: etwa einer Hängebrücke über einem Kanal, einer riesigen Pyramide mit Wänden aus farbigem Plexiglas, Spielen mit optischen Veränderungen, interaktiven Beobachtungsspielen und Wasserbecken (Abb. 165–170). Unser formales Vokabular erweiterte sich, die Kenntnis über das soziale Umfeld der Projekte wuchs und wir wurden uns der Wichtigkeit bewusst, auf die Bedeutung der Regionen, Kulturen und Traditionen, ihre alltäglichen Lebensgewohnheiten und Verhaltensweisen einzugehen, damit die Bewohner des Orts sich die Innovationen, unabhängig von technischen und sozialen Aspekten, tatsächlich aneignen konnten.

Die Einsicht, dass Anerkennung nicht Erfolg bedeutet

Da wir mit unserem neuen Bekanntheitsgrad, den gesammelten Erfahrungen, Erfolgen und „Geländegewinnen" zuverlässigere und überzeugendere Kompetenzen erworben hatten, fingen wir an, unsere Methoden, Ansätze und Referenzen wichtigen Entscheidungsträgern zu präsentieren. Wir hofften, auf diese Weise eine neue Denk- und Handlungsweise zu begründen: Qualität und Flexibilität der Formen, gesellschaftliche Relevanz der Räume, Benutzerfreundlichkeit der Materialien, Bereicherung gesellschaftlicher Verbindungen, Qualität des Raumes, kurz all unsere Methoden und erworbenen Fertigkeiten sollten einen Schritt in Richtung eines besseren sozialen Klimas bedeuten.

Doch das waren Illusionen, nichts als Illusionen! Nur weil Lob und Bewunderung geäussert wurden, hiess das noch lange nicht, dass diese auch gehört wurden. Die Tatsache, dass Fachpersonen und die Medien uns zu unseren Errungenschaften gratulierten, half uns nicht dabei, die Hürden der

field—surrounded on every side by a huge void—convinced his boss to ask us to devise a play area designed to unify the zone shared by several buildings. Drawn up after numerous stays on the site and even during construction, this playground project—erected by the team on the site during the completion phase of construction, as residents of the first-completed units were moving in—demonstrated the richness of close collaboration between designers and residents, both in the incorporation of functional details provided by everyday users, and in their appropriation of what would become their public space.

That was the source of the set of participatory guidelines subsequently followed by the team, which were the object of reflection on the practices and relationships involved in concerted, participatory efforts on the part of designers and residents, yielding simple and efficient rules for project management.

A Remarkable Encounter

That is the only way to describe the fact that we met François Mathey, who headed the Centre de Création Industrielle at the Musée des Arts Décoratifs in Paris, just when he was planning to open the new Centre de Création Industrielle (CCI) assisted by François Barré—that young, brilliant scout in the field of new design initiatives. Together they commissioned us to plan, organize, and implement a forerunner show in one of the pavilions of Les Halles (the central market hall designed by Victor Baltard), slated for demolition just when all eyes were focused on the building of the current Centre Pompidou. The pair were struck not just by the design of our projects, but also by the social issues raised by the intention to install them in public spaces.

They gave us free reign to occupy this exclusive piece of real estate (tens of thousands of square feet), and they provided media coverage and total official recognition of the project by backing a full-scale display of our work that not only addressed the handling of public spaces for children, but actually allowed tens of thousands of them to "go and play at Les Halles" on their own or with their parents (who remained present and visible, but outside the play zone, in order to give the children complete freedom). This exhibition of different approaches furthermore sought to demonstrate the absurdity of certain taboos and prohibitions arising from fears of risk, danger, the unknown, and the mixing of age groups.

From the creative standpoint, Les Halles was also the project in which, at Simon's urging, we appropriated industrial equipment. That is to say, we took displaced industrial objects

Zurückhaltung der Institutionen und Entscheidungsträger und deren tief verwurzelten Konservatismus zu überwinden.

Dies hinderte uns freilich nicht daran, im folgenden Jahrzehnt Dutzende von Projekten zu realisieren, einige davon mit Unterstützung der „Société Aires et Volumes". Der Verleger Jean-Jacques Nathan hatte diese gegründet, um unsere Forschungen und Aktionen zu unterstützen, und um einige kleinere, für Kindergärten bestimmte Spielmodule zu vermarkten. Sein bemerkenswerter Vorschlag sagte uns zu und ermöglichte uns, unsere Energie voll und ganz für die Krise der Stadt einzusetzen.

Was 1979 nicht gesagt werden konnte, dem Internationalen Jahr des Kindes

Diese Phase des Forschens / Handelns / Umsetzens war nicht nur sehr lehrreich, sondern gipfelte Anfang 1979 in einer Anfrage der Abteilung für Lebensqualität (Délégation à la Qualité de la Vie) des Umweltministeriums, im Botanischen Garten von Paris auf einer von einem Zeltdach überspannten, ein Hektar grossen Fläche eine Ausstellung zu organisieren. Die Ausstellung sollte sich mit der Welt der Kinder, ihrer Umwelt und der Wahrnehmung derselben befassen. Die Hauptanliegen (Tiere, Wasser, Luft, Umweltverschmutzung, Abfall, Raum, Architektur) sollten auf verschiedene Weisen behandelt werden: in Form von kleinen Themenausstellungen, Workshops, Darbietungen, Spaziergängen, einem von Kindern geleiteten (und von Journalisten mitbetreuten) Presseraum und der Veröffentlichung einer vierseitigen illustrierten Tageszeitung, Entdeckungstouren sowie Diskussionsrunden inklusive Befragung „bemerkenswerter Persönlichkeiten" (des damaligen Umweltministers Michel d'Ornano, des Architekten Jean Prouvé, der pazifistischen Politikerin Louise Weiss usw.) seitens der Kinder. Es kam eine Reihe von Werkzeugen und Techniken zum Einsatz, die - mit Unterstützung der Erwachsenen - die produktiven Kapazitäten der Welt der Kindheit veranschaulichen sollten. Dies betraf nicht nur die Fragen und Erwartungen der Kinder, sondern auch ihre einfallsreichen, positiven Beiträge, die sie lieferten, sobald die Begleitung durch Erwachsene nicht mehr eine ständige Infantilisierung oder Verblödungstaktik bedeutete und man sie wirklich im Sinne des „Kindes als Vater des Menschen" behandelte (Abb. 173–174).

Diese neue Aktivitätsphase hielt einige Jahre an und dauerte bis etwa 1995. Wir entwickelten neue Aktionsformen wie etwa eine stärkere Partizipation von Bewohnern an der Umgestaltung der Spielplätze und Freizeitstätten sowie eine zunehmende Beteiligung von Kindern an spezifischen Teilen eines Projekts (Wahl der Themen und des Programms der Raumgestaltung, Zeichnungen auf dem Boden, Dekoration, Errichtung einfacher Mauern usw.).

Doch unmerklich und schleichend kam es zu mehreren notorischen Veränderungen, die auf subtile Weise Folgen zeigten. Die besondere Aufmerksamkeit, die Kindern in den 1970ern zuteil geworden war, liess nach. Wie bereits zwanzig Jahre früher in den USA wurde klar, dass die Kindheit kein beliebtes, vielversprechendes Thema mehr ist. Das heranwachsende, sich entwickelnde Kind, also das Kind, um das es uns ging, war faktisch eliminiert worden. Die Aufmerksamkeit, die wir ihm schenkten, sowie die Umwelt dieses Kindes interessierte die Gesellschaft nicht mehr.

and assigned a different use to them. For example, the extremely large inflatable cushions used to get an airplane out of the mud (somebody had to come up with that one!) were transformed into a giant jumping pit, the forerunner of today's bouncy castles (ill. 171–172).

During that time, David was overseeing four construction projects in Holland—in Amsterdam, Rotterdam, Eindhoven, and The Hague. The De Bijenkorf store in each of those cities was celebrating the anniversary of the firm's founding by offering the town a vast playground featuring previously unknown attractions such as a suspension bridge over a canal, a giant pyramid with walls of colored transparent Plexiglas, games involving optical transformation, interactive games of observation, and pools of water (ill. 165–170). The formal vocabulary was expanded, and knowledge of environments of human intervention grew, as did awareness of a need not just to listen, but to grasp the input of local regions with their cultures and traditions, their everyday lifestyles and behavior, in order that, quite apart from the technical and social aspects, local inhabitants would truly appropriate the innovations, enabling a true graft to occur.

Realizing that Recognition Does Not Mean Success

Considering that, along with our new fame, experience, and successes in the field, we had acquired more reliable and convincing skills, we began presenting our methods, approaches, and references to key decision-makers in the hope of creating a trend in ideas and action in which the quality and flexibility of forms, the sociability of developed areas, the user-friendliness of materials, the reinforcement of social links, the quality of space—in short, all of our methods and acquired skills—would constitute a step toward the creation of a better sense of social wellbeing.

Illusion, illusion, illusion. Just because praiseworthy, positive, admirable information has been provided, does not mean it will be adopted, incorporated, established. The congratulations of specialist authorities and the media for our accomplishments did not help us over the hurdles of institutional reticence and the deeply anchored conservatism of decision-makers.

That did not prevent us, however, from carrying out several dozen projects in the following decade, some of which were implemented, under our supervision, by the Aires et Volumes firm founded by publisher Jean-Jacques Nathan, who wanted to back our research and our efforts even as he marketed certain smaller play items destined for nursery schools. His honorable proposal suited us, and enabled us to focus on the realm of the urban crisis.

171–172 Group Ludic, *jouer aux halles*, Les Halles, Paris 1970, Auftrag des / commissioned by Centre de Création Industrielle (CCI)

An seine Stelle trat nun das „Kind als Konsument", auf das sich alle Blicke richteten. Man denke nur daran, wie Hochsicherheitsdesigner Kinderwagen als rollende Festungen entwarfen, die an SUVs mit hydropneumatischen Radaufhängungen erinnern. Was Spiele im Aussenraum betraf, so trat zunehmend sicherheitstechnischer Schnickschnack an die Stelle des Spielerischen, ja man war häufig versucht, diese „neuen" Kinder zunächst mit Rettungsbojen auszustatten, bevor man sie zum Händewaschen schickte.

In den grossen städtischen Siedlungen, für die wir besonders nach besseren Lösungen gesucht hatten, stiessen wir im letzten Jahrzehnt unserer Interventionen auf eine regelrechte Weigerung, die wahren Ursachen und Gründe der urbanen Dysfunktion und Unordnung anzugehen, obwohl diese eindeutig identifiziert waren, sodass sie aus Nachlässigkeit und mangelndem Interesse zu einer dauerhaften Erscheinung wurden.

Die Kombination all dieser Faktoren hatte eine gravierende Folge: Die Errichtung städtischer Spielplätze im Aussenraum von Wohnsiedlungen und Quartieren hatte keine Priorität mehr, und die finanziellen Mittel für ihre praktische Umsetzung (Planung, Teilnahme, Vorstudien, Integration, Anpassung, fachliche Betreuung) wurden nicht mehr zur Verfügung gestellt. Unsere Vorgehensweise, die auf akrobatisch geschnürten Finanzierungspaketen beruhte, die jedes Mal einen wahren Drahtseilakt erforderten, wurde immer riskanter und ungewisser, sodass sich die Projekte schliesslich nicht mehr realisieren liessen.

Eine gemischte, aber zuversichtliche Bilanz

Wir drei haben uns für einen Bereich entschieden, von dem wir uns angezogen fühlten, aus Lust, kreativ zu sein, aus Überzeugung für mehr Solidarität, dem Enthusiasmus für das Machen und Argumentieren, aber wahrscheinlich ebenso - ohne uns dies einzugestehen - aus Vergnügen beim Anblick unserer eigenen Schöpfungen. Da wir keine anerkannten Spezialisten waren, akzeptierten wir bereitwillig, von denen zu lernen, die uns vorausgegangen waren und bei denen wir wohl oder übel Ähnlichkeiten mit uns selbst erkannten. Etwas erschaffen bedeutet in erster Linie zu lernen und dann in die Richtung vorwärts zu gehen, die andere vorgegeben haben.

Vom freudigen Lachen auf den Baustellen von Reims oder Hérouville Saint-Clair bis zu den Rufen der Kinder von Les Halles haben wir zwar gelernt, dass das Kind der Vater des Menschen ist, aber auch, dass das Kind nicht der Vater seines Vaters werden soll und die Rollenverteilung klar bleiben muss. Von den Einwohnern von Asnières haben wir gelernt, dass Vorschlagen auch am Ball bleiben heisst, aber auch, dass man eine Stadt manchmal erst richtig erleben muss, um zu wissen, wie man sie bewohnt.

Von all den Designern, Künstlern und Architekten, die sich wie wir auf die Entwicklung des öffentlichen Raums konzentriert haben, haben wir gelernt, dass die räumlichen Qualitäten bei einem erfolgreich geführten Bauvorhaben immer emotional aufgeladen sind, und dass kein Pflichtenheft dies zu berücksichtigen vermag.

Indem diese Ausstellung das Feld des Möglichen absteckt, hat sie den Vorteil, nicht nur die Bandbreite der bereits

What Could Not Be Said in 1979, the International Year of the Child

That period of research / action / execution not only provided additional input, but culminated early in 1979 with a request from the Ministry of the Environment's "Quality of Life Department" (Délégation à la Qualité de Vie) to organize a show in the botanical gardens in Paris, beneath a tent-covered space of some two and a half acres. The exhibition had to address the World of Children, their environment, and their perception of it. Key topics—animals, water, air, pollution, detritus, space, architecture—had to be addressed in the form of small thematic displays, workshops, performances, promenades, a press room jointly run by children (under the guidance of journalists) who published a four-page illustrated daily, discovery walks, panel discussions in which children questioned "notable figures" (such as Environment Minister Michel d'Ornano, architect Jean Prouvé, pacifist politician Louise Weiss), and so on. A set of tools and techniques were employed in order to reveal—with the help of adults who assisted in using them—the productive capacities of the world of childhood, including not only their questions and expectations, but also their own inventive, positive contributions, which they made once adult accompaniment did not mean a constant infantilization or dumbing down, once they were truly treated in the spirit of "child as father to the man." (ill. 173–174)

This new period of activity continued for a number of years, until roughly 1995. We developed new forms of action, such as extending the participation of inhabitants when revamping the recreational zones in their neighborhood, plus the increasing participation of children in specific aspects of the construction project (choice of renovation theme and topics, drawings on the ground, decorative elements, the erection of low supporting walls, etc.).

Yet several notorious changes were underway, insidiously and imperceptibly producing their subtle effects. The spotlight placed on children during the 1970s faded—people realized, as they had 20 years earlier in the United States, that childhood is no longer a fashionable, promising subject. The child undergoing development, the one we were concerned with, had in fact been eliminated; our attentiveness to children and the childhood environment was no longer of interest to society.

In contrast, the prime target became "the child as consumer," toward whom all eyes turned. Just recall how designers of total safety, when simply taking small children for a walk, came up with strolling fortresses that were still dubbed baby strollers, but resembled SUVs

von Tausenden von Benutzern getesteten und ausprobierten Möglichkeiten zu zeigen. Sie kann auch Wege aus heutiger Sicht und aus dem aktuellen Kontext heraus erkunden, um sich dabei immer in Erinnerung zu rufen, dass jeder Ort, jeder Platz, jeder Häuserblock seine eigene spezifische Identität hat und der Geist des Ortes darauf wartet, zum Leben erweckt zu werden.

Xavier de la Salle diente von 1954 bis 1958 als Schiffsjunge und Matrose in der Handelsmarine und drei weitere Jahre im Militärdienst der französischen Marine. Nach dem Baccalauréat begann er das Studium der Politik- und Wirtschaftswissenschaften an der Université de Bordeaux. Er stellte erste Zeichnungen und Aquarelle aus. Nach Abschluss des Studiums zog er 1964 nach Paris; er arbeitete neben seiner Tätigkeit als Maler und Bildhauer als Presseassistent bei der Europäischen Gemeinschaft (EG) und assistierte Künstlern wie den Brüdern Baschet oder Joël Stein. 1967 gründete er zusammen mit David Roditi und Simon Koszel Group Ludic. 1975 bis 1979 führte er Group Ludic alleine weiter. Gleichzeitig schrieb er seine Dissertation zur Planung der städtischen öffentlichen Räume an der Universität Paris 8 Vincennes. Von 1973 bis 2001 war er Professor für Design, Umwelt und Urbanismus an der École d'Architecture de Paris La Défense. Von 1979 bis 1985 führte er Interventionen in Problemquartieren in den Pariser Banlieues durch und veröffentlichte in dieser Zeit *Espace de jeux, espace de vie* (Bordas, Paris 1982). Bis 2000 bearbeitete er Aufträge in Raumplanung und Regionalwirtschaft und widmete sich seiner künstlerischen Tätigkeit. Nach der Übersiedelung in den Südosten Frankreichs ist er hauptsächlich als Maler und Bildhauer tätig und ist als Kommunalpolitiker aktiv.

with oleo-pneumatic suspensions. As to outdoor games, safety gadgets slowly got the better of playfulness itself—people were often tempted to supply this new species of children with lifesavers before allowing them to go and wash their hands.

In vast urban zones (the very ones we most wished to provide with suitable solutions), the final decade of our career met with a veritable refusal to deal with the true causes and reasons—although clearly identified—of the rise of urban dysfunction and disorder, allowing them to take permanent hold through negligence and laxity.

The combination of all these factors had one major consequence: the creation of urban outdoor play areas in dense neighborhoods and housing projects was no longer on the agenda; the funds required to make everything click—planning, participation, preliminary studies, incorporation, adaptation, technical maintenance—were no longer made available. Our approach, based on acrobatic financial packaging that called for a high-wire act with each operation, became increasingly risky and uncertain, and could no longer be carried out.

Mixed Yet Sure Results

The three of us had committed ourselves to a field that appealed to us, spurred by a need for creativity, indeed by a conviction of the need for a fairer social deal, by enthusiasm for doing as well as saying, and also probably—without admitting it—for the pleasure of dazzling ourselves with our own creations. Since we were not established specialists, we were open to learning from the people who had preceded us, in whom we necessarily recognized similarities with ourselves. Creating means above all learning, then pursuing paths already blazed by others before.

From the delighted smiles we saw on the sites of places like Reims and Hérouville Saint-Clair to the shouts of the children at Les Halles, we learned that while the child is father to the man, the child must not become his father's father. The proper division of roles should remain clear. From the inhabitants of Asnières we learned that making suggestions implied following up, over time and through time, and that sometimes you must also learn to experience the city in order to know how to inhabit it.

From all the designers, artists, and architects who, like us, have focused on developing public spaces, we learned that, in a successfully mastered operation, spatial qualities always carry an emotional charge that no project guidelines can ever include in their description.

By revealing the realm of the possible, this exhibition has the advantage of showing

Groupd Ludic, *Atelier cordes*, Veranstaltung zum Internationalen Jahr des Kindes / Event for the International Year of the Child, Jardin des Plantes, Paris, 1979

173

not only a range of possibilities already explored, implemented, tested, and tried by thousands of users, but also paths that can be explored from the standpoint of the present-day context, the current environment, all the while recalling that every location, every place, every block has its own specific identity, that the spirit of the place is there to be awakened.

From 1954–1958 Xavier de la Salle served as cabin boy and sailor in the mercantile navy. He served in the French marines for an additional three years. He began his studies in political science and economics at the University of Bordeaux in 1961. At the same time, the first exhibitions of his drawings and watercolor works took place. In 1964 he moved to Paris and worked as press assistant for the European Community (EC), assisted artists such as the Baschet brothers and Joël Stein alongside his artistic practice as a painter and sculptor. Together with David Roditi and Simon Koszel he founded Group Ludic in 1967. Between 1975 and 1979 he continued Group Ludic on his own. During that time he wrote his thesis on the design of urban

public space at the University Paris-8 Vincennes. From 1973 to 2001 he was professor of design, environment, and urbanism at the École d'Architecture de Paris-La Défense. Between 1979 and 1985 he carried out interventions in problematic areas in the Parisian suburbs. He published *Espace de jeux, espace de vie* (Bordas, Paris) in 1982. He then executed mandates in spatial planning and regional economy until 2000 in parallel with his artistic practice. In 2000 he moved to the southeast of France where he mainly works as a painter and sculptor and has been active as a community politician.

Visionen erzählen und teilen. Das Projekt *The Park* (2008–2009)

Narrating Community Vision. *The Park* Project (2008–2009)

Sreejata Roy

Der urbane Kontext

Gegenwärtig lebt fast die Hälfte der siebzehn Millionen Einwohner von Delhi in Slums und Resettlement Colonies, Kolonien umgesiedelter Slum-Bewohner. Die Anwohner dieser Bezirke erbringen mit ihrer Arbeit für die Stadt unentbehrliche Dienstleistungen; sie selbst sind jedoch in hohem Masse unterversorgt und leben in ärmlichen Verhältnissen mit sehr schlechter Abwasser- und Abfallentsorgung sowie schlechter Versorgung mit Wasser und Elektrizität. Diese Bevölkerungsgruppen werden als renitent, störend und illegal, als Eindringlinge, Gesetzesbrecher, Umweltverschmutzer und schädlich für die Gesellschaft betrachtet und tauchen bei Debatten – etwa über „öffentliche Sicherheit", „kulturelles Erbe", „Entwicklung", „Stadtplanung/Städtebau" und „Fortschritt" – nur als statistische Variablen auf. Die Öffentlichkeit und die Medien nehmen unterprivilegierte Communities nur dann zur Kenntnis, wenn ihre Stimmen für lokale und nationale Wahlen gebraucht werden, oder in urbanen Krisensituationen – bei Auseinandersetzungen mit städtischen Behörden und Ordnungskräften (etwa bei Krawallen, Protesten, Kundgebungen, Zerstörungen, Streiks, krimineller und sexueller Gewalt, Zwangsräumungen). Die Stadt – ein offener und zugleich ablehnender Ort verführerischer Moderne und boomenden Kapitals – ist eine soziale Schnittstelle und erlaubt es Personen und Gruppen, sich über Klassen- und Einkommensgrenzen hinweg auszudrücken. Hier werden Einfallsreichtum, enge Alltagsbeziehungen und informelle lokale Netzwerke gefördert, was es einer entrechteten, „umgesiedelten" Bevölkerungsgruppe nicht nur ermöglicht, die Not zu überwinden, sondern sogar zu gedeihen. Die vielschichtigen Realitäten dieser gesellschaftlichen Konstellationen kommen in der gängigen Berichterstattung der Medien kaum vor.

Als Vertreter einer sozial engagierten Kunst visualisieren und realisieren wir Projekte, die ein breites Spektrum von Beteiligten aus Delhis unterversorgten Siedlungen dazu einladen, ihre persönlichen Erfahrungen in einem sich verändernden urbanen Umfeld individuell und kollektiv in unterschiedlichen medialen und künstlerischen Formen zu schildern. Wir sind durch unsere Praxis zu der Erkenntnis gelangt, dass eine gesellschaftlich engagierte Kunst, insbesondere, wenn sie auf Dialog beruht, nicht anhand der empirischen Parameter konkreter „Ergebnisse", „Nutzen" und „Produkte" für die Community beurteilt, belegt oder bestätigt werden kann. Unser Ziel besteht immer darin, innerhalb von vorhandenen lokalen Netzwerken und Notwendigkeiten gemeinsam neue künstlerische Formen zu prägen sowie die städtischen Muster und die ihnen innewohnenden ästhetischen Konsequenzen – ihre vielfältigen Kartografien, Ökologien und Kulturen – aufzudecken, freizusetzen und zu unterstützen. Angesichts der komplexen Geschichte der Slums und Resettlement Colonies sowie ihrer systematischen Einbettung und Neueinschreibung in die autoritäre, hochpolitische Stadtentwicklung gewinnen die Begriffe „Stadt", „Stadtteil" (locality) und „Gemeinschaft" (community) eine besondere Resonanz als zentrale Grössen für künstlerische Praktiken, die auf städtischen Alltagserfahrungen aufbauen.

Die Geschichte des Ortes und die Interventionen

Der Park, Eigentum der Municipal Corporation of Delhi (MCD), liegt im Block J von Dakshinpuri. Die Anwohner hatten ihn seit

The Urban Context

At present, nearly 50% of Delhi's 17 million inhabitants live in slums and resettlement colonies. The residents of these areas provide essential services to the city through their labor, but are themselves grossly under-served and live in squalid conditions with very poor drainage, sanitation, water supply, and electricity. Such populations are perceived as unruly, disruptive, illegal, encroachers, trespassers, polluters, and social contaminants, and valued only as a statistic/ variable within different larger discourses such as "public safety and security," "heritage," "development," "urban planning/design," "progress." Underprivileged communities come to public and media notice only when votes are needed during local and national elections, or during urban crises—clashes with civic authorities and law enforcement (riots, protests, rallies, demolitions, strikes, criminal and sexual violence, evictions). However, the "developing" urban habitat (paradoxically both hostile and hospitable) of seductive modernity and burgeoning capital also significantly enables personal and collective expression, across class and circumstance, through its function as a social interface—one that fosters ingenuity, strong pragmatic relationships, and informal local networks that crucially allow a disenfranchised "resettled" demographic to not only survive conditions of deprivation, but in fact to thrive. The layered realities of these social constellations are largely absent from popular media narratives.

As practitioners of socially engaged art, we visualize and render projects that invite a range of participants from Delhi's under-served colonies to individually and collectively narrate their personal experiences of the changing urban milieu through a variety of media and art forms. We have come to understand through our practice that socially engaged art, especially when based on dialogic principles, cannot be evaluated, substantiated, or validated through the empirical parameters of concrete "outcomes," "benefits," and "products" for the community. Our objective in each context is to collaboratively shape new art forms within given local nodes and imperatives, as well as to catalyze/release/ uncover the aesthetic logic inherent in the urban existential template, its diverse cartographies, ecologies, and cultures. Given the complex history of slums and resettlement colonies, their systematic embedment and reinscription within the authoritarian and highly politicized blueprint of urban development, the terms "city," "locality," and "community" acquire a special resonance as core variables in creative practices based on the experiential truths of urban life.

längerer Zeit als gemeinsames Erholungsgebiet aufgegeben. Stattdessen wurde er von der lokalen Bevölkerung, darunter auch den Markthändlern, benutzt, um sich bequem Hausmüll und anderer Abfälle zu entledigen. Obwohl es sich um die einzige Freifläche in Block J handelte, wurde sie dem Verfall überlassen, und die MCD glänzte durch Abwesenheit. Trotz der Verschmutzung diente der Ort immer noch als Abkürzung zur Hauptstrasse, und Kinder nutzten ihn als Spielplatz.

Das Projekt *The Park*, das von der Foundation for Indian Contemporary Art gefördert und in Zusammenarbeit mit der Ankur Society for Alternatives in Education durchgeführt wurde, zielte von Anfang an darauf ab, die Anwohner zu einem dauerhaften Engagement einzuladen.

Als wir begannen, erste Schritte zur Reinigung des Parks zu unternehmen, stiessen wir auf Klagen unterschiedlicher Akteure, die Ansprüche auf den Park erhoben. Die MCD, Ortsansässige, die den Park für ihre eigenen spezifischen Zwecke nutzten, und misstrauische Anwohner begannen, unsere Absichten infrage zu stellen. Aus der Sicht jener, die uns skeptisch und gelegentlich mit offener Aggression beobachteten – überwiegend Mitglieder lokaler Jugendgruppen, die den Park gewöhnlich als Treffpunkt nutzten –, erschien die Logik hinter unserer Reinigungsaktion und unserer Forderung, den Park sauber zu halten, sinnlos. Es kam täglich zu Störungen – unterschiedlichen unverhohlenen und geschickten Blockaden, Behinderungen und Widerständen. Nachdem in der Gegend zunehmend das Gerücht „Qabza kar rahe hain" („sie eignen sich den Park an/übernehmen ihn") kursierte, wiederholten wir jeden Tag unablässig unsere Argumente.

Wir brachten einige *charpais*, transportable Sitz- und Liegemöbel, in den Park, postierten uns darauf und appellierten an alle, die den Ort betraten, ihn nicht zu verschmutzen. Durch diese spürbare Präsenz konnten wir eine intensive Beziehung mit den Anwohnern aufbauen. Wir sprachen auch mit Gärtnern, die in Dakshinpuri leben. Sie schlugen vor, dass wir uns bei der MCD in Green Park für eine Verpachtung bewerben sollten, wenn wir den Park tatsächlich neu gestalten wollten. Durch andere Leute erfuhren wir auch von dem *Bhagidari* (Kooperations)-Programm, das es NGOs und privaten Organisationen erlaubt, städtischen Besitz wie Park- und Gemeinschaftsanlagen zu verwalten und zu unterhalten.

Es ist eigentlich unmöglich, unsere Interaktion mit der MCD treffend zu beschreiben; diese begann im Oktober 2008 mit dem Ziel, einen offiziellen Pachtvertrag zu erhalten, der es dem Ankur Bal Club ermöglichen sollte, im Park von Dakshinpuri ein öffentliches Kunstprojekt durchzuführen. Als wir den Vertrag endlich erhielten, waren wir zu erschöpft, um uns über dieses Wunder zu freuen. Wir konnten uns nur noch an das monatelange Rennen von einem Schreibtisch zum nächsten erinnern, an die dringenden Bitten um Termine und Unterschriften. Erfüllt von der Sorge um das Schicksal unserer Akte, die zwischen Tausenden anderer Akten im Labyrinth der kommunalen Verwaltung willkürlich hervorgeholt wurde oder wieder in Vergessenheit geriet, vergassen wir, wer wir waren. Wir wurden zu einem weiteren bedeutungslosen, irrelevanten, unsichtbaren Rädchen im Getriebe unserer lokalen Regierung – einer höhlenartigen, scheinbar unbeweglichen Mühle, die jedoch langsam und übertrieben gründlich mahlt.

Site History and Interventions

Property of the Municipal Corporation of Delhi (MCD), the park is situated in Block J of Dakshinpuri. For quite a while residents had abandoned it as a common recreational area. Instead it was used by locals, including shopkeepers from the market, as a convenient place to dump household and other garbage. Although it was the only open space in Block J, it was allowed to decay, and the MCD was simply absent. Though filthy, the site was still frequented as a shortcut to the main road, and children used it as a playground.

From the inception of *The Park* project, supported by Foundation for Indian Contemporary Art and in collaboration with Ankur Society for Alternatives in Education, our intention was to invite continuous engagement from the neighborhood.

As soon as we began to take steps toward cleaning up the park, we encountered various claimants regarding the space. The MCD, locals who used the park for their own specific purposes, and suspicious residents all began to question our intent. The logic behind our cleaning up and insistence on the park being kept clean did not seem to make sense to those who observed us with skepticism and, occasionally, outright aggression—mostly from groups of local youths accustomed to using the park for their own socializing. Daily interruptions began to manifest—various kinds of overt and subtle blockings, obstacles, and resistance. It was a struggle to repeat our arguments daily, once the rumor "Qabza kar rahe hain" ("They are appropriating/taking over") began to circulate with increased momentum in the neighborhood.

We brought a couple of *charpais* (rope cots) into the park and posted ourselves on these, appealing to everyone who came in not to litter the space. Making our presence felt in this direct manner enabled a continuous interaction with the neighborhood. We also spoke to local gardeners who live in Dakshinpuri. They suggested that if we really wished to do any actual reshaping of the park, we would have to apply for a lease from the Municipal Corporation of Delhi (MCD) office in Green Park. We also came to know, through other people, about the government's *Bhagidari* (collaboration) program that permits NGOs and private organizations to manage and maintain municipal assets such as parks, community halls, etc.

It is not really possible to adequately describe our interaction with the MCD, beginning in October 2008, during the process of acquiring an official lease that would enable Ankur Bal Club to intervene in the park in Dakshinpuri as part of a public art project. By the time we got the lease,

Nachdem wir in einem mühsamen Verfahren von der MCD die Genehmigung erhalten hatten, organisierten wir eine Reihe von Workshops mit verschiedenen Anwohnergruppen, um einen echten Dialog zu ermöglichen und die gemeinsamen Ziele und Vorstellungen der Bewohner von Block J herauszufinden.

Der Park ist ein gemeinsam genutzter Raum innerhalb des Stadtteils. Um zu untersuchen, was ein gemeinsam genutzter Raum bedeutet und welche Rolle er im Alltag der Anwohner spielt, beschlossen wir, in einem ersten Schritt zu dokumentieren, wie die Ortsansässigen das Konzept des kollektiven / gemeinsam genutzten Raumes verstehen. Um aus dem Park einen Raum des offenen Dialogs und für experimentelle Kulturproduktion zu machen und um den Wert des Parks für seine Anwohner besser einschätzen zu können, wählten wir für unsere Interventionen das Verfahren einer kollektiven Entscheidungsfindung. *Saanjhi jagah* – der gemeinsam genutzte Raum – soll ein Ort sein, wo die Verbreitung von gemeinschaftlichen Bräuchen unterstützt wird, Kommunikationskanäle geschaffen werden sowie die Möglichkeit geboten wird, Forderungen zu formulieren und Beziehungen zu knüpfen und zu vertiefen. Die Anwohner schienen Vergnügen daran zu finden, Geschichten aus der Gegenwart und der Vergangenheit zum gemeinsam genutzten Raum zu erzählen und führten aus, was sie darunter verstanden. Oft waren sie leidenschaftlich und besitzergreifend, was den gemeinsam genutzten Raum und die darin befindlichen Objekte betraf.

Zahlreiche Anwohner bestätigten und beklagten die Art und Weise, wie sich der gemeinsame öffentliche Raum im Stadtteil gewandelt hatte. Diese Veränderungen deuteten auch auf erheblich veränderte Verhaltensmuster hin. Es war nicht leicht, ein Vertrauensverhältnis aufzubauen, das eine solche Offenheit förderte. Unsere ersten Interventionen im Park hatten Reaktionen ausgelöst, die von Feindseligkeiten über Apathie bis zu Aggressionen reichten. Ständig tauchten in unseren Gesprächen mit den Anwohnern neue Widerstände auf. Selbst jetzt gibt es noch Schwierigkeiten. Doch die Texte einiger Jugendlicher aus dem Quartier zeigten freimütige, aufschlussreiche Meinungen. Die folgenden Auszüge veranschaulichen, wie die Grenzen zwischen öffentlichem und privatem Raum, ebenso wie die Aktivitäten und Formen des Widerstands in öffentlichen und häuslichen Bereichen verwischt wurden:

„Als Amma schliesslich erkannte, dass wir ihre Anwesenheit ignorierten, versuchte sie um Mitternacht mithilfe ihres Sohnes den Baum zu fällen. Sie begann zu weinen und zu schreien, während es ihrem Sohn gelang, einen der Äste abzusägen. Sie rief nach allen Anwohnern in der Nachbarschaft, um den Baum vor der Hand ihres Sohnes zu retten; sie tat so, als könne sie diesen brutalen Akt nicht ertragen, obwohl sie selbst hinter seiner Aktion steckte. Die Nachbarn riefen die Polizei. Ihr Sohn wurde auf die Polizeistation mitgenommen, und die MCD belegte ihn mit einer Strafe von 4'000 Rupien. Das war eine wirklich übertriebene Summe für eine arme Frau."
- Tina

„Eines Tages weckte die unbebaute Fläche an unserer Strasse unsere Aufmerksamkeit. Wir hatten gehört, dass dort ein Park entstehen sollte. Einige Meter weiter wurde ein Haus gebaut.

we were too exhausted to appreciate the miracle. All we could remember were months of rushing from one desk to another, pleading for appointments and signatures. Consumed with anxiety over the fate of our file among the thousands of others being arbitrarily resuscitated and obfuscated in the labyrinth of the municipality office, we forgot who we were. We became just another insignificant, irrelevant, invisible cog in our local government machinery—a cavernous, apparently unmoving mill that, however, does indeed grind slowly and exceedingly finely.

After laboriously extracting permission from the MCD, we organized a series of workshops with various neighborhood groups in order to facilitate regular dialogue and explore the collective aspirations and imaginings of Block J residents.

The park is a shared space in the locality. To explore the meaning of a shared space and how it integrates with the daily life of the local neighborhood, we decided, as a first step, to document the understandings of local residents with regard to the concept of collective/shared space. To make the park a space for exploratory dialogue and experimental creation, and to assess how much the residents inherently value the space, we chose the process of collective decision making within the framework of our interventions. *Saanjhi jagah* (shared space) is seen as vehicle of community practices and systems of transaction, claims, and relationships. The residents seemed to enjoy narrating stories linked to their understanding of shared space, from the present as well as the past. Residents were often passionate and possessive about shared space and the objects located therein.

Many residents testified to and lamented the change in the modes of usage of common public areas in the locality. These changes also indicated significantly transformed patterns of sociality. It was not easy to reach this point of trust that fostered such a flow of narration. Our early interventions in the park had aroused reactions ranging from hostile to apathetic to aggressive. Obstacle after obstacle came up when we began our dialogues with the residents. It is difficult even now. However, the pens of some local youngsters freely offered insightful perspectives. The excerpts below illustrate the blurring of private/public spatial boundaries, as well as the activity and modes of resistance in both public and domestic spheres:

"Eventually, when Amma could see that we were ignoring her presence, she attempted to cut the tree down at midnight with the help of her son. She started weeping and shouting while her son managed to cut one of the branches. She started

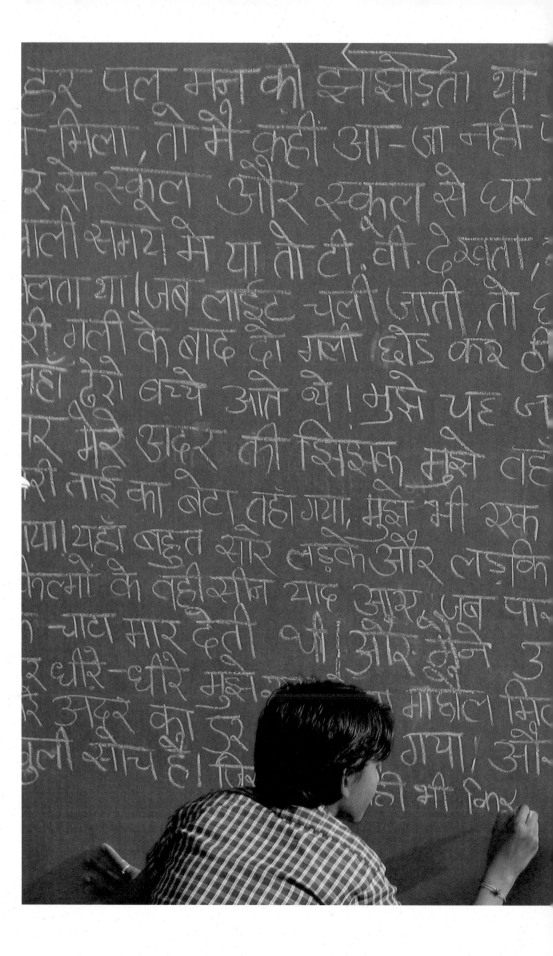

र, कही कोई साथी

।मेरा दायरा सिर्फ

ो सीमित था। मै अपने

र बहन-भाइयो के साथ

ो देहलीज पर जा बैठता

ामने एक समूह चलता था।

ारी तो पहले से ही थी।

का मौका न देती। पर जब

त मिली और मै वहा पहुँच

। ये नजारा देखकर मुझे

गुजरने पर भी लडकिया लडको

र बैठना शुरू कर दिया

ाघ मेरी इच्छाएँ और

न मेरे पास वो हौसला और

225

Wir holten einen Spaten und gruben auf der unbebauten Fläche einen Bereich aus, um daraus eine *akhada* zu machen, das Spielfeld, auf dem man *kabaddi* spielt. Und dann haben wir Sand von einem beladenen Lastwagen gestohlen, den ausgehobenen Raum damit gefüllt und ihn wirklich in eine *akhada* verwandelt."

– Uttam

„Sogar heute habe ich noch Lust darauf, dieses Spiel zu spielen, obwohl mein Alter und mein Zustand das nicht mehr zulassen. Wenn ich Zeit habe, sitze ich auf der *chabutra* an der Bushaltestelle der Linie 17, weil ich dort die Möglichkeit habe, mich an unser Spiel zu erinnern. Ich habe das Gefühl, dass ich den alten Fahrradreifen meiner Kindheit nachjage, wenn ich mir die Busse, Roller und Fahrräder ansehe und die Leute, die sie fahren. Sogar heute mag ich noch die Kreisbewegungen der Reifen. Wenn ich auf der *chabutra* an der Bushaltestelle von Linie 17 sitze, beobachte ich diese Reifen und verbringe auch Zeit mit meinen Freunden."

– Aniket

„Aus dem städtischen Wasserhahn in Talkatora Garden kam gelbliches Wasser, aber er wurde genutzt, weil er den Frauen die Möglichkeit bot, sich dort zu treffen. Die Frauen, die kamen, um Wasser zu holen, genossen einen Moment der Freiheit, liessen sich um den Hahn herum nieder und unterhielten sich, während sie auf das Wasser warteten. Manche sprachen über ihre Pflichten in der Küche und am Herd und über verschiedene Gerichte, andere machten ihrem Ärger über den Druck durch die Familie oder angeheiratete Verwandte Luft. Manchmal führte jemand neue Kleider vor; bei anderen Gelegenheiten kamen zwischen Kichern und Gelächter plötzlich die ernsten Tatsachen eines häuslichen Problems zur Sprache. Wir jungen Mädchen, die mit solchen Themen nichts anfangen konnten, begannen zu spielen, während wir auf das Wasser warteten."

– Aarti

Mit der grundlegenden Kritik daran, dass der Park als Müllkippe benutzt wurde, entstand ein wertvoller Dialog - manchmal konfliktreich und feindselig, manchmal in Übereinstimmung. Die Menschen beschrieben ihren „Traum"-Park, ein Bild, das in ihrem hektischen und schwierigen Alltag nur selten oder nie zum Ausdruck gebracht wurde. Sie waren sich einig, dass der Park als gemeinsam genutzter öffentlicher Raum für die Community von entscheidender Bedeutung war - um Kontakte zu knüpfen, für Spiele und Freizeitaktivitäten, als ein angenehmer Ort, um am Ende eines Arbeitstages zu entspannen, als psychologische Stütze (eine Quelle frischer Luft in einer sehr dicht bebauten Umgebung); in einem extrem verdichteten, von Umweltverschmutzung geprägten, aggressiven Umfeld verkörperte der Park ein umfassenderes abstraktes Ideal von zutiefst ersehnter Ruhe, Sicherheit, Gesundheit, Ausgeglichenheit und Wohlbefinden.

Wir besprachen alters- und genderspezifische Meinungsunterschiede. Die meisten Frauen in Dakshinpuri brachten das Thema der Privatsphäre auf und formulierten sehr nachdrücklich den Wunsch, einen Raum zu haben, der offen und doch abgesondert ist und für Männer unzugänglich bleibt; einen sicheren, durch Hecken oder Büsche abgetrennten Be-

calling everybody in the neighborhood to save the tree from the hand of her son; she acted as if she could not tolerate this brutality, whereas she herself was behind his action. The neighbors called the police. Her son was taken to the police station and the MCD fined him 4,000 rupees. This was a really exorbitant sum for a poor woman."

—Tina

"One day the open space by our lane drew our attention. We had heard that a park would be coming up there. A few yards away, a house was under construction. We brought a spade and dug up a section in the open space to turn it into a *akhada*, the arena where *kabaddi* is played. And then, stealing sand from a loaded truck, we filled in the dug-up space and really turned it into an *akhada*."

—Uttam

"Even today, I feel like playing that game, though my age and circumstances do not allow me to do so. When I have time, I sit on the *chabutra* by the bus stop of lane 17 because there I get the opportunity to recollect that game of ours. I feel I am chasing the old cycle tires of my childhood when I look at the buses, scooters, or cycles and the people riding them. Even today, I am fond of the circular movements of tires. Sitting on the *chabutra* by the bus stop of lane 17, I watch these tires as well as spend time with my friends."

—Aniket

"The municipal tap in Talkatora Garden gave yellowish water, but it was used because it allowed women to socialize there. Women who came to get water enjoyed the moment of freedom, to sit around the tap and talk while waiting for the water to come. Some talked about their kitchens and cooking duties and kinds of food, others vented anger at family pressures or in-laws. Sometimes someone would be showing off new clothes; at other times, amid giggling and laughter, the serious fact of a domestic problem would suddenly come up. We young girls, not able to empathize with such issues, would start playing while waiting for the water."

—Aarti

Along with the fundamental criticism of the park being used as a garbage dump, there slowly emerged a valuable exchange of views, at times conflicted and hostile, at times congruent. People described their "dream" park, an image rarely or never articulated within their hectic and difficult daily lives. They agreed that the park as shared public space was vital to the community—for socializing; for games and leisure activities; as a convenient place to relax after the day's work; as a psychological support (source of fresh air in

reich, ergänzt durch einen weiteren für Kinder. Sie wollten, dass ein Teil des Bereichs unter dem grossen Banyan-Baum des Parks Frauen vorbehalten sein sollte.

Die Jugendlichen von Dakshinpuri wollten die konventionelle Parknutzung erweitern, um ihnen mehr Mobilität und Autonomie zu gewähren; sie stellten sich den Park als einen Raum vor, an dem sie jenseits der Einschränkungen durch ihre Familien und unbeobachtet von wachsamen Erwachsenen interagieren können, und sahen ihn als Ort für kreative Aufführungen, Musik, Versammlungen und ungezwungene Spiele. Sie schlugen vor, ein Schwarzes Brett anzubringen, um die Leute über lokale Veranstaltungen und Neuigkeiten im Quartier zu informieren, und die Mauern des Parks zu nutzen, um darauf die lokale Geschichte in bunt gemalten Erzählungen festzuhalten.

Die erwachsenen männlichen Anwohner reagierten bei jedem Fortschritt negativ auf unsere Anwesenheit. Sie versuchten, unter unserer Gruppe Panik zu verbreiten, und kritisierten die Leute heftig wegen der Teilnahme an unseren Versammlungen. Die älteren Männer, die von allen mit „Onkel" angesprochen werden, verhielten sich jedoch ziemlich kooperativ. Die meisten waren im Ruhestand oder hatten einen kleinen Laden; man sah regelmässig, wie sie unter den kleinen Bäumen der Siedlung Siesta machten oder Karten spielten. Ihnen war bewusst, dass eine Verschmutzung des Parks verhindert werden sollte, und abends halfen sie dem Ankur Bal Club, die Pflanzen zu giessen und die Anwohner zu ermahnen, keine Abfälle dort abzuladen. Ihr grösster Wunsch war, einen sauberen, vor Regen und Sonne geschützten Ort zu haben, um dort möglichst viel Zeit miteinander zu verbringen.

In Städten werden Mauern meistens als Barrieren betrachtet, die Räume voneinander abgrenzen und als Mittel der Exklusion/Inklusion fungieren. Mauern um urbane öffentliche Räume wie Parks gehören allen und niemandem. Als gebaute Struktur bieten sie eine Fläche, die für kollektive Ausdrucksformen – Graffiti, Neuigkeiten, Proteste, ideologische Statements und so weiter – genutzt werden kann. Wir haben einen Parkmauer-Blog als detailreiches Tagebuch des Lebens in der Nachbarschaft geschaffen, als Zeuge für die Lebensmuster im Quartier und als Archiv für seine Wünsche. Viele Darstellungen bezeugen, dass sich die Nutzung öffentlicher Flächen im Stadtteil umfassend verändert hat. Diese Geschichten wurden auf einer Website zusammengestellt, die zu einer vertieften und breiteren Auseinandersetzung mit solchen Fragen einlädt.[1]

Die Neugestaltung des Dakshinpuri-Parks entstand durch eine gemeinsame Vision sowie durch die Entwicklung und Herstellung von ortsspezifischen und dreidimensionalen Arbeiten, die den Raum neu erfahrbar machten. Wir gingen dabei immer von den Ansprüchen an den Raum jeder einzelnen Gruppe aus, mit der wir in Dialog getreten waren. Im neu gestalteten Park widerspiegelte jedes Element die lokale Geschichte oder die Wünsche der Gemeinschaft, aufbauend auf einer Idee des Teilens und dem Einbezug der individuellen Ansprüche der Bewohner. So funktionierte der Park als solcher gleichzeitig als Ort und Installation, Subjekt und Objekt, Prozess und Produkt, Frage und Antwort.

Im Rahmen ihres Masterstudiengangs in Medienkunst (Coventry School of Art and Design, Coventry University GB, 2001–2005), entwickelte

a very densely built environment); and within an extremely pressured, polluted, and aggressive urban ethos, the park embodied the residents' larger abstract ideal of keenly-desired serenity, safety, health, equilibrium, and well-being.

We negotiated age and gender-related differences of opinion. Most Dakshinpuri women raised the issue of privacy and the very strong wish to have a space that was open and yet sequestered, into which men could not intrude; a safe area segregated by hedges or bushes and with an accessible adjacent area designated for children. They wanted part of the area under the park's large banyan tree to be designated for women only.

Dakshinpuri's youth segment wanted conventional park usage to be altered to provide greater mobility and autonomy; they visualized the park as a space where they could interact away from familial restrictions and vigilant adults; and as a space for creative performances, music, meetings, and informal games. They suggested putting up a notice board to inform people of local events and neighborhood news, and using the park's walls to document local history via colorful painted narratives.

The local adult men reacted negatively to our presence every step of the way in this project. They tried to spread panic among the people who supported us, castigating them for coming to our meetings. However, the elderly men, generically addressed as "Uncle," were quite cooperative. Most were either retired or running small shops; they could be regularly seen taking siestas and playing cards under small trees in the colony. They were more conscious of the need to prevent littering, and in the evenings joined the Ankur Bal Club in watering the ground and reminding locals to not throw garbage there. Their main desire was to have a clean space protected from rain and sun, where they could spend the maximum time with each other.

Walls in cities are primarily seen as barriers, delineating and legitimizing spaces, and functioning as a means of exclusion / inclusion. Walls around urban public spaces such as parks belong to everybody and to nobody. As a built structure they offer themselves as a common canvas for collective self-expression, in the form of graffiti, news, protest, ideology, etc. We created a park wall blog as a detailed log of neighborhood life, a testament of patterns of sociality and an archive of community aspirations. Many accounts bore witness to overall changes in usage of the locality's public areas. These narratives are compiled on a website that invites deeper and wider engagement with the issues.[1]

The re-landscaping of the Dakshinpuri park through the collaborative envisioning and

227

181

Sreejata Roy eine künstlerische Praxis, die sich dezidiert über Untersuchungen zu soziokulturellen Fragen artikuliert. Zentral für ihr Vorgehen sind dabei Oral History, Subjektivität, Volkskunde und Alltagserzählungen. Seit einigen Jahren arbeitet Roy vermehrt mit jungen Menschen, seit 2007 realisiert sie in einkommensschwachen Siedlungen Neu-Delhis verschiedene Kunstprojekte, die unterschiedliche Vorstellungen vom öffentlichen Raum ausnutzen. Als Stipendiatin für „Kunst im öffentlichen Raum" von der Foundation for Indian Contemporary Art (FICA) hat sie die Neugestaltung eines Parks in Neu-Delhi initiiert. Für ihr innovatives Vorgehen bei *The Park* wurde Roy 2015 für den International Public Art Award nominiert. Zur Zeit arbeitet sie an einem von der Khoj International Artists' Association New Delhi unterstützten Projekt in Khirkee, das sich mit dem Frauenbild im öffentlichen Raum befasst.

Anmerkungen:

1   http:// www.parkdpuri.blogspot.com (zuletzt aufgerufen am 15. September 2015).

creation of locality-specific, three-dimensional works designed to transform the experience of a space, was undertaken keeping in mind the repurposing of that space as desired by each group we had engaged in dialogue. Based on an ethic of sharing, and in accordance with residents' subjectivities and knowledge bases, each object in the "reformed" park was conceptualized to embody local traces and community imaginings. Thus, the park itself functioned as simultaneous site and installation, subject and object, process and product, question and answer.

During her MPhil studies in media art at the Coventry School of Art and Design, Coventry University, between 2001 and 2005, Sreejata Roy evolved a culturally embedded form of personal practice within her larger investigation of socio-cultural issues via oral history, ethnography, the narration of daily life, and the formation of subjectivity. For the past several years Roy's practice has involved working with young people; since 2007 this has been through a variety of art practices connecting the ideas of public spaces in the low-income colonies in New Delhi.

She was awarded a Public Art grant from FICA, and completed reshaping a community park in one of these colonies. *The Park* project from India has been selected for final jury in International Public Art Award 2015. She is currently working on a project hosted and funded by Khoj International Artists' Association, New Delhi, in the urban village Khirkee, which explores the idea of women in public space.

Notes:

1   http://www.parkdpuri.blogspot.com (last accessed October, 2015).

184–185　Mitsuru Senda, *Fortress of Winds*, Toriidaira Yamabiko Park, Okaya, Nagano Prefecture, 1982

Ruinen und Reform. Spielplätze in Japan nach dem Zweiten Weltkrieg

Vincent Romagny

Renewal and Ruins. Post-World War II Playgrounds in Japan

Wie in anderen Ländern, die die Zerstörungen des Zweiten Weltkriegs erlitten hatten, wurden in Japan in den Jahren des starken Wirtschaftswachstums nach dem Krieg zahlreiche Spielplätze errichtet. Die treibende Kraft hinter dieser Erneuerung war der Wunsch, Zerstörtes wieder aufzubauen und mögliche weitere Szenarien dieser Art in Zukunft zu verhindern. Tatsächlich waren bereits nach einer früheren Katastrophe – dem schrecklichen Erdbeben von Kanto 1923 – Spielplätze angelegt worden. Nach diesem Beben, bei dem die Ballungsräume von Tokyo und Yokohama zerstört worden waren, setzten japanische Städtebauer die Schaffung öffentlicher Plätze durch, auf denen sich die Bevölkerung im Falle einer Naturkatastrophe versammeln konnte. Nach und nach wurden in allen Städten solche Plätze angelegt.[1] Da Kindergärten (*yochien*) und Kindertagesstätten (*hoikuen*) ebenfalls über Spieleinrichtungen verfügen, gibt es sogar noch mehr solcher Plätze. Im Anschluss an das grosse Beben vor der Pazifikküste der Region Tōhoku im Jahr 2011 (der durch dieses Beben ausgelöste Tsunami führte zum Unfall im Atomkraftwerk von Fukushima) wurde die Ausstattung dieser öffentlichen Räume im Hinblick auf das Überleben der Bevölkerung verändert (so gibt es beispielsweise Bänke, die sich in Feuerschalen umfunktionieren lassen, ausfaltbare Toiletten usw.).

Die zweite japanische Besonderheit ist die Offenheit gegenüber ausländischen Einflüssen und der Import westlicher Modelle. Die städtischen Grünämter bestückten die Spielplätze in Absprache mit den Anwohnern mit Geräten, die amerikanischen Standardgeräten nachempfunden waren. Die sogenannten „4S" – *sandbox* (Sandkasten), *see-saw* (Wippe), *slide* (Rutsche) und *swing* (Schaukel) – wie sie die Playground Association of America propagierte, verbreiteten sich ab Beginn des 20. Jahrhunderts in Japan. Die dürftige Qualität dieser hauptsächlich nach dem Krieg entstandenen Geräte – in Kyoto sind die Bahnen der Rutschen aus Beton – ist auf die wirtschaftlich schwierige Lage in der Wiederaufbauzeit zurückzuführen.[2] Da der Unterhalt dieser zahlreichen Parks (allein in Kyoto gibt es etwa 900 davon) ungenügend ist, sind sie oft in einem erbärmlichen Zustand (Abb. 193–194).

Auch wenn diese öffentlichen Parks nicht primär eine erzieherische Funktion haben, wurde diese doch vor allem von Kuro Kaneko (1902–1982) erkannt und weiterentwickelt. Wie schon Reijo Oya[3] (1890–1934) vor ihm betonte er den Zusammenhang zwischen einer bestimmten japanischen Park- und Gartenkultur und verbreitete das Wissen um die soziale und pädagogische Rolle der Parks in der modernen Stadt, die aus seiner Sicht vor allem durch die *play leaders* (*jidoshidoin*) zum Tragen kommen muss. Kaneko selbst begann seine Karriere, indem er in Parks ein *kamishibai*[4] betrieb (ein kleines Papiertheater, das hinten auf einem Fahrrad installiert wird und eine erzieherische Funktion hat), bevor er Beamter in der Parkverwaltung wurde. Als Universitätsprofessor und danach als Gartenamtdirektor von Yokohama und Direktor des Japanese Institute of Landscape Architects baute er sein Engagement auf der Beziehung zwischen Kind und Natur auf, ein Aspekt, der aus seiner Sicht in Japan bedauerlicherweise wenig präsent war.[5] Dabei wollte er keineswegs ein strenges pädagogisches Prinzip einführen, sondern er kämpfte, insbesondere in der International Federation of Landscape Architects (IFLA), für die Erneuerung städtischer Parks, *zoen*, sowie öffentlicher

Postwar Japan saw the development of playgrounds in parallel with its years of fast economic growth, as did other countries that had suffered the ravages of World War II. The driving force behind this renewal was the concern both for regeneration after the destruction and for the prevention of potential future scenarios. Indeed, playgrounds had also developed in the wake of a previous disaster, the Great Kanto Earthquake of 1923. Following this quake, which devastated the Tokyo-Yokohama urban area, Japanese town planners enforced the creation of public areas where people could gather if natural disasters struck. Gradually every city had its own playground.[1] As preschools / kindergartens (*yochien*) and nursery schools (*hoikuen*) routinely feature play facilities, this makes for even more such grounds. Following the recent earthquake in 2011 off the Pacific coast of the Tohoku region (where the tsunami led to the nuclear accident at the Fukushima power plant), the fittings of these public spaces (items such as benches that can be converted into braziers and fold-out portable toilets) have been tailored to human survival.

The second point specific to Japan is its permeability to foreign influence and the importing of Western models. The public parks' municipal departments, in consultation with local residents, selected the playground equipment in these places from vendor catalogues whose play equipment was originally styled on American models. In fact, playgrounds in their standard "4S format" (*sandbox*, *see-saw*, *slide*, and *swing*) arrived in Japan in the early 20th century, as a result of the efforts of the Playground Association of America which theorized about—and fixed—form and function. Economic difficulties during the reconstruction explain the mediocre quality of the playgrounds produced in the immediate postwar period (toboggan runs in Kyoto are made of concrete).[2] These numerous parks (almost 900 in Kyoto, for example) now appear quite outdated given their irregular upkeep (ill. 193–194).

While an educational function may not be the primary purpose of public parks, their educational dimension has been recognized and developed, particularly by Kuro Kaneko (1902–1982). Like Reijo Oya[3] (1890–1934) before him, Kaneko established a link between a certain Japanese park and garden culture and its social and instructive implications for the modern city, which he felt were conveyed in particular through the presence of play leaders (*jidoshidoin*). In fact it was in this capacity that he began his own career in parks, working a *kamishibai*[4] (a small paper theater set on the back of a bicycle as an instructive and civic billboard) before becoming a park administration official, university professor just after the war, and head of Yokohama Park Department

Gärten, die häufig nur aus rein technischer Sicht betrachtet wurden, statt im Zusammenhang mit Natur oder Landschaft. Ihm ging es vor allem darum, die positiven Eigenschaften der Gärten mit einer ästhetischen Aufgabe (der *teien*, in der japanischen Tradition der Zeremonial- oder Meditationsgärten), auf Natur und Landschaft auszudehnen oder umgekehrt die *teien* „als weiter gefasste Gesellschaftsräume"[6] zu öffnen. So trug er in den 1960er Jahren, nachdem der Wiederaufbau nach dem Krieg abgeschlossen und das Land wirtschaftlich gestärkt war, zur Neuorganisation der Spielplätze bei.

Auf den städtischen Grünflächen (wenn auch nicht in den für die Evakuierung der Bevölkerung vorgesehenen Parks, wo bis heute nur die gleichen trostlosen Geräte stehen) oder in Schulhöfen befinden sich einige innovative Einrichtungen. So zeugen etwa die Spielinstallationen, die Yoshiyasu Ishii (geb. 1938) für NIDO Industrial Design Office errichtet hat – *Riesenrutsche, Wald aus Stäben* (*Kinoboribayashi*) (1968, Kindergarten in Keisho, Tokyo) – von einem wirklichen Bemühen, die Natur des kindlichen Spielens zu begreifen, da der Gestalter hier von der natürlichen Faszination des Kindes für Formen und Farben ausgeht (Abb. 192).

Die Abenteuerspielplätze[7] waren bei der Wiederbelebung der Spielplätze im Japan der 1960er Jahre ein wichtiges Vorbild. Die Idee wurde ebenfalls aus dem Ausland importiert, jedoch wurde sie nicht zwangsläufig verändert, der Grundge-danke blieb über die Jahre erhalten. 1979 errichtete Kenichi Omura (1938–2014)[8] im Hanegi Park in der Agglomeration von Tokyo ein Gelände für gemeinsames Bauen oder andere Aktivitäten (Lagerfeuer, improvisierte Schwimmbecken, Baumhütten usw.) (Abb. 188–189). Mittlerweile gibt es in Japan mehr als 400 derartige Abenteuerspielplätze, die sporadisch oder ganzjährig geöffnet sind.

Zwei Persönlichkeiten nahmen in den 1960er Jahren auf dem Gebiet des Spielplatzplanung eine herausragende Rolle ein: Isamu Noguchi (1904–1988) und Mitsuru Senda (geb. 1941).

Der 1965 eingeweihte Park Kodomo no Kuni (Welt der Kinder) in Yokohama wurde auf dem Gelände einer ehemaligen Waffenfabrik errichtet. Eine Gruppe von Architekten – Kisho Kurokawa, Kiyonori Kikutake, Masato Otaka sowie Sachio Otani, die der Bewegung des Metabolismus angehörten – arbeiteten dort unter der Regie von Takashi Asada mit Isamu Noguchi zusammen. Während der Spielplatz von Noguchi stammt, handelt es sich bei Kodomo no Kuni um einen Treffpunkt herausragender Akteure, die von architektonischen und künstlerischen Vorstellungen motiviert waren (Abb. 187). Statt für reine Funktionalität interessierten sie sich für die Frage, wie Formen auf das Verhalten ihrer Benutzer wirkten und bevorzugten in diesem Zusammenhang eine an der Biologie statt an Maschinen und Technik orientierte Metaphorik, sowohl auf individueller (Noguchi) als auch auf kollektiver Ebene (die Metabolisten definierten „die menschliche Gesellschaft als lebendigen Prozess"[9]). So schuf Noguchi hier 1966 seinen ersten Spielplatz, nachdem er bereits mehrere Jahrzehnte lang an Spielplatzprojekten gearbeitet hatte, die nie realisiert worden waren: *Play Mountain* (1933), *Contoured Playground* (1941), ein Projekt für den Sitz der UNO (1952) und schliesslich der Adele Levy Memorial Playground im New Yorker Riverside Park in Zusammenarbeit mit Louis I. Kahn (1966) (s. S. 154). Im

and of the Japanese Institute of Landscape Architects.[5] Kaneko's underlying vision was children's relationship to nature, and he deplored the fact that Japan afforded so little opportunity for developing this. Far from establishing a strict educational system, he pushed for the renewal of urban parks, *zoen*, and public parks, mainly through the International Federation of Landscapes Architects (IFLA), motivated mainly by purely technical considerations rather than issues relating to nature or landscape. For him it was a matter of extending to public parks the qualities of an essentially aesthetic garden (the *teien* according to the Japanese tradition of ceremonial gardens or those intended for contemplative viewing), or conversely of opening up the *teien* to a "sociological milieu and wider area."[6] In this way he contributed to the reorganization of playgrounds in the 1960s, following the completion of postwar rebuilding programs and the nation's economic recovery.

A number of innovative features are therefore found in urban green parkland zones (but not in areas intended for human evacuation where facilities remain outdated) or in schoolyards. For example, the play apparatus created at the NIDO Industrial Design Office by Yoshiyasu Ishii (born 1938)—*Giant Slide, Tree-like Poles* (*Kinoboribayashi*) (Keisho kindergarten, Tokyo, 1968)—show a real interest in understanding children's play, as the designer works from a child's natural attraction to shapes and colors (ill. 192).

Adventure playgrounds[7] formed an important role model in initiatives to revitalize play areas in the 1960s. They were also imported to Japan, but did not necessarily undergo many alterations, carefully perpetuated in form and spirit. In 1979, Kenichi Omura (1938–2014)[8] fitted out a sloping area of Hanegi Park (adjacent to Tokyo) with a ground that has since been open to collaborative constructions and a host of quirky and exciting activities (bonfires, makeshift swimming pools, tree houses, etc.) in this urban context of the Tokyo Metropolitan area (ill. 188–189). There are now over 400 adventure playgrounds, open from once a month to all year round.

Two major figures deserve a mention for their central role and the scope of their work in the area of playgrounds from that period onward. They are Isamu Noguchi (1904–1988) and Mitsuru Senda (born 1941).

Opened in 1965, Kodomo no Kuni (Children's Land), a park in Yokohama, stands on the site of what used to be an armaments plant. In 1966 the project, coordinated by Takashi Asada, brought together architects from the Metabolism movement, Kisho Kurokawa, Kiyonori Kikutake, Masato Otaka, as well as Sachio Otani with Isamu Noguchi. While the playground itself is the work

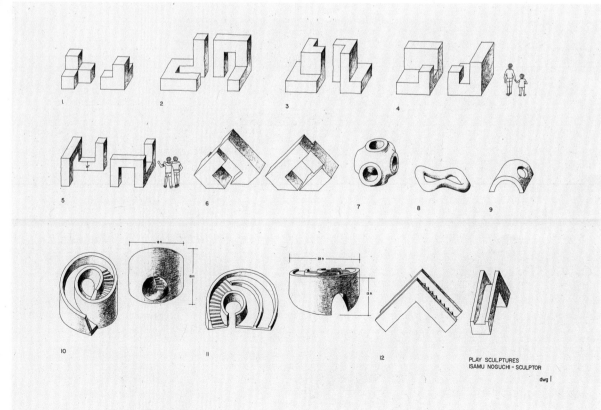

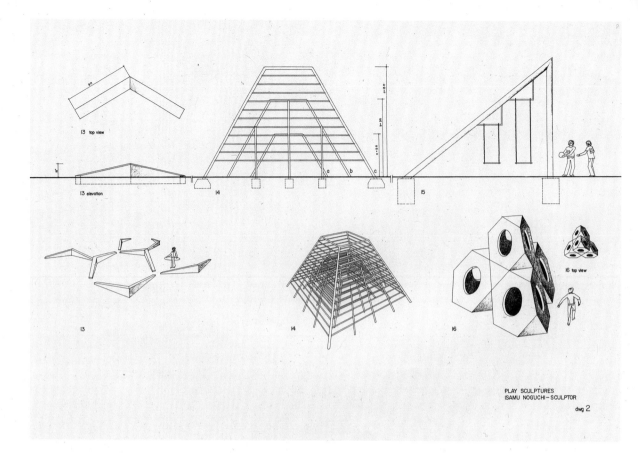

190–191 Isamu Noguchi, Entwürfe für Spielgeräte / Architectural drawings for play equipment, c. 1965

238

Einklang mit seiner Auffassung, derzufolge „alles Skulptur ist, ob es sich dabei um einen Garten, ein Theater oder einen Spielplatz handelt", und seiner Sorge, dass die Kunst „nicht nur auf einer visuellen Ebene existiert"[10], sind die Formen, die er dem Kinderspiel verleiht, nicht einfach nur auf dem Boden platzierte Objekte, sondern tauchen aus diesem auf: Der Park wird Skulptur, und die Skulptur ruft Wirkungen hervor (deren Verständnis ihre Form bestimmt hat). Im selben Jahr wurde im Odori Park in Sapporo sein *Slide Mantra* installiert. Diese spielerische Skulptur verbindet in einer abgerundeten Form Rutsche und Stufen. Mit den Worten des Künstlers: „Der Kinderpo vollendet die Skulptur." Ebenfalls in Sapporo wurde 2005 der Moerenuma Park eröffnet, mit dessen Bau 1989, ein Jahr nach dem Tod des amerikanisch-japanischen Künstlers und gemäss seinen Plänen, begonnen wurde. Während die zur Landschaft werdende Skulptur sich mit der Monumentalität verträgt, trifft dies beim Spiel nur bedingt zu: 120 Spielelemente sind auf sieben „Wälder blühender Kirschbäume" verteilt. Ähnlich wie die Spielgeräte, die er erstmals 1976 für Playscape im Piedmont Park Atlanta realisiert hatte (und von denen er einige 1939 für den Ala Moana Park von Honolulu entworfen hatte), bestehen sie aus verschiedenen Modellen von Klettergerüsten, Skulpturen aus Kuben und Quadern in Form von ineinander verschachtelten L-Trägern (*Play Cubes*), *Octetra*, Schaukeln in Form eines Dreiecks, Sandkästen (*Play Maze*), Rutschen in breiten Zylindern mit wendelförmigem Aufgang, schwenkbaren Wippen sowie röhrenförmigen, gebogenen und in sich geschlossenen Spielskulpturen (*Play sculptures*) (Abb. 190–191).

Während Noguchi seinen Spielplatz in Kodomo no Kuni errichtete, plante der 1941 geborene Mitsuru Senda im Auftrag des Metabolisten Kiyonori Kikutake im selben Park die Errichtung von Landschulheimen.[11] 1968 eröffnete er sein eigenes Büro, das Environment Design Institute. Seither kann er zu Recht als der bedeutendste japanische Gestalter von Spielplätzen bezeichnet werden (s. S. 174). Dabei ging es ihm nicht darum, die herkömmlichen Formen von Spielgeräten neu zu interpretieren, sondern er hat vielmehr eine neue Methode definiert, mit der spannende Spielumgebungen mit viel Handlungs- und Interpretationsspielraum geschaffen werden: „Ich bin überzeugt, dass die Mehrdeutigkeit der Funktionen [...] es den Kindern erlaubt, frei neue Spiele zu erfinden."[12] Die Gestaltung seiner Spielplätze geht auch auf Erinnerungen an seine Kindheit zurück, wo er in jenen Tunnels spielte, die die japanische Bevölkerung in den Hügeln von Yokohama angelegt hatte, um sich gegen die Bombardierung durch die Amerikaner zu schützen. In seiner „Circular Play System Theory"[13], Sendas Hauptbeitrag zum Verständnis des kindlichen Spielens, formuliert er die Bedingungen, die seine Spielplätze erfüllen: kreisförmige Wege, vielfältige Aktivitäten, Elemente mit starker Symbolik (erhöhte Aussichtspunkte, Versteckmöglichkeiten usw.), Abkürzungen, Treffpunkte, und alle Strukturen sollen aus „porösem" Materialien hergestellt sein (zum Hindurchschauen oder -gehen).[14] Während er bei seinen ersten Entwürfen Metall verwendete, bevorzugte er später Holz, da dieses kaum Wärme leitet. Ausserdem überdachte er seine hölzernen Spielparcours, um sie besser vor dem feuchten Klima seines Landes zu schützen (Abb. 184–186).

Darüber hinaus entwarf Senda eine Reihe von Schulen und Kindergärten. Die Vitalität der Architektur dieser

of Noguchi, Kodomo no Kuni is the meeting point for major players fired by architectural and artistic conceptions with a common focus on the effect of forms on their users' behavior, the biological metaphor on the notion of pure functionality, and the metaphor of machines at both individual (Noguchi) and collective level (the Metabolists define "human society as a living process"[9]) (ill. 187). It was here that Isamu Noguchi created his first playground in 1966, after several decades of playground projects that had never materialized: *Play Mountain* in 1933, *Contoured Playground* in 1941, a project for the UN headquarters in 1952, and finally the Adele Levy Memorial Playground in 1966 at the Riverside Park in New York, in collaboration with Louis I. Kahn (see p. 154). In keeping with his vision that "everything is sculpture, whether it is a garden, a theater, or a playground," and his concern that art is "not only on a visual level,"[10] the forms given to children's play are not merely objects placed on the ground, but emerge at ground level: the park becomes sculpture and the sculpture has effects (their understanding having determined its form). The same year saw the installation of his *Slide Mantra* in Odori Park, Sapporo. This playful sculpture combines steps and a slide run in a rounded form. To quote the artist, "The completion of this sculpture will be when children polish it with their bottoms as they slide down." Also in Sapporo, the Moerenuma Park opened in 2005; work had begun in 1989, a year after the Japanese-American artist died, in accordance with designs he had completed in his lifetime. While sculpture extended to landscape is well matched in terms of monumentality, we should acknowledge that the same does not go for play facilities: 120 playground elements are set among seven "forests of cherry blossoms." Similar to the play apparatus he had seen produced for the first time in 1976 in the Playscape in the Piedmont Park, Atlanta (some of which was designed in 1939 for the Ala Moana Park in Honolulu), they include several models of jungle gyms, sculptures made from cubes and rectangular parallelepipeds forming interlinked "L-Beams" (*Play Cubes*), *Octetra*, swings triangular in shape, sandboxes (*Play Maze*), slides built around a large column containing the access ramp, swivel swings, and playful sculptures in the form of curved self-sealed tubes (*Play Sculpture*) (ill. 190–191).

While Noguchi was setting up his Kodomo no Kuni playground, Mitsuru Senda (born 1941), who was working for the agency of Metabolist architect Kiyonori Kikutake, oversaw the construction of buildings in the same park designed to accommodate students on field trips.[11] In 1968 he created his own agency, the Environment Design Institute. Thereafter he may be considered Japan's most important designer of Japanese

für Kinder bestimmten Einrichtungen verdeutlicht das Anliegen, neue Formen zum Experimentieren nicht mehr nur ausschliesslich auf Spielplätzen zur Verfügung zu stellen. In Japan weitet sich die Erkenntnis, dass auch nicht explizit fürs Spiel geschaffene Formen einen erzieherischen Effekt haben, auf andere Einrichtungen für Kinder aus. So wird der Wunsch Kuro Kanekos, den dieser in einem gemeinsam mit Mary Mitchell verfassten Text formulierte, erfüllt: „[...] die Spielplätze sollten die Kinder zunächst mit einer kreativen Aktivität anziehen, die einer natürlichen Neigung des Kindes entspricht".[15]

Unter den kürzlich realisierten Projekten ist der Kindergarten von Hibinosekkei in Kumamoto auf der Insel Kyushu erwähnenswert, in dessen vertieftem Innenhof sich das Regenwasser sammeln kann (Abb. 195). Neben dem Fuji Kindergarten von Takaharu Tezuka versuchen auch die Architekten Sugawaradaisuke mit dem Yutaka Kindergarten (Saitama) eine Umgebung zu schaffen, die durch passive Beeinflussung (Veränderung der Deckenfarbe oder der Formen der Raumaufteilung) oder durch aktive Motivation die Konzentration und Aktivität erleichtern (grosse, mit den Klassenzimmern verbundene Spielzimmer). Diese Umgebungen, die in einem starken Gegensatz zu den maroden Spielplätzen stehen, werfen allerdings auch die Frage auf, ob die Beherrschung ihrer Formen nicht auch zu einer Beherrschung ihrer Benutzer führt. Sind daher gerade die trostlosesten Spielplätze diejenigen, die eine grössere Freiheit zulassen? Vielleicht ist dieser Verdacht nicht nur eine nostalgische Schwärmerei für diese Spielplätze, auch wenn sie möglicherweise den Blick trübt.

Vincent Romagny ist Herausgeber und freier Kurator. Er unterrichtet Kunsttheorie an der École des Beaux-Arts in Marseille und verfasst eine Doktorarbeit *Epistemologie der Spielplätze* an der Université Paris 8 Vincennes. 2015 war er Stipendiat der Villa Kujoyama in Kyoto.

Anmerkungen:

1   Nicholas Blanchard, „Le Séisme de 1923 et l'urbanisme à Tôkyo", in: *Ebisu*, Tokyo, Nr. 21 (*Le Japon des séismes*), 1999, S. 137–167.
2   Hirao Kazuhiro, „La politique de la ville de Kyoto en matière de parcs et d'espaces verts", in: Nicolas Fiévé (Hg.), *Atlas historique de Kyoto. Analyse des systèmes d'une ville, de son architecture et de son paysage urbain*, UNESCO / Les éditions de l'Amateur, Paris 2008, S. 274.
3   Dieser Gestalter öffentlicher Parks in Osaka versuchte, den Naturraum sowie Baseball- und Sportplätze miteinander in Einklang zu bringen; 1928 widmete er dem Thema der Spielplätze eine Doktorarbeit mit dem Titel *Toshi no jido asobiba no kenkyu* (*Untersuchung zu Kinderspielplätzen in Japan*), veröffentlicht im *Journal of the Japanese Society for Horticultural Science* (Nr. 4, 1933). Siehe auch: Masayuki Shimizu, „Oya Reijo. The First Green Planner of the City", in: *J. JILA* 60 (3), 1997.
4   Edith Montelle, *La Boîte Magique, le théâtre d'images ou kamishibaï. Histoire, utilisation, perspectives*, Callicéphale éditions, Strassburg 2007, und Eric Peter Nash, *Manga Kamishibai. The Art of Japanese Paper Theater*, Abrams, New York 2009.

playgrounds (see p. 174). Far from revamping the forms of conventional play apparatus, he took a new approach by seeking to offer real environments to children that would allow them great inventive leeway in their deeds and actions: "the ambiguity of the functions [...] would give children the opportunity to freely invent new games."[12] But his playground design also draws on his own memories of childhood games in the tunnels for protection against American bombing dug into Yokohama hillsides by the people of Japan. Indeed Senda's main contribution to the understanding of children's games lies in his "Circular Play System Theory,"[13] which sets out the conditions underlying his playgrounds: offering circular passageways, a variety of activities, strong symbolic features (high vantage points, hiding places), short-cuts, areas for multiple occupation, and a "porous" structure (that may be seen or moved through).[14] Though his early designs used metal, Senda later favored wood, as it is a poor conductor of heat. He also added a roof to the wooden play circuits for greater resistance to Japan's humid climate (ill. 184–186).

In addition Senda designed a number of schools and kindergartens. The architectural vibrancy of structures intended for children in Japan shows that efforts to provide children with new forms to experiment with are no longer confined to playgrounds. Recognition of the fundamental educational effect of forms that are not given in play but that are able to generate play extends to other child-oriented facilities in Japan, in fulfillment of the wish expressed by Kuro Kaneko, in an essay co-authored with Mary Mitchell, whereby "playgrounds should attract children first, along the line of creative activity which is a child's natural tendency." [15]

We might mention some more recent designs, including the preschool by Hibinosekkei in Kumamoto, on the island of Kyushu, where the hollowed central courtyard, surrounded by buildings, is designed to accumulate rainwater (ill. 195). In addition to Takaharu Tezuka's Fuji Kindergarten, architectural offerings like the one recently designed by Sugawaradaisuke for Yutaka Kindergarten (Saitama) endeavor to provide an environment conducive to concentration and activity through passive inference (by changing the ceiling color, or based on the forms of space division) or active motivation (large play areas communicating with all classrooms). In sharp contrast to those playgrounds that encumber Japan's urban areas, these environments do however raise the question of whether controlling their shape and form also leads to controlling those who use them. Are the most desolate playgrounds therefore the ones that allow greater freedom? This suspicion is perhaps not entirely a by-product of the nostalgia

240

5   Kaneko war für die Realisierung des Gartens des japanischen Pavillons auf der Weltausstellung 1958 in Brüssel zuständig.

6   Historical View of IFLA (IFLA-Kongress in Japan), „Von Israel bis Japan", Tagungsakten, *Zoen zasshi* (Zeitschrift des Japanischen Instituts für Landschaftsarchitektur), Februar 1963.

7   Die 1931 in Dänemark von Carl Theodor Sørensen erfundenen und 1943 in Kopenhagen erprobten Abenteuer-spielplätze für Kinder in Kriegszeiten wurden von Lady Allen of Hurtwood unterstützt. Siehe hierzu auch Roy Kozlovsky, „Les terrains d'aventure et la reconstruction d'après-guerre", in: Vincent Romagny (Hg.), *Anthologie Aires de jeux d'artistes*, Infolio, Gollion 2010, S. 33–67, sowie Marjory Allen, *Planning for Play*, MIT Press, Cambridge, Massachusetts 1969. Vgl. auch den Text zu Marjory Allen in dieser Publikation, S. 51.

8   Zusammen mit seiner Frau Shoko Omura über-setzte er *Planning for Play* von Marjory Allen sowie *Adventure Playgrounds* von Arvid Bengtsson. Beide Bücher erschienen bei Kajima Publishing und wurden seither immer wieder neu aufgelegt.

9   Yann Nussaume, *Anthologie critique de la théorie architecturale japonaise. Le Regard du milieu*, Editions Ousia, Brüssel 2004, S. 281–282. Wie Benoît Jacquet und Takamatsu Shin in demselben Werk schreiben, hatten die erwähnten Architekten, die „[in den 1950er Jahren] Studenten am Beginn ihrer Karriere waren, jetzt die Möglichkeit, mit den neuen, aus dem wissenschaftlichen Fortschritt der Nachkriegszeit her-vorgegangenen Technologien zu experimentieren und über die Theorien der Moderne hinauszugehen, um die Expansion der Städte einzudämmen". In: „L'Expo '70 comme achèvement de l'architecture moderne japonaise", ebd., S. 339.

10   Robert Tracy, *Spaces of the Mind. Isamu's Noguchi's Dance Designs*, Proscenium Publishers, New York 2000, S. 5.

11   Der junge Architekt zeichnete sich übrigens durch sein Präzisionsbewusstsein als Bildhauer und Gestalter aus. Vgl. das Interview zwischen Terunobu Fujimori und Mitsuru Senda, „How Mitsuru Senda has accumulated his career", in: *SENDA MAN 1000*, Bijutsu Shuppan-Sha, Tokyo 2011, S. 957.

12   Mitsuru Senda, *Design of Children's Play Environ-ment*, McGraw-Hill Inc, New York 1992, S. 21.

13   Ebd., S. 19–20.

14   Mitsuru Senda, „Circular Play System Theory", in: *SENDA MAN* (s. Anm. 11), S. 13.

15   Kuro Kaneko und Mary Mitchell, „Children's Playgrounds in Japan", in: Clifford R. V. Tandy (Hg.), *Landscape and Human Life. The Impact of Landscape Architecture upon Human Activities*, Djambata publishers and cartographers, Amsterdam 1966, S. 59.

that these playgrounds inspire, and which may color the way we see them.

Vincent Romagny is an editor and independent curator. He teaches art theory at the École des Beaux-Arts in Marseille and is currently working on a PhD in aesthetics (thesis titled *Epistemology of the Playground*, Université Paris 8 Vincennes). In 2015 he was a resident at the Villa Kujoyama in Kyoto, Japan.

Notes:

1   Nicolas Blanchard, "Le Séisme de 1923 et l'urbanisme à Tôkyô," in *Ebisu*, Tokyo, no. 21 (*Le Japon des séismes*), 1999, p. 137–167.

2   Hirao Kazuhiro, "La politique de la ville de Kyoto en matière de parcs et d'espaces verts," in Nicolas Fiévé (ed.), *Atlas historique de Kyoto. Analyse des systèmes d'une ville, de son architecture et de son paysage urbain*, UNESCO / Les editions de l'Amateur, Paris 2008, p. 274.

3   A designer of public parks in Osaka, Oya sought to balance natural environment with baseball and athletics pitches. In 1928 he wrote the thesis *Toshi no jido asobiba no kenkyu* (Research on Children's Play Spaces in Cities) published in the *Journal of the Japanese Society for Horticultural Science* (no. 4, 1933) on the issue of playgrounds. See also: Masayuki Shimizu, "Oya Reijo. The First Green Planner of City," in *J.JILA*, 60 (3), 1997.

4   Edith Montelle, *La Boîte Magique, le théâtre d'images ou kamishibaï. Histoire, utilisation, perspectives*, Callicéphale éditions, Strasbourg 2007; and Eric Peter Nash, *Manga Kamishibai. The Art of Japanese Paper Theater*, Abrams, New York 2009.

5   Kaneko was in charge of designing the garden of the Japan Pavilion at *Expo 58*, the Brussels World's Fair in 1958.

6   Kuro Kaneko, *International Federation of Landscape Architects*, conference report, Jerusalem, 1962, published 1963, in: Historical View of IFLA (IFLA Congress in Japan), "From Israel to Japan," conference proceedings, *Zoen zasshi* (Japanese Institute of Landscape Architecture periodical), February 1963).

7   Conceptualized in Denmark in 1931 by Carl Theodor Sørensen, and later tested in Copenhagen in 1943, the social and psychological virtues of adventure playgrounds for children in times of warfare were promoted by Lady Allen of Hurtwood. For further reading on this subject see Roy Kozlovsky, "Les terrains d'aventure et la re-construction d'après-guerre," in Vincent Romagny (ed.), *Anthologie, Aires de jeux d'artistes*, Les

Éditions Infolio, Gollion 2010, p. 33–67; as well as Marjory Allen, *Planning for Play*, MIT Press, Cambridge, Massachusetts 1969, and the text to Marjory Allen in this publication, p. 51.

8   Together with his wife Shoko Omura, he translated *Planning for Play* by Marjory Allen, and *Adventure Playgrounds* by Arvid Bengtsson, Kajima Publishing, still in print.

9   Yann Nussaume, *Anthologie critique de la théorie architecturale japonaise. Le Regard du milieu*, Editions Ousia, Brussels 2004, p. 281–282. As indicated by Benoît Jacquet and Takamatsu Shin in the same work, the architects concerned—"students who began their careers [in the 1950s] then had the opportunity to experiment with new technology born of postwar scientific progress and to go beyond the theories of the Modern Movement to curb urban expansion," in "L'Expo '70 comme achèvement de l'architecture moderne japonaise," ibid. p. 339.

10   Robert Tracy, *Spaces of the Mind. Isamu's Noguchi's Dance Designs*, Proscenium Publishers, New York 2000, p. 5.

11   The young architect was in fact marked by the sculptor/designer's meticulous sense of precision. See the interview with Terunobu Fujimori and Mitsuru Senda, "How Mitsuru Senda has accumulated his career," in *SENDA MAN 1000*, Bijutsu Shuppan-Sha, Tokyo 2011, p. 957.

12   Mitsuru Senda, *Design of Children's Play Environment*, McGraw-Hill, New York 1992, p. 21.

13   Ibid., p. 19–20.

14   Mitsuru Senda, "Circular Play System Theory," in *SENDA MAN* (see note 11), p. 13.

15   Kuro Kaneko and Mary Mitchell, "Children's Playgrounds in Japan," in Clifford R. V. Tandy (ed.), *Landscape and Human Life. The Impact of Landscape Architecture upon Human Activities*, Djambata Publishers and Cartographers, Amsterdam 1966, p. 59.

⑤

⑥

⑦

192   Yoshiyasu Ishii / Nido Industrial Design Office, riesige Kinder–
gartenrutsche / Giant slide for kindergarten, Keisho, Tokyo, 1968

243

195 Hibinosekkei, Innenhof der Dai-Ichi Grundschule / Dai-Ichi
Preschool courtyard, Kumamoto, Kyushu Island, 2015

Bibliografie / Bibliography

• Marjory Allen, *Design for Play. The Youngest Children*, Housing Centre Trust, London 1965.

• Marjory Allen, *Planning for Play*, MIT Press, Cambridge, Massachusetts 1969.

• Marjory Allen and Susan Jellicoe, *The New Small Garden*, Architectural Press, London 1956.

• Marjory Allen and Mary Nicholson, *Memoirs of an Uneducated Lady. Lady Allen of Hurtwood*, Thames and Hudson, London 1975.

• Lady Allen of Hurtwood, "Why Not Use Our Bomb Sites Like This?" in *Picture Post*, London, November 16, 1946, p. 26–27.

• Ursula Ambord (et al.), *Projekt 73*, Schule für Sozialarbeit, Solothurn 1973.

• Thorbjörn Andersson, "Erik Glemme and the Stockholm Park System," in Marc Treib (ed.), *Modern Landscape Architecture. A Critical Review*, MIT Press, Cambridge, Massachusetts 1993, p. 114–133.

• Alfred Auer, "Das öffentliche Grün," in Stadtbauamt Wien (ed.), *Der Aufbau. Fachschrift für Planen, Bauen, Wohnen und Umweltschutz der Stadtbaudirektion Wien & Fachschrift der Stadtbaudirektion Wien*, Vienna, no. 9, 1954, p. 212.

• Autorengruppe Abenteuerspielplatz Märkisches Viertel, *Abenteuerspielplatz – Wo verbieten verboten ist. Experiment und Erfahrung*, Rowohlt Taschenbuch Verlag, Reinbek near Hamburg 1973.

• Tanja Baar, *Die Gruppe KEKS. Aufbrüche der Aktionistischen Kunstpädagogik*, kopaed, Munich 2014.

• Hilary Ballon and Kenneth T. Jackson, *Robert Moses and the Modern City. The Transformation of New York*, W.W. Norton and Company Inc., New York 2007.

• Ole Bang and Dea Trier Mørch, *Legepladser* (special issue of *Arkitektens*), Arkitektens Forlag, Copenhagen 1952.

• Ernst Baumann, *Lebende Gärten. Pflanze, Holz und Stein als Verbindungselemente zur Naturlandschaft*, Verlag für Architektur, Zurich 1980.

• Arvid Bengtsson, *Adventure Playgrounds*, Crosby Lockwood, London, 1972.

• Arvid Bengtsson, *Environmental Planning for Children's Play*, Crosby Lockwood, London 1970.

• Arvid Bengtsson, *Vom Schulhof zum Spielhof. Anregungen zur vielfältigen Gestaltung und Nutzung für Spiel, Unterricht und Freizeit*, Bauverlag, Wiesbaden / Berlin 1978.

• Charles A. Birnbaum (ed.), *Preserving Modern Landscape Architecture. Papers from the Wave Hill National Park Service Conference*, Spacemaker Press, Cambridge, Massachusetts 1999.

• Nicholas Blanchard, "Le Séisme de 1923 et l'urbanisme à Tôkyo," in *Ebisu*, Tokyo, no. 21 (*Le Japon des séismes*), 1999, p. 137–167.

• Bonnefantenmuseum, Maastricht (ed.), *Paweł Althamer. The Vincent Award 2004*, Hatje Cantz, Ostfildern 2004.

• Joseph Brown Papers, 1933–1990, MS 1884. University of Tennessee Libraries, Knoxville, Special Collections.

• Catherine Burke and Ken Jones (ed.), *Education, Childhood and Anarchism. Talking Colin Ward*, Routledge, London 2014.

• Gabriela Burkhalter, "Kunst und Bau – Schulhauskunst und Spielskulptur," in *Kunstbulletin*, Zurich, no. 3, 2015, p. 44–47.

• Gabriela Burkhalter, "Offensiva de la comunicaciòn / Communication Offensive," in *paisea. Landscape Architecture Magazine*, Valencia, no. 022 (*Playscapes*), September 2012, p. 96–99.

• Gabriela Burkhalter, "Spielplätze – Labor, Landschaft, Kunst?," in *Kunstbulletin*, Zurich, no. 10, 2010, p. 36–41.

• Gabriela Burkhalter, "The Playground Project," in Daniel Baumann, Dan Byers, and Tina Kukielski (eds.), *2013 Carnegie International*, Carnegie Museum of Art, Pittsburgh 2013, p. 278–295.

• Gabriela Burkhalter, "When Play Got Serious," in *Tate Etc.*, London, no. 31, Summer 2014, p. 102–109.

• Roger Caillois, *Die Spiele und die Menschen. Maske und Rausch*, Ullstein, Berlin 1982 (1958).

• Centre national d'art et de culture Georges Pompidou and Centre de Création Industrielle (eds.), *Enfants, à vous de jouer! Terrains d'aventure, transformations d'espaces urbains*, Culture au Quotidien, Paris 1980.

• Central Park Conservancy, *Plan for Play. A Framework for Rebuilding and Managing Central Park Playgrounds*, New York 2012, http://www.planforplay.org (last accessed November, 2015).

• Ning de Coninck-Smith, *Natural Play in Natural Surroundings. Urban Childhood and Playground Planning in Denmark, c. 1930-1950*, Working Paper 6, Department of Contemporary Cultural Studies, The University of Southern Denmark, Odense 1999, http://www.static.sdu.dk/mediafiles/Files/Information_til/Studerende_ved_SDU/Din_uddannelse/Kultur_og_formidling/WorkingPapers/06_NaturalPlayIn-NaturalSurroundings%20pdf.pdf (last accessed November, 2015).

• Galen Cranz, *The Politics of Park Design. A History of Urban Parks in America*, MIT Press, Cambridge, Massachusetts 1982.

• Sylvia Crowe and Geoffrey Jellicoe, *Space for Living. Landscape Architecture and the Allied Arts and Professions*, Djambatan, Amsterdam 1961.

• Riccardo Dalisi, *Architettura d'animazione. Cultura di proletariato e lavoro di quartiere a Napoli*, B. Carucci, Assisi 1974.

• *Riccardo Dalisi. In-arch, Istituto nazionale di architettura, Roma, Palazzo Taverna, 7–14 febbraio 1977*, Centro Di, Florence 1977.

• Riccardo Dalisi, "La partecipazione creativa è possibile / Creative Participation is Possible," in *Casabella. International Architecture Magazine*, Ed. Domus, Milan, no. 368–369, 1972, p. 93–99.

• Riccardo Dalisi, *L'architettura della imprevedibilità. Glossario delle varianti*, Argalià, Urbino 1970.

• Riccardo Dalisi, "La tecnica povera in rivolta / Minimal Technology in Revolt," in *Casabella. International Architecture Magazine*, Ed. Domus, Milan, no. 365, 1972, p. 28–34.

• Riccardo Dalisi, "Technica povera partecipazione creatività / Poor Technique Participation Creativity," in *Casabella. International Architecture Magazine*, Ed. Domus, Milan, no. 371, 1972, p. 40–41.

• Riccardo Dalisi, "Technica povera e produttività disperata / Minimal Technology and Disparate Productivity," in *Casabella. International Architecture Magazine*, Ed. Domus, Milan, no. 382, 1973, p. 46–47.

• Riccardo Dalisi, "Usucapione infantile negli scheltri urbani / Children's Usucapion [sic!] in Urban Skeletons," in *Casabella. International Architecture Magazine*, Ed. Domus, Milan, no. 373–378, 1973, p. 30–35.

• Richard Dattner AIA, *Design for Play*, Van Nostrand Reinhold Company, New York 1969.

• Hans Dragehjelm, *Das Spielen der Kinder im Sande. Praktische Ratschläge und Winke zur Förderung des Sandspielens für Haus, Schule, Spielplatz und Behörde, zusammengestellt auf Grundlage amtlicher und anderer Berichte aus den verschiedenen Ländern*, authorized transl. from the Danish by Alf. Dietrich, Tillge, Copenhagen 1909.

• *European seminar on playground activities, objectives and leadership, Bergendal (Stockholm), Sweden, May 27–June 7, 1958*, United Nations, Geneva 1958.

• Annie Fourcaut, "Les premiers grands ensembles en région parisienne. Ne pas refaire la banlieue?," in *French Historical Studies*, Duke University Press, Durham, vol. 27, no. 1 (*New Perspectives on Modern Paris*), Winter 2004, p. 195–218.

• Andrew Freear, Elena Barthel, Andrea Oppenheimer Dean, and Timothy Hursley, *Rural Studio at Twenty. Designing and Building in Hale County, Alabama*, Princeton Architectural Press, New York 2014.

• Chad Freidrichs, *The Pruitt-Igoe Myth* [DVD], First Run Features, New York 2011.

• M. Paul Friedberg, *Do It Yourself Playgrounds*, The Architectural Press Ltd., London 1976.

• M. Paul Friedberg, *Playgrounds for City Children*, Association for Childhood Education International, Washington 1969.

• M. Paul Friedberg and Ellen Perry Berkeley, *Play and Interplay. A Manifesto for New Design in Urban Recreational Environment*, The Macmillian Company, London 1970.

• Terunobu Fujimori and Mitsuru Senda, "How Mitsuru Senda Has Accumulated his Career," in *SENDA MAN 1000*, Bijutsu Shuppan-Sha, Tokyo 2011, p. 957.

• "Glasgow kids rediscover adventure in shadow of the Commonwealth Games," in *The Guardian*, London, July 25, 2014, http://www.theguardian.com/cities/scotland-blog/2014/jul/25/glasgow-kids-rediscover-adventure-shadow-commonwealth-games (last accessed November, 2015).

• Brian Goldstein, *A City within a City. Community Development and the Struggle Over Harlem, 1961–2001*, Ph.D. Harvard University Thesis, Cambridge, Massachusetts 2012.

• Gerda Gollwitzer (ed.), *Kinderspielplätze* (in collaboration with Rudolf Ortner), Callwey, Munich 1957.

• Michael Gotkin, "The Politics of Play. The Adventure Playground in Central Park," in Charles A. Birnbaum (ed.), *Preserving Modern Landscape Architecture. Papers from the Wave Hill National Park Service Conference*, Spacemaker Press, Cambridge, Massachusetts 1999, p. 60–75.

• Group Ludic, "aire de jeux: espace de libre connaissance," in *L'Architecture d'Aujourd'hui*, Paris, no. 154 (*L'architecture et l'enfance*), February–March 1971, p. 80–84.

• Marta Gutman and Ning de Coninck-Smith (eds.), *Designing Modern Childhoods. History, Space, and the Material Culture of Children*, Rutgers University Press, New Brunswick 2008.

• Susan Herrington, *Cornelia Hahn Oberlander. Making the Modern Landscape*, University of Virginia Press, Charlottesville 2013.

• Jeremy Joan Hewes, *Build Your Own Playground. A Sourcebook of Play Sculptures, Design and Concepts from the Work of Jay Beckwith*, San Francisco Book Company / Houghton Mifflin, Boston 1974.

• Paul Hogan, *Playgrounds for Free. The Utilization of Used and Surplus Materials in*

Playground Construction, MIT Press, Cambridge, Massachusetts 1974.
- Jane Jacobs, *The Death and Life of Great American Cities*, Vintage Books / Random House, New York 1961.
- Daniel Jost, "Changing Places. Resurrecting the 'Adventure-Style' Playground," in *Landscape Architecture Magazine*, Washington, no. 3, March 2010, p. 44–63.
- Kuro Kaneko, *International Federation of Landscape Architects'* conference report, in Jerusalem in 1962, published in: Historical View of IFLA (IFLA Congress in Japan), "From Israel to Japan," conference proceedings, *Zoen zasshi* (Japanese Institute of Landscape Architecture periodical), February 1963.
- Kuro Kaneko and Mary Mitchell, "Children's playgrounds in Japan," in Clifford R. V. Tandy (ed.), *Landscape and Human Life. The Impact of Landscape Architecture upon Human Activities*, Djambata Publishers and Cartographers, Amsterdam 1966, p. 57–65.
- Hirao Kazuhiro, "La politique de la ville de Kyoto en matière de parcs et d'espaces verts," in Nicolas Fiévé (ed.), *Atlas historique de Kyoto, Analyse des systèmes d'une ville, de son architecture et de son paysage urbain*, UNESCO / Les editions de l'Amateur, Paris 2008, p. 274.
- Wolfgang Keim and Ulrich Schwerdt (eds.), *Handbuch der Reformpädagogik in Deutschland (1890–1933). Teil 1: Gesellschaftliche Kontexte, Leitideen und Diskurse*, Peter Lang, Frankfurt a. Main 2013.
- G. E. Kidder Smith, *Sweden Builds*, Reinhold Publishing Corporation, New York 1957 (1950).
- Juliet Kinchin (ed.), *Century of the Child. Growing by Design 1900–2000*, The Museum of Modern Art, New York 2012.
- Richard F. Knapp, "The National Recreation Association, 1906–1950, Part II From Ideas to Association. Founding and Early Years," in *Parks and Recreation*, Ashburn, October 1972, p. 20.
- Shaina D. Larrivee, "Playscapes. Isamu Noguchi's Designs for Play," in *Public Art Dialogue*, vol. 1, no. 1, 2011, p. 54–80.
- Lars Bang Larsen, "Child's Play. Toying with the White Cube," in *Frieze*, London, no. 51, March–April 2000, p. 59–61.
- Lars Bang Larsen (ed.), *Palle Nielsen. The Model. A Model for a Qualitative Society (1968)*, Museu d'art contemporani de Barcelona, 2009, print and http://www.macba.cat/PDFs/lars_bang_larsen_eng.pdf (last accessed November, 2015).
- Alfred Ledermann, "Robinson kommt nach Zürich... Tagebuchnotizen von Dr. A. Ledermann," in *Neue Zürcher Zeitung*, Zurich, May 21, 1954.
- Alfred Ledermann, *Schilebinggis und Sozialclochard. Erinnerungen an ein reiches Leben*, 2 vols., self-publishing, Zurich 1997.
- Alfred Ledermann and Alfred Trachsel (eds.), *Spielplatz und Gemeinschaftszentrum*, Gerd Hatje Verlag, Stuttgart 1959.
- Liane Lefaivre and Alexander Tzotis, *Aldo van Eyck, Humanist Rebel. In-betweening in a Postwar World*, 010 Publishers, Rotterdam 1999.
- Jack Lambert and Jenny Pearson, *Adventure Playgrounds. A Personal Account of a Play-Leader's Work, as Told to Jenny Pearson*, Jonathan Cape, London 1974.
- Walter Leimgruber, Thomas Meier, and Roger Sablonier, *Das „Hilfswerk für die Kinder der Landstrasse". Historische Studie aufgrund der Akten der Stiftung Pro Juventute im Schweizerischen Bundesarchiv* (federal archive dossier 9), Bern 1998.
- Vincent Ligtelijn and Francis Strauven (eds.), *Aldo van Eyck. Collected articles and other writings 1947–1998*, SUN, Amsterdam 2008.
- Karl Linn, *Building Commons and Community*, New Village Press, Oakland 2007.
- Cordula Loidl-Reisch, "Im Freien. Von Spielorten, Spielplätzen und der bespielbaren Stadt," in Ernst Strouhal, Manfred Zollinger, and Brigitte Felderer (eds.), *Spiele der Stadt. Glück, Gewinn und Zeitvertreib*, Springer, Vienna 2012, p. 202–213.
- Richard Louv, *Last Child in the Woods. Saving Our Children From Nature-Deficit Disorder*, Algonquin Books, Chapel Hill 2006.
- Hans Mayrhofer and Wolfgang Zacharias, *Aktion Spielbus*, Belz Verlag, Weinheim / Basel 1973.
- Georges Mesmin and Karl Hermann Koch, "L'achitecture et l'enfance," in *L'Architecture d'Aujourd'hui*, Paris, no. 154, February–March 1971.
- E. Müller-Kraus, "Der Bildhauer, der spielen kann," in *Abstrakte Kunst: Querschnitt 1953* (special issue of the magazine *Das Kunstwerk*), Woldemar Klein, Baden-Baden 1954, p. 82–83.
- Gustav Mugglin and Alfred Trachsel, *Spielräume – Spielplätze*, Pro Juventute, Zurich 1972.
- "Neighborhood Playgrounds and Parks," in Hilary Ballon and Kenneth T. Jackson (eds.), *Robert Moses and the Modern City. The Transformation of New York*, W.W. Norton and Company Inc., New York 2007, p. 174–189.
- Irene Nierhaus, *Kunst-am-Bau im Wiener kommunalen Wohnbau der fünfziger Jahre*, Böhlau Verlag, Vienna 1993.
- Yann Nussaume, *Anthologie critique de la théorie architecturale japonaise. Le Regard du milieu*, Editions Ousia, Brussels 2004.

- Amy F. Ogata, *Creative Playthings. Educational Toys and Postwar American Culture*, Winterthur portfolio 39, 2/3, 2004.
- Amy F. Ogata, *Designing the Creative Child. Playthings and Places in Midcentury America*, University of Minnesota Press, Minneapolis 2013.
- Andrea Oppenheimer Dean and Timothy Hursley, *Rural Studio. Samuel Mockbee and an Architecture of Decency*, Princeton Architectural Press, New York 2002.
- Adolf Portmann, Richard Arioli (et al.), *Gärten, Menschen, Spiele. Festschrift zum hundertjährigen Bestehen der Stadtgärtnerei Basel*, Pharos-Verlag, Basel 1960.
- Neil Postman, *The Disappearance of Childhood*, Delacorte Press, New York 1982.
- *Process: Architecture. M. Paul Friedberg: Landscape Design*, Tokyo, no. 82, 1989.
- *Process: Architecture. Playgrounds and Play Apparatus*, Tokyo, no. 30, 1982.
- *Process: Architecture. Strategies of Man Senda*, Tokyo, no. 79, 1988.
- Robert Rauschenberg, "Proposal for Public Parks," presented at a meeting of the New York City Cultural Commission in spring 1968, published in *TECHNE 1*, New York, no. 1, April 14, 1969.
- Jasia Reichardt (ed.), *Play Orbit*, Studio International, London 1969.
- Ingrid Rösli and Heidi Roth, *30 Jahre im Dienst der Jugend. Zum Abschied von Zentralsekretär Dr. Alfred Ledermann. Chronik 1948–1978*, Pro Juventute, Zurich 1979.
- Vincent Romagny (ed.), *Anthologie, Aires de jeux d'artistes*, Les Éditions Infolio, Gollion 2010.
- Hanna Rosin, "The Overprotected Kid," in *The Atlantic*, Washington, April 2014, http://www.theatlantic.com/magazine/archive/2014/04/hey-parents-leave-those-kids-alone/358631 (last accessed December, 2015).
- Marguerite Rouard and Jacques Simon, *Spielraum für Kinder. Von der Sandkiste zum Abenteuer-Spielplatz*, Verlag Gerd Hatje, Stuttgart 1976.
- Xavier de la Salle, *Espaces de jeux, espace de vie*, Dunod, Paris 1982.
- Mitsuru Senda, *Design of Children's Play Environments*, McGraw-Hill, New York 1992.
- Mitsuru Senda, "Playground Types in Japan," in *Process: Architecture. Playgrounds and Play Apparatus*, Tokyo, no. 30, 1982, p. 19–20.
- Mitsuru Senda and Mitsumasa Fujitsuka, *Play Structure. Design of Play Environments for Children*, Shuichi Watanabe, Tokyo 1998.
- Whitney North Seymour (ed.), *Small Urban Spaces. The Philosophy, Design, Sociology and Politics of Vest-Pocket Parks and Other Small Urban Open Spaces*, New York University Press, New York 1969.
- Jacques Simon (ed.), *Plans d'éxécution d'ouvrages divers d'aménagements*, no. 15 of *Aménagement des espaces libres*, illustrations by Simon Koszel, Turny 1990.
- "Strategy and Tactics in Public Space," *a + t architecture publishers*, Vitoria-Gasteiz, no. 38, 2011.
- Jacques Simon, "400 terrains de jeux. Aménagement des espaces libres," in *Revue Espaces Verts*, Saint-Michel-sur-Orge, no. 4, 1975.
- Susan G. Solomon, *American Playgrounds. Revitalizing Community Space*, University Press of New England, Hanover 2005.
- Susan G. Solomon, *The Science of Play. How to Build Playgrounds that Enhance Children's Development*, University Press of New England, Lebanon 2014.
- Carl Theodor Sørensen and Ole Thomassen, *Parkpolitik I Sogn Og Købstad*, Christian Ejlers, Copenhagen 1931.
- Francis Strauven, "Wasted pearls in the fabric of the city," in Liane Lefaivre, Ingeborg de Roode, and Rudolf Herman Fuchs (eds.), *Aldo van Eyck. The Playgrounds and the City*, Stedelijk Museum Amsterdam, NAi Publishers, Rotterdam 2002.
- Ernst Strouhal, Manfred Zollinger, and Brigitte Felderer (eds.), *Spiele der Stadt. Glück, Gewinn und Zeitvertreib*, Springer, Vienna 2012.
- Sveriges Arkitekturmuseum (ed.), *Aufbruch und Krise des Funktionalismus. Bauen und Wohnen in Schweden 1930–80*, Stockholm 1976.
- J. Thaler, "Kinderspielplätze in den öffentlichen Gartenanlagen der Stadt Wien," in Stadtbauamt Wien (ed.), *Der Aufbau. Fachschrift für Planen, Bauen, Wohnen und Umweltschutz der Stadtbaudirektion Wien & Fachschrift der Stadtbaudirektion Wien*, Vienna, no. 9, 1954, p. 210–212.
- Ana Maria Torres, *Isamu Noguchi. A Study of Space*, The Monacelli Press, New York 2000.
- Alfred Trachsel, "Kinderspielplatz Bergwiesen der Baugenossenschaft Sonnengarten im Triemli, Zürich," in *Schweizerische Bauzeitung*, vol. 70, no. 37, September 13, 1952, p. 536–538.
- Alfred Trachsel, "Spielplätze und Gemeinschaftszentren," in *Bauen und Wohnen 11*, Städteheft Zürich, November 1957, p. 397–404.
- Alfred Trachsel, "Vom Spielplatz zum Freizeitzentrum," in *(Das) Werk*, Zurich, vol. 46, no. 7 (*Mensch und Stadt*), 1959, p. 229–233.
- Robert Tracy, *Spaces of the Mind, Isamu's Noguchi's Dance Designs*, Proscenium Publishers, New York 2000.

• Lianne Verstrate and Lia Karsten, "The Creation of Play Spaces in Twentieth-Century Amsterdam. From an Intervention of Civil Actors to a Public Policy," in *Landscape Research*, Oxford, vol. 36, no. 1, January 2011, p. 85–109.
• Colin Ward, "Adventure Playground. A Parable of Anarchy", in *Anarchy. A Journal of Anarchist Ideas*, London, no. 7 (*Adventure Playground. A Parable of Anarchy*), September 1961.
• Colin Ward, *The Child in the City*, Pantheon, New York 1979.
• Watari Museum of Contemporary Art and The Isamu Noguchi Foundation (eds.), *Play Mountain. Isamu Noguchi + Louis Kahn*, Watari-Um, Tokyo 1996.
• Hans-Ulrich Weber, "Gedanken zu 'La Grande Borne' in Grigny," in *Anthos. Zeitschrift für Landschaftsarchitektur / Une revue pour le paysage*, Wabern, vol. 13, no. 3, 1974, p. 2–7.
• D.W. Winnicott, *Playing and Reality*, Routledge, London / New York 2005 (1971).
• Ken Worpole, *Here Comes the Sun. Architecture and Public Space in Twentieth-Century European Culture*, Reaktion Books, London 2000.

Erscheint anlässlich der Ausstellung / Published on the occasion of the exhibition
The Playground Project
Kunsthalle Zürich
20.2.-15.5.2016

Ausstellung / Exhibition

Ausstellungskuratorin / Exhibition Curator:
Gabriela Burkhalter
Direktor und Kurator / Director and Curator:
Daniel Baumann
Leitung Administration / Head of Administration:
Monika Milakovic
Ausstellungsmanagement / Exhibition
Management: Rebecka Domig
Kuratorin Theorie und Vermittlung / Curator
Theory and Programs: Julia Moritz
Presse, Kommunikation und Veranstaltungen /
Press, Communication, and Events: Michelle Akanji
Sponsorship and Development: Barbara Gerber
Administrative Assistenz / Assistance to the
Administration: Lily-Pauline Koper
Cheftechniker / Chief Technician: Attila Panczel
Techniker / Technicians: Jöelle Allet, Adrian
Eberhard, Boris Knorpp, Gregory Polony,
Jessica Pooch, Roland Rüegg, Florian Wagner,
Herbert Weber
Führungen / Guided Tours: Yannic Joray,
Andreas Selg
Kinderprogramm / Children's Programs:
Seline Fülscher
Kasse / Cashiers: Julia-Faye Mangisch,
Konstantinos Manolakis, Joke Schmidt, Karin Schuh
Aufsicht / Supervision: Sveta Bürki, Sharon Ehbel,
Hani Jahangiri, Eunkyung Jeong, Ben Rosenthal,
Sally Schonfeldt, Naima Trabelsi, Michael
Zimmermann

Wir danken den grosszügigen Leihgebern der
Ausstellung / We are grateful to the generous
exhibition lenders:
Amsterdam City Archives;
Arkitekturoch Designcentrum, Stockholm;
Baugenossenschaft Sonnengarten, Zurich;
Baugeschichtliches Archiv der Stadt Zürich;
Leonardo Bezzola; Canadian Centre for
Architecture; Analivia Cordeiro; Riccardo Dalisi;
Danish Film Institute; Richard Dattner; Det
Kongelige Bibliotek, Copenhagen; Free To Be
Foundation, Inc.; M. Paul Friedberg; Kasumi
Fujisawa; Adrian Gasser; Gabriel Grossert; Sara
Grossert; gta Archiv, ETH Zurich; gta Exhibitions,
ETH Zurich; Heinz History Center Pittsburgh;
Hibinosekkei; Alfred Ledermann; Library of
Congress, Washington; Modern Records Centre
and the Lady Allen of Hurtwood papers, University
of Warwick, Coventry; Musée d'art et d'histoire
Fribourg; Museu d'Art Contemporani de Barcelona;
Museum of London; New Jerseyy, Basel;
Niederösterreichische Landessammlungen,
St. Pölten; Cornelia Hahn Oberlander; Pace Gallery,
London; Yvan Pestalozzi; Playworld; Brigitta
Raimann and Andreas Ledermann; Robi-Spiel-
Aktionen, Basel; David Roditi; Vincent Romagny;

253

Emanuel Rossetti; Sreejata Roy; Xavier de la Salle; Josef and Gertrude Schagerl; Mitsuru Senda; SIK-ISEA, Schweizerisches Kunstarchiv; The University of Tennessee Libraries, Knoxville; The Noguchi Museum and Archives, Long Island City; Tinguely Museum Basel und den privaten Leihgebern, die nicht genannt werden wollen / as well as the private lenders who do not wish to be named.

Wir danken herzlich für die Hilfe und Unterstützung / We very much appreciate the help and support of:

Hideaki Amano, Ei Arakawa, artgenève, Ralph Bänziger, basurama, Susi Berger, Bernhard Luginbühl Stiftung, Lionel Bovier, Julien Donada, Deke Dusinberre, Nicolas Eigeneer, Deborah Favre, Nicolas Fiévé, Fredi Fischli, Diana Gatani, Elisabeth Gaus, Michael Gotkin, Michael Grossert †, Lukas Haller, Andi Hanslin, Susan Herrington, Barbara Hess, Masato Hirano, Benoit Jacquet, Vera Kaspar, Simon Koszel, Masako Kotera, Rie Kodera, Anna Komorowska, Wolfgang Krug, Timothée Lecaudey, Tobias Madison, Clare Manchester, Takayuki Mashiyama, Rudolf Meyer, Hirotoshi Ogashiwa, Paulina Olowska, Niels Olson, Tadashi Ono, Gela Patashuri, Eléonor de Pesters, Karin Prätorius, Naomi Pritchard, Pamela Quick, Carla Rabuffetti, Marie Thérèse Régnier, Philip Reinartz, Vincent Romagny, Grégoire Romefort, Sreejata Roy, Marilyn Russell, Nana Saïto, Xavier de la Salle, Nikolaus G. Schneider, Susan Schneider, Andrew Shields, Dan Solbach, Susan G. Solomon, Daniel Sommer, Paul Stalder, Manuel Tardits, Sofie Thorsen, Reiko Tsubaki, Mutsumi Tsuda, Filine Wagner, Pascal Werner

Kunsthalle Zürich dankt für die kontinuierliche Unterstützung / Kunsthalle Zürich would like to thank for their continuous support:

LUMA STIFTUNG

Ein spezieller Dank für die grosszügige Unterstützung der Ausstellung und der Publikation an / Special thanks for the generous support of the exhibition and the publication to:

ERNST GÖHNER STIFTUNG   Graham Foundation

Kunsthalle Zürich
Limmatstrasse 270
CH-8005 Zürich
T + 41 (0) 44 272 15 15
info@kunsthallezurich.ch
www.kunsthallezurich.ch

Publikation / Publication

Herausgeberin / Editor: Gabriela Burkhalter
Redaktion / Editorial Coordination: Rahel Blättler
Gestaltung / Graphic Design: Dan Solbach
Satz / Typesetting: Dan Solbach, Philip Reinartz
Lektorat und Korrektorat / Copyediting and Proofreading: Rahel Blättler, Clare Manchester, Karin Prätorius
Übersetzungen (Deutsch-Englisch) / Translations (German-English): Andrew Shields, Anthony DePasquale (Foreword)
Übersetzungen (Englisch-Deutsch) / Translations (English-German): Barbara Hess
Übersetzungen (Französisch-Deutsch) / Translations (French-German): Nikolaus G. Schneider
Übersetzungen (Französisch-Englisch) / Translations (French-English): Deke Dusinberre (de la Salle), Susan Schneider (Romagny)
Lithografie und Druck / Color Separation and Print: Musumeci S.p.A. Quart (Aosta)

Umschlag / Cover: Group Ludic, *jouer aux halles*, Paris, 1970
Deckblatt / Endpaper: Maurice Guillon, "Le toboggan psychédélique enlève aux cadres leurs complexes," in *Le Figaro*, Paris, August 8, 1968. Schrift / Font: Rauchwaren, Rauchwaren Custom (Titel / titles)

Erschienen bei / Published by

JRP|Ringier
Limmatstrasse 270
CH-8005 Zürich
T +41 (0) 43 311 27 50
F +41 (0) 43 311 27 51
E info@jrp-ringier.com
www.jrp-ringier.com

ISBN 978-3-03764-454-6

Bücher von JRP|Ringier sind weltweit in spezia-
lisierten Buchhandlungen erhältlich und werden
von den unten aufgeführten Distributionspartnern
vertrieben / JRP|Ringier publications are available
internationally at selected bookstores and from
the following distribution partners:
        Schweiz / Switzerland
AVA Verlagsauslieferung AG, Centralweg 16,
CH-8910 Affoltern a.A., verlagsservice@ava.ch,
www.ava.ch
        Deutschland und Österreich /
Germany and Austria
Vice Versa Distribution GmbH, Immanuelkirch-
strasse 12, D-10405 Berlin, info@vice-versa-
distribution.com, www.vice-versa-distribution.com
        Frankreich / France
Les presses du réel, 35 rue Colson, F-21000 Dijon,
info@lespressesdureel.com,
www.lespressesdureel.com
        Grossbritannien und andere euro-
päische Länder / UK and other European countries
Cornerhouse Publications, HOME,
2 Tony Wilson Place, UK-Manchester M15 4FN,
publications@corner-house.org,
www.cornerhousepublications.org
        USA, Kanada, Asien und Australien /
USA, Canada, Asia, and Australia
ARTBOOK|D.A.P., 155 Sixth Avenue, 2nd Floor,
USA-New York, NY 10013, orders@dapinc.com,
www.artbook.com

Eine aktualisierte Liste unserer Partnerbuch-
handlungen und weitere Informationen über unser
Programm finden Sie unter www.jrp-ringier.com.
Für weitergehende Informationen wenden Sie
sich bitte an info@jrp-ringier.com. / For a list of
our partner bookshops or for any general
questions, please contact JRP|Ringier directly
at info@jrp-ringier.com, or visit our homepage
www.jrp-ringier.com for further information about
our program.

r bien si, après
de griserie au
sse soixante mi-
rfondre en atten-
épublique ait fini

lippe Bouvard.

htique d'un marché encore limité à
l'Europe, mais qui doit faire rapi-
dement tache d'huile. A quoi ser-
virait en effet la conquête de
dizaines d'hectares sur la mer si ces
terres rapportées ne devaient fina-
lement rien rapporter de sérieux ?
Si l'on ne se mettait pas tout de

s l'Ouest et le Midi
s continue ailleurs

ETAT DU CIEL : PREVISION POUR LE 8 AOUT A 13 H.   LE FIGARO

t orageux. Les seules
fera assez beau se-
ituées de la Vendée
anée ou, malgré une
tabilité, de belles
développeront.

S EN FRANCE, AU-
8 AOUT. — Zone
s et bas, localement
ute la journée avec
passagères, prenant
caractère orageux
Vents faibles a mo-
10 nœuds), de sud-
empératures station-

◆

: Temps légèrement
matin, ciel générale-
gé partout. Dévelop-
nuages ensuite, res-
abord isolés, puis
x nombreux l'après-
Vendée aux Pyrénées
es locales sont pos-
de la Méditerranée,
, les éclaircies reste-
ment prédominante
urnée. Temperatures
stationnaires, maxi-
gère hausse. Vents
(force moyenne 10
nord-ouest à ouest.

— Du sud de la

Clermont-Ferrand, 13, 20 ; Di-
jon, 15, 21 ; Dinard, 15, 14 ;
Embrun, 11, 23 ; Lille, 16, 17 ;
Limoges, 14, 17 ; Lorient, 13,
17 ; Lyon, 16, 21 ; Marseille-
Marignane, 18, 26 ; Nancy, 14,
20 ; Nice, 18, 26 ; Paris-Mont-
souris, 16, 18 ; Perpignan, 16,
26 ; Rennes, 14, 16 ; Rouen,
14, 15 ; Strasbourg, 12, 21 ;
Toulouse, 12, 22 ; Tours, 14, 21.
TEMPERATURES RELEVEES,
A L'ETRANGER, LE 7 AOUT,
A 7 HEURES ET A 13 HEURES.
— « Alert », 1, 0 ; Londres,
14, 16 ; Copenhague, 16, 24 ;
Oslo, 16, 23 ; Stockholm, 18,
27 ; Bonn, 16, 19 ; Bruxelles,
16, 18 ; Genève, 14, 20 ; Lis-
bonne, 16, 24 ; Rome, 23, 26 ;
Milan, 16, 23 ; Madrid, 14,
22 ; Barcelone, 19, 27 ; Palma
de Majorque, 20, 26 ; Séville,
25, 28 ; Athènes, 24, 25 ; Ma-
dère, 20, 25 ; Las Palmas (Ca-
naries), 21, 25 ; Le Caire, 24,
31 ; Tunis, 25, 29 ; Djerba, 27,
30 ; Eilath, 28, 27 ; Casablanca,
17, 23 ; Rhodes, 25, 31 ; Dakar,
26, 29.

PRESSION BAROMETRIQUE,
A PARIS, LE 7 AOUT, A
16 HEURES. — 757,3 milli-
mètres de mercure, soit 1.009,6
millibars.

◆

RENSEIGNEMENTS ASTRO-

Le débarquement
du Corse
aux cheveux plats

Cannes, 7 août. (De notre en-
voyée spéciale.) — En guise de
vacances, **Tino Rossi** prend, en
ce moment, des leçons particu-
lières d'anglais et suit un régi-
me spécial pour maigrir de
10 kilos. Savoir son rôle dans
la langue de **Frank Sinatra** et
rester mince constituent les
deux clauses principales du
contrat qu'il compte signer en
octobre, aux Etats-Unis, pour
creer à Broadway une opérette
de **Francis Lopez.**

Les impresarios d'outre-Atlan-
tique ont choisi Tino Rossi par-
ce qu'il est, à leurs yeux, le
seul chanteu. français qui n'es-
saie pas d'imiter les Améri-
cains. Pour l'inoubliable créateur de « Marinella », ce séjour
dans le Nouveau Monde sera
une découverte.

Il n'a mis les pieds à New
York qu'une fois en 1937, au dé-
but de sa carrière. Mais touché
par la nostalgie du pays natal,
il repartit au bout de quinze
jours pour la France. Cette fois-
ci, il prend ses précautions : il
emmène toute sa famille en
Amérique.

NOTE DE LECTURE
« La presqu'ile du Cotentin »

La presqu'ile du Cotentin,
ouvrage heureusement édi-
té par l'Office départemental
du tourisme sur l'initiative de
son directeur, M. Elie Guene,
enrichi de nombreuses illustrations, est le premier volet
d'un triptyque consacré à la
Manche. En effet, doivent pa-
raître l'an prochain dans cette
collection deux volumes consa-
crés, l'un au pays de Cou-
tances et de Saint-Lô, le second
aux régions d'Avranches et de
Mortain. Les bibliophiles appre-
cieront La Presqu'ile du Cotentin, les amis de la Normandie
et de ses richesses naturelles ou
artistiques y puiseront de nouvelles raisons de leur rester
fidèles.

Maurice GUILLON, à
Le toboggan
enlève aux ca

Royan, 7 août. (De notre en-
voyé spécial.)

LORSQU'UN vacancier, « ca-
dre » dans le civil, arrive
aux « Pins de Cordouan »,
près de Royan, le nouveau village réalisé par la Caisse des
Cadres du groupe Mornav et
géré par le Touring Club, on lui
attribue tout de suite un em-
placement de parking numéroté
que personne n'a le droit de
lui emprunter. Il le paie 28 F
par jour, ce qui n'est pas cher
puisque, pour le même prix,
on lui donne aussi le gite, la
nourriture, les jeux et l'anima-
tion. Après avoir déposé ses
valises dans l'un des 162 bun-
galows étincelants de blancheur
qui semblent semés au hasard
de la pinède, il suit le chemin
dallé qui, en pente douce, con-
duit au restaurant, au bar et,
accessoirement, à la plage de
sable qui borde l'océan sur
7 kilomètres.
Là, l'attend une surprise qui
peut être celle de sa vie : il
découvre l'« Objet ». Extérieu-
rement, cet objet est constitué
par une trentaine de tuyaux de
couleurs et de diamètre diffe-
rents qui se dressent à quel
ques centimètres les uns des
autres. Trois ou quatre d'entre
eux sont munis intérieurement
d'échelles et l'on voit une foule
d'enfants y jouer les petits ra-
moneurs. Le nouveau villageois
se renseigne et apprend que
cette étrange construction se
nomme le « sous-marin ». En le
contournant, il s'aperçoit qu'on
peut aussi y entrer par deux
tunnels aménagés, l'un en toboggan, l'autre en escalier.

◆

La faim, trois fois par jour,
la soif à intervalles plus ou
moins fréquents ramènent l'enfant devant le monstre inquié-
tant. Il le détaille, l'observe,
le photographie, en plaisante
avec ses amis et puis, le soir,
lorsque les enfants sont cou-
chés, de plus en plus troublé
et ne pouvant résister plus long-
temps, il se glisse à l'intérieur
de ce sous-marin à demi im-

LA FRANCE TOURISTIQUE DE PIEM